GLOBAL HISTORY OF PHILOSOPHY

Global History of Philosophy

VOLUME I

The Axial Age

JOHN C. PLOTT

with

James Michael Dolin
Russell E. Hatton

edited by
Robert C. Richmond

MOTILAL BANARSIDASS PUBLISHERS
PRIVATE LIMITED • DELHI

First Edition : Delhi, 1963
Reprint : Delhi, 1987, 1993

ISBN : 81-208-0158-x (VOL. I)
ISBN : 81-208-0549-6 (Set)

Also available at:

MOTILAL BANARSIDASS

41 U.A. Bungalow Road, Jawahar Nagar, Delhi 110 007
120 Royapettah High Road, Mylapore, Madras 600 004
16 St. Mark's Road, Bangalore 560 001
Ashok Rajpath, Patna 800 004
Chowk, Varanasi 221 001

PRINTED IN INDIA

BY JAINENDRA PRAKASH JAIN AT SHRI JAINENDRA PRESS,
A-45 NARAINA, PHASE I, NEW DELHI 110 028
AND PUBLISHED BY NARENDRA PRAKASH JAIN FOR
MOTILAL BANARSIDASS PUBLISHERS PVT. LTD,
BUNGALOW ROAD, DELHI 110 007

CONTENTS

FOREWORD

Readers will find here a pioneering work of quite unique character, to the completion of which the author has devoted his whole life.

Comparative Philosophy has made remarkable progress in this century. Beginning with the masterpiece by Paul Deussen, *Die all-gemeinische Geschichte der Philosophie*, many scholars of East and West have made various significant contributions. The works by Rudolf Otto Max Weber, T.W. Rhys Davids, Friedrich Max Müller, Paul Masson-Oursel, Helmuth von Glasenapp, Sarvepalli Radhakrishnan, and others, are well known. The East-West Philosophers' Conferences held under the directorship of Charles A. Moore and Abraham Kaplan, which Professor Plott never failed to attend, gave an enormous impetus to the development of endeavors in this field. In recent years very valuable works in Comparative Philosophy were published by the topmost scholars. Among the names of such great scholars one might mention, for example, Professors Robert H.L. Slater, P. T. Raju, Van Meter Ames, Huston, Smith, E.A. Burtt, and others.

All these works in the past were excellent and meritorious. But they are not *History*. Some attempts to compile a world history of philosophy were made in the West, but they are mere collections of articles by different contributors. This is very regrettable, since they necessarily lack an integrated perspective, such as Professor Plott has attempted in the present work. Some remarkable books which were written systematically, on the other hand, by single authors are, for example :

Kurt Schilling, *Weltgeschichte der Philosophie*, Berlin :

Duncker und Humblot, 1964, 579 pp.

Hans Joachim Storig : *Kliene Weltgeschichte der Philosophie.*

Stuttgart usw : W. Kohlhammer Verlag. Zehnte überarbeitete

Auflage, 1968. 467 pp.

These tried to be as universal and impartial as possible in terms of different traditions. I fully admit their intentions and value. But, in the eyes of an Easterner like myself, Eastern philosophy was taken into consideration very little, indeed almost negligibly. Also, alas, they are not truly what they claim to be, since they treat the histories of philosophy in each area separately rather than in a synchronologically integrated perspective such as Professor Plott has attempted in the present work. That is to say, they are really only further exercises in traditional Comparative Philosophy, and not truly integrated *world histories* of Philosophy. Moreover, I cannot help expressing the impression that many such works thus far published are limited by philosophical provincialism; and this is deeply to be regretted.

That is why I ventured to publish my own work :

Hajime Nakamura : *Parallel Developments: A Comparative History of Ideas*. Tokyo : Kodansha, 1975. 576 pp. (Agency : Harper and Row, New York)

Now we see a colossal, gigantic work by Professor Plott. He has traced the development of philosophy in a wider scope than my work, referring to numerous countries, this feature being most conspicuous in the last part of this work. Although he is a Westerner, he has paid due attention to non-Western traditions.

Of course, it may be easy to find faults with minor points in various passages, which can easily be corrected or improved by specialists. But this work has something which ordinary scholars cannot effectuate, and which his indefatigable assiduity and diligence alone have made possible. Wherever he might go in his travels to many parts of the world, he was and is always studying for this Global History of Philosophy.

Thus, readers of this book will find richness and abundance of ideas in the world history of philosophy of all mankind, and will derive helpful ideas in human life very relevant for the present time, when the emergence of peaceful World Community can come about only through mutual understanding of the Traditions of all lands on a basis of complete equality with each other.

Hajime Nakamura
Director, The Eastern Institute,
Tokyo.

PREFACE

If we were to employ the Rectification of Names principle, this work might be more informatively entitled 'The Essence of a Global History of Philosophy'. We believe that the essence of aglobal history of philosophy is not so much the history itself as the "global perspective" which may result from studying such a history. Global perspective means absence of provincialisms—geographical, cultural, temporal, dimensional. It is sincerely hoped that this present volume, as well as all subsequent volumes, will help to eliminate provincialisms. Perhaps the most difficult provincialism to remove is what we have called "dimensional" provincialism. Most of us tend to myopia: we can 'see' only that which is right in front of us and we refuse to look anywhere else. In short, we have a monodimensional perspective concerning what is, ever was, and ever will be. Multidimensionality or a multidimensional perspective may be partially developed by meeting, all together, Buddhists, Jainas, Sāṃkhyans, Confucianists, as well as Aristotelians.

In attempting to treat in any way such vast expanses and depths of knowledge and wisdom as one finds in the Axial Age, one must determine whether to consider extensive details and thus produce a "resource book" or instead endeavor to get to "the heart of the matter". No doubt this should not be posed as a strictly either/or choice, still there is at least the tendency toward one side or the other. And this volume tends toward the latter side. A large number of sentences in this volume set forth comparisons, contrasts, or simply insights the development of which could be taken as an objective for the student himself. But the scholarly development of these comparisons, contrasts, and insights must be preceded by the development of the global perspective, and that development is our primary concern. We know that a more elaborate and academic global history of philosophy can be (and hopefully soon will be) written; but we believe that the essence of a global history of philosophy, the global perspective, can be found in this present volume.

No doubt the present effort will receive criticism on many fronts. The scholar-specialists in the many areas herein brought into a single focus will complain about technicalities and perhaps more serious matters. Students may complain at first about the number of unfamiliar names and terms confronting them, at least until they begin to get the 'feel' of the global perspective. One of the greatest barriers to attaining this global perspective is the lack of background in world history, without which a global history of philosophy may not make much sense. It should be remembered that this work is designed, not for the experts—although for some of them it is hoped that at least a new pattern of procedure towards historical, and indeed synchronological, integration has been set—but for students who are concerned with problems of peace and international, intercultural, and interfaith relations, and especially students who have begun to realize that there are no short-cut solutions for the planetary crises that have beset mankind in the twentieth century and are therefore willing to work more thoroughly towards the One World goal which have become not just an ideal but a necessity.

Concerning some more technical aspects of this volume, let us first note that no bibliography is presented here. The reader is referred to *Sarva-Darśana-Saṅgraha*: *A Bibliographical Guide to the Global History of Philosophy* (Brill, Leiden, 1969) which was specifically designed to accompany this and the following volumes. This first volume is not as chronologically precise as was originally hoped would be possible. In many cases a philosopher of the Axial Age can, at best, be placed in a 200 year niche. Therefore, for the present, we must be content with allowing a wide margin of consideration more according to typology rather than strict chronology. Finally, extensive documentation of sources, opinions, counter-opinions, and insights has been purposefully avoided, not only because such documentation could be endless, but also because this work is not aimed primarily at professional scholars but at concerned students.

J.C.P.

ACKNOWLEDGMENTS

After work at Banaras Hindu University, Annamalai and Mysore, on the Rāmānuja tradition in comparison with the Bonaventuran—this having been done as a sort of pilot project in comparing contemporaries in global history—it was decided to attempt a restructuring of the whole of the range of what has been called comparative philosophy on a synchronological basis. That decision was made in 1959, and work on this project is continuing, although not always under favorable circumstances. Research for volumes one to ten was done at Northwestern University and the University of Chicago. The rest was put into first draft at the University of Hawaii in the early 1960s and some emendations were made at the University of Michigan in 1964. This present volume was completely re-written at Marshall University during 1972-73.

For constant encouragement sincerest thanks go to many scholars, Philosophers, and friends, including Prof. Hajime Nakamura of the Univ. of Tokyo, Prof. R. C. Pandeya of the Univ. of Delhi, the late Prof. Charles A. Moore of the Univ. of Hawaii, Prof. Paul A. Schilpp of Southern Illinois University, Prof. Swan-liat Kwee of the Univ. of Leiden, Prof. Richard McKeon of the Univ. of Chicago, Prof. Wing-tsit Chan of Chatham College—and a long list of others. A special thanks is due to Prof. Howard A. Slatte, Chairman of the Department of Philosophy of Marshall University, for his generous support of efforts directed towards the publication of this volume.

Encouragement and assistance from students has been most gratifying and sometimes has proven more important in the daily grind of university life. Martha Johnson Coen, Kenneth Gallagher, Bill Pinkney, and Paul D. Mays should be mentioned, as, indeed, should many others.

Finally, due credit must be given to the Benedum Foundation, and to those responsible for its distribution on the Marshall University Campus, for a modest grant which was quite helpful in making the publication of this volume possible.

John C. Plott

INTRODUCTION

Types of Philosophy of History

The humility of a scholar is not necessarily that of a saint, but the virtue is essential to both. The historian must have detachment or he becomes a propagandist, for in historical matters the problem of the observer remains the crucial one. Openness is about the best we can hope for.

The facts of history are so numerous that it scarcely makes sense to string them together without some orientation wherein they are selected and put into meaningful form. Thus, as Hegel not so long ago observed, a history of anything presupposes a philosophy of history. The dialectics between philosophy of history and history of philosophy are unavoidable and he who tries to do one without the other will end up in either dogmatism or nonsense.

In spite of all the subjective factors that enter in, it is possible to designate Types among man's theorizing efforts towards understanding his place in the cosmos. We suggest the following scheme of classification: Organic, Mechanistic, Panpsychic, Dialectical, Theogonic, Prophetic, and Revelational. The arrangement is more or less in a hierarchical progression. We cannot be detained for long by these for they are only introductory to our chief burden even though they are an extremely important field in themselves.

The *Organic* view always presupposes that man in relation to nature has no particular vocation or destiny, but, being part of the process by which the cycles and seasons, cosmic and atomic, continue, he does best by cultivating harmony with them. All things are more or less 'alive', and therefore not only the merely biological realm but the whole of nature, and therefore the whole of human history, is perceived as operating according to 'laws' of birth and death, growth and decay. Cultures, nations, movements, societies, and civilizations, according tc this view, are not exempt from these laws. Religions also may be an expression of this process, even while they seek some awareness of it. This view cannot be very advanced, although there is some argument that when man tries to extrapolate himself too far from his organic roots, he tends to "dry up" and abstract himself out of existence. Thus it has a qualified validity. But it cannot be the whole picture because man is also an inventor, a fabricator, opposing himself to his natural limitations, *striving towards an end* that is not organic, but conquering organic limitations.

Thus, the generalization from this fabricating faculty of man also gives an alluring key to man's role in the universe in the *Mechanistic* view. From Archimedes to Edison man's increasing use of mechanistic principles appears to be the key to his progressive domination over his environment. The mind also is considered as subject to mechanical ('logical') principles. However, 'the mechanical man', not quite transcending his machines, tends to see only mechanistic principles at work in history. Thus, instead of growth and decay, birth and death, etc., we hear of stresses and strains, thrusts and counterthrusts, forces and drives. The striving for ultra-objectivity only reinforces the subjective commitment to the ideal of 'objectivity'. Mechanized warfare is too easily the ultimate outcome of this view. Amoral, value-free science too easily becomes the ultimate ideal and mechanistic scientism becomes the new dogma.

The Panpsychic view tries to remedy this extreme by placing unseen, immaterial Intelligence at the helm. The cosmos itself is thus seen as the material embodiment of Spirit working according to principles that are at once moral and aesthetic and intellectual—knowable, but not by mere abstraction from observation of the senses. Intuition enters, and sense of Presence governs everything. Thus each level of existence is seen not as a 'level' strictly designated but as an analogical signification of the total panoply. Microcosm and macrocosm adumbrate each other according to this view, and each integral individual retains a participated autonomy which is unaccountable according to fixed laws. Freedom enters, in other words, and man is at the fulcrum of the realization of this freedom which gives him awareness of his relatedness to the whole. Thus history is the working out of this awareness, the unfolding of a complete wisdom that has always been inherent but not quite in overt governance of the whole. Unity, nevertheless, is seen as an ideal, and *ideas* become the dominating concern.

But ideas also eventually prove inadequate, for they tend to cancel each other out. Nevertheless, their interplay is not a foolishness entirely, for at each level of cancellation a new emergent, a synthesis, is produced or introduced, and process is thus pushed into the realm of formality along with other efforts at reducing observables into universal principles. This is what is meant by *Dialectic*. Thus if one culture or period is confronted with another, comparison and contrast challenge the mind towards still more inclusive comprehension. Comprehension is needed not only of wholeness in the abstract, but even of the concept of wholeness as determinable among other concepts. These concepts may or may not be contributory to the attainment of the ideal as already conceived, but there must be a critical examination of ideals in the effort to arrive at a Single Principle whereby all ideals, actions, possible programs, possible theories, achievable ends and seeming impossibilities can be viewed for what they really are in themselves, while being understood from outside by the judging, evaluative faculty as well as the faculty of understanding and comprehension. Thus in history, man is not only concerned with his own betterment and the right utilization of his control over ever-widening areas of nature, and again not only with his capacity for contemplation of his position within the whole of nature, but also with speculation as to what is beyond himself and beyond nature. Determinism and freedom both give place to the concept of destiny, and the question of the end towards which all processes tend comes into focus as being a *challenge* and not an ideal only. Something is at work both within, around, and above man which he must admit is beyond his reach, and yet is impinging upon him inexorably.

Thus, man has learned to distinguish between his gods and God, who/which is this 'Something' which he can't avoid and yet which he cannot quite comprehend. The crisis of the admission of incomprehensibility as the source of all efforts at comprehension is the beginning of the entrance into faith. Not just faith in the sense of believing in the invisible and supernatural, but faith in the sense of engagement in the commitment to bring forth new orders of affairs responsibly. Thus the *Theogonic* theory comes to the foreground: history is the triumph of more than mere intelligibility; it is the spiritual burden of man wherein he is, or is increasingly becoming, the instrument of Deity in achieving the complete elimination of all falsehood and error and imperfection even in the cosmos itself. Man, in short, acknowledges God as not only Creator in the primitive sense of Cause Supreme, but as incarnate and inspiriting towards the achievement of completely incorporeal Existence. Being becomes distinct as supra-rational and yet as the ultimate entelechy of the infra-rational and rational alike. Immortality, the Second Birth, becomes then not a mere cultic reason for rites and ceremonies, but the primary goal of Godmanhood. Man realizes that he is only *viator*, a being on the way, but a Way that is also end-and-means in realizable togetherness. Grace then completes faith, openness surmounts system, and love becomes the supreme bond of union of all things and persons present and distant, the exigent mystery of reconciliation of all that is not God to the supreme identity that God is then known to be. Thenceforth, no longer conflict but the 'Good News', the Second Birth, the Gospel becomes man's concern. Man shares in resurrection and hopes for ascension; heaven becomes more real than the best that earth can support. Man learns to praise as well as to pray.

Some might challenge the next distinction, that of the *Prophetic* from the Theogonic. The chief characteristic of this distinction is that, beyond man's rising up to God, God speaks in a metalogical mode, even though through man. Herein time and space are set aside, and the cosmic ego has no part to play. Usually there is no need of demiurge or mediator between God and creation. Loveliness is set aside and the rugged prophet invades the sanctuary with rather devastating pronouncements, especially on hypocrisy. "Thus saith the Lord" is a hard word to hear, but values are set up by such men which last and live beyond all sociometric expectations. When a William Penn or a John Woolman or a Mahatma Gandhi gets a Concern, something is going to break.

For philosophy in the speculative sense, this is a double challenge. The prophet, if he begins to analyze his message, will have to admit that it is rationally absurd. "Impossible" is always the objection, and "Do you have the adequate means, the right sort of program to bring this about?" is the usual query. The prophet will answer directly, "None is needed; go and do!" The Islamic Empire was built and maintained on this basis through the several khalifates, unmotivated by anything less than the categorical OUGHT—and not merely 'categorical' either, for God will not allow His Law to be classified, coded, or speculated about; it must be *obeyed* without question. To the objection that this prophetic "go and do" often breeds fanaticism, it may readily be replied that without some measure of fanaticism, *in* history *nothing happens*. The fanatic lends some hybrid vigor, so to speak, to the pure stock of motivating ideas. This is probably why the United Nations has not been so effective as it ought to be. The abolition of slavery must be followed by the abolition of war as a human institution and the obliteration of national boundaries in the achievement of the unification of mankind. But it may well be that this will not happen until an almost fanatic zeal is created for it in the hearts of all, until some prophet, *mahatma* (great soul), or charismatic leader arises—or until he is adequately heard.

To the objection that we do not know which prophet to follow since all claim authentic inspiration but some contradict others and a few even speak an 'atheistic' language (prophets are often dubbed as atheists because they do not hold tradition, whether in morals or in theology, as sacrosanct), the answer should be simple: insofar as their vision points toward liberation from the bondage of the beast and toward the unification of humanity under supra-human goals, they must be followed. It may not be that prophets rise above conflict since there is almost always conflict between new and old, between temporal and eternal. The final resolution of this problematic situation is reserved to the next type, the *Revelational*. The prophet upsets the easy dissolution of conflict, allows no 'opiates', and depends on no theories, but deals with the hard realities of history. The other types of philosophies of history deal with history *ab extra*, theorizing *about* the whys and the wherefores; the prophet becomes the why and the therefore. It is wrong in a sense to include the prophetic as a type of philosophy of history; it almost negates philosophy of history as such. For above all, the prophet may be a prophet of doom, of the Judgment of God, as well as a promiser of good to the faithful.

The pre-prophetic works *within* history, the prophetic works *on* history, but the *Revelational* works *from beyond* history. It has been generally doubted or denied that the mystical life, or even the values and experiences that concern the mystic, have any place in societal application. But quite the reverse is actually the case, except that the intensity of effectiveness is in inverse ratio to the extensiveness of the field of operation. However, even this mystical revelational perspective, although it may be the ultimate attainable in our hierarchy of orientations from which we must view the operations of ideas in world history, nevertheless remains only one node in the nexus of interpretations in which our hierarchical structuring operates. The other factors or nodes in the nexus, even the following of a prophet, operate rather directly; but the authentic mystic to whom is always open the Mind of God in true immediacy almost always will live in complete secrecy and will leave behind no trace of himself but only the Vision he has had of what will be. The prophet is a man of super-ego, the mystic is a man with no ego at all. But the philosopher must attain the perspective wherein these are also seen as interrelated with the panpsychist, mechanist, and organicist. Whereas the theologian, like the prophet, claims to supersede the philosopher, the philosopher must be sufficiently all-inclusive not to omit even those who claim to have transcended him.

Revelation, of course, *ab extra*, is still not unproblematical. Not all 'revelations' harmonize; some are merely visionary, others are truly wise—wise, that is, with the wisdom that is not of man or of the demiurge but from the Divine Light, not romantically or metaphorically talked about, but actually experienced. The revelational, in short, is not concerned with ends and means but only with the Goal, which becomes all-consuming. Immortality—whatever the type, whatever the qualification that may be placed upon it—and the nature of God have been the chief infatuations of mankind through all cultures in a way that remains completely unaccountable by any naive naturalistic hypothesis. The revelationist, therefore, may be concerned with history, not as material out of which to mold hypotheses or against which to posit new values, but as containing material to illustrate his message of the nature of trans-finite possibilities that remain beyond mere worldly existence. Like the prophet, he will probably be an incredible ascetic, exacting from himself much more than he would ever ask others; but unlike the prophet, he will not usually disturb the crowd but will merely wait in constantly purged humility until the time when he has gained sufficient grace from God to give his—or rather God's, for he will have nothing for himself—devastatingly simple blessing. But he will ordinarily keep silence and become at least a positing-place for God's presence. He will never command, but to those who approach him he may say, "You may do thus and so" or "If God wills, it will take place". The revelational view of history, therefore, is also not strictly a 'philosophy' of history; it is rather an *opening* of history to its hidden spiritual content. It is God's striving to give man understanding both of himself and of Himself as the absolutely Unlimitable, as the Giver of Beatitude, before Whom the whole of the created cosmos, much less the affairs of men on this little waif of a planet, 'dances' the rhythm of the Eternal Return, seeking release from selfhood and the limitations of embodiment.

PART ONE

ONE

The Age of Myth

The primitive age of man need not detain us for long; it remains a matter for specialists. The beginning of literary forms is what really concerns us, and we need not become involved in the artifacts that concern anthropologists and archeologists. Man's *emergence out of nature*, nevertheless, is of extreme significance. Although Egyptian civilisation may have preceded the rest of the planet in some respects, particularly in regard to the theological transition from henotheism to monotheism, one must be cautious for the trend seems to be to push origins elsewhere (Mohenjo-Daro, for example), further and further back. External communication or not, there seems to be some psychic (as well as material) unity among mankind at a very early period.

This emergence out of nature, however, has been costly and is not yet complete. Dialectically, of course, it means first of ali the setting aside of the concept of "nature". Before civilizations can emerge from nature (or philosophy from mythology) the concept of the natural has to be set off in phenomenological perspective. Certainly this was the work of the Greeks. Although some European scholars will claim that this work was uniquely of the Greeks, this is simply not true as any unprejudiced historical survey of the early developments of Indian and Chinese civilizations will demonstrate. Even a superficial scanning of the *Mahābhārata* or cursory knowledge of the Vedas will show this incorrect as far as India is concerned; and in China similarly, the earliest odes vie with any Greek lyrics or epics in designating the place of man in the macrocosm. The worship of sun and moon, the beginnings of astrology, and the tendency toward abstract symbols (geometrical symbols in particular) seem to be quite universal and are found, for example, in an excellent mode of development—perhaps strangely contemporaneous, on the larger scale, with the Eurasian beginnings—in the Central and South American civilizations. It is difficult to say just where and when the first concept of nature arose, but there were certainly presages of it long before systematic speculation began.

The greater difficulty is in getting at an adequate definition of what is meant by "primitive". Do we mean (a) superstition in confusion of magic and religion ? (b) lack of self-awareness ? (c) lack of technical skill ? (d) lack of aesthetic refinement ? (e) lack of established domain ? (f) confusion of natural and divine operations ? (g) lack of communication ? (h) lack of the capacity to handle complexity ? As to this last point, it may well be, on the contrary, that the primitive, by reason of freedom from complexity, is closer than the more sophisticated to the basic components that distinguish the intuitive aspects of the comprehension of truth. To say the least, there is much that is 'primitive' as far as moral conduct is concerned still surviving in our most advanced technological societies. Man still murders, rapes, steals, lies, and carries on the general perpetuation of things that increase his misery in spite of the fact that these things are forbidden even in the earliest epics and codes—the Laws of Manu, the Code of Hamurabbi, the Ten Commandments, the Code of Solon, the Hsio Ching. Materialism linked with hedonism in any culture is best interpreted as a reversion to primitivism; therefore, in all the great epics—Indic, Norse, Germanic, Hellenic, Semitic—we find at least a concern for the 'unseen' and the great possibility of man's conquest not only of demonic forces but of himself.

It makes a considerable difference whether one takes the orientation of designating the primitive in terms of *privation* or in terms of nascent *beginnings*. In the latter perspective, for one thing, the distinction between the primitive and the primordial becomes all-important. The primitive may be surpassed. A primitive machine is no more advanced than a primitive drum; but a drum, no matter how refined, tends to preserve the primordial, whereas the machine tends to destroy and/or transcend the primordial. The most sophisticated gentleman or monk may have terribly primordial dreams, and share the same biophysical limitations and challenges with the mechanic—and there have been all three types from the beginnings of civilization—but their attitudes toward them may be quite different from the 'primitive' man, who may have a better intuitive grasp of their meaning. Karl Jung has explored this region well, and his popularity may be due largely to the implicit foundation of most of his work in elaborating this distinction.

Perhaps the best designation of man's emergence out of the primitive is the *refusal to acknowledge limitation.* To some this may sound too much like Nietzsche. To others it may need the qualification that the achievement of objectivity is either parallel to or a *sine qua non* of that refusal since refusal remains subjective and uncritical. To still others, however, objectivity is not the principal criterion since the subjective is not inherently 'primitive', but rather the entrance of the factors of form and structure into the subjective in order to make it communicable. At any rate, the transition from the merely primitive to the mythological seems to carry with it something of this achievement of detachment from the merely biophysical as its major characteristic. Man, in short, gains the freedom of affirmation and denial. The power to say *no* may have some beginnings at the sub-human level—the ass remains the paradigm of stubbornness—but the strictly moral aspects of it remain the source both of man's separation from paradise and the beginnings of the struggle towards better skies.

Nevertheless, the moral and the aesthetic are not the only realms in which this power to say no may be demonstrated. Man begins to want to *know.* The earliest myths are speculations about creation and the problem of causation, maintenance and destruction, past, present, and future. They are also evidence of the moral and aesthetic, and perhaps quite independently, but more likely these myths are expressions of the full nexus embraced by the religious drive: the vision of unity, the relation of man to nature, the gods or God, and the necessity of self-transcendence—indeed, the search for the ultimately or really real. The great question here is whether this transition from myth to philosophy is purely emergent, or whether it comes from God as actual and literal revelation, or whether it is merely concomitant with astronomical and meteorological factors such as the variation of the icecaps and the availability of means of survival. The last hypothesis is obviously the weakest because there does seem to be a shift of intelligence that cannot be accounted for in merely naturalistic terms. The strictly theological explanation, however, is admittedly subject to some qualifications, although the qualifications may be only in terms of our presuppositions in regard to the strict delimitations of the realms of nature, man, and God.

But whatever our superimposed interpretation may or may not be, the empirical fact is there : wisdom begins with the same questions that still plague us ; and if the answers take mythological form at the outset, it is still an open question whether our sense of wonder, which ever increases as we learn more of the cosmos, is not better communicated in ever-enlarging mythopoetic form. Perhaps we are only enlarging the questions, not answering them. This then is the chief qualification of the revelational theory: revelation does not expose truth; rather than being final, it only *opens* the realm of investigation further. Hence the Hindu *Purāṇas*, the early books of the Old Testament, the early traditions of the Inca and Maya civilizations, the early Babylonian myths, the early Shinto myths, the Chinese dragon motif—all of these still fascinate us, and there is the suspicion that they share some coincidence of origin and end.

These early and persistent questions are closely followed by the sagas and epics of man's achievements. Homer and Hesiod are not unique. The *Mahābhārata* and *Rāmāyaṇa*, early Mesopotamian literature such as the *Epic of Gilgamesh*, the exaltation of the early sage-kings of China, the Old Testament account of Abraham and his descendents, the legends of the American Indians, not to mention the Germanic and Norse sagas, all carry the same basic characteristics, the same basic challenges of human existence: life and death, the virtues, the response to calamity, the problem of suffering, the challenge of conquest, the endurance of danger, the battle with the elements, the evocation of inventiveness, the engagement with the opposites—light and darkness, good and evil, high and low, male and female, war and peace, beauty and ugliness, demonic and divine—and, above all, the strange enthralment to the achievement of immortality, whether seen as the coveted possession of demi-gods or something gained by transcendence of the round of metempsychosis or given as divine reward for merit acquired in the struggle. Chronologically they may be a little more scattered as far as concerns their final literary form, but the oral traditions may very well stem from the same era for the whole of humanity.

The freshness and vitality of these early literary enterprises, which take on a charismatic importance, remain unrivalled. Is there an inherent 'law' that the ability to inspire and the permanence of value lie in inverse proportion to the abstruseness of sophistication of expression ? The mythopoetic genius of man defies even the most rigorous of logicians, as it inspires the saint.

One difficulty that is extremely vexing is the relation of myth to history. When does a historical record take on mythological overtones; and obversely, when does a myth, ungrounded in event at all, take on the power to mold history? For some myths are definitely eschatological, like the concept of the Messiah of the Old Testament, and the figure of Kalki Avatar in Vaiṣṇava Hinduism or the Maitreya Bodhisattva of Mahāyāna Buddhism. Is there within each civilization a beginning in the mythological, an evocation of the strictly logical in dialectical opposition to this, and finally, with the beginnings of decline, an existentialization of the myth that was the original orientation ? May we not discern this dialectical movement through the history of mankind as a whole thus far ? For example, the conquest of time and space has been a dream ever since man began to move at all. Jealous of the birds, man, instead of rejecting myth and rationally admitting his earthbound condition, invented tools which enabled him to travel through the air. Imagination is unlimitable; is achievement also unlimitable ? But again, has our mythologizing in terms of *deity* kept pace with our mythologizing in terms of man ?

TWO

The Classical Age : The Openers

The transition out of the purely mythological to the classical consciousness, which has its analogue not only in all other periods but in the lives of philosophic individuals in every time and place, seems to begin approximately in the sixth century B.C. The sense of system enters and the need for codification becomes predominant. Thus Confucius, Lao Tzu, Socrates, Gautama Buddha, Mahāvīra, Second Isaiah, and Zoroaster appear on the scene roughly in the same era. How much difference there may or may not be between them is still a matter for careful discernment; but rather than differences, perhaps it is better to seek a common denominator that unites them. Are they reformers only or are they *initiators* introducing new gods, more humane, less bound to the old cultic ties of race and blood ? Is their wisdom basically intuitive even though Socrates expressed it in the form of exhaustive questioning, Lao Tzu used primarily the form of paradox, Confucius the form of precept and example, Zoroaster the form of poetic expression of Divine Love, Second Isaiah the form of prophecy of the suffering Savior, the Buddha the form of Supreme Compassion, and Mahāvīra the form of pre-eminent ascetic prowess ? Together they had a Vision of a better humanity and of a theology that was not limited to nature symbolism but constrained to the limits of rational investigation. Together, the moral values come to the foreground over investigation and speculation about the nature of the universe. Together, nevertheless, they did not intend to destroy the old order but to submit it to critical scrutiny. Together they met with considerable opposition, yet together they still hold up a standard that is scarcely put into practice even today. And together they were soon followed by rival schools attempting comprehensive and systematic formulation and application of their teachings. Although in almost direct opposition to the mythological consciousness, they themselves became almost a myth. Critical of anthropomorphic conceptions of Deity, with the exception of Second Isaiah, they themselves became almost deified. From them we inherit the right to question, but perhaps our answers are no better than their answers. They are supremely the Openers.

Nevertheless, to deny the specific differences between them would be foolish. Socrates had the Eleatics and the Milesians and Pythagoras behind him. Although accused of being a Sophist, he only used the Sophists' method against them. Man cannot know without committing *hybris*. Self-knowledge is the best he can attain to, for this will encompass all, including nature and the gods and the manner of conducting human education and government. Socrates died in complete detachment, speculating about the immortal aspect of human existence, not necessarily bewailing the inherent evil in history and man's failure to achieve perfection in the here and now, but forgiving his accusers as being, not through any fault of their own, unwise.

With Lao Tzu man discovers the joy of naturalness and the possibility of achieving harmony without first struggling against himself and the universe. Socrates felt the need to question the nature of man, society, and the cosmos in order to prevent the undermining of ethics, but Lao Tzu has a more *laissez faire* attitude since he realised that behind the manifestations which are constantly "reversing", behind the play of opposites—and even within them if one could but see it—there is the eternal Tao. Once one realized the Tao, or the *teh* which is the Tao in one, the fluctuations of *yin* and *yang* are seen as but a harmonious playing of which man is a part. Spontaneity and naturalness, rather than struggle and 'survival', are the goals to be attained, not through social virtue and rational ordering so much as through spontaneity and naturalness themselves.

Confucius, on the other hand, was primarily concerned with the ethical ordering of the empire and his emphasis on self-culture and filial piety was directed towards this end. He seems to have been unconcerned with immortality. Heaven will be auspicious if men rectify their ways according to *jen* (genuineness). His way was not that of dialectical investigation so much as the cultivation of the virtues; neither radical pessimism nor foolish optimism, but the doctrine of the mean; not renunciation nor abandonment of responsibility, but the setting of a good example through self-purification; not theological speculation but the conduct of rites and ceremonies in due keeping with the things that will stabilize and harmonize human affairs Music and the arts and the promotion of classical learning in particular are enjoined as good discipline for the soul. And above all, not just supreme detachment and stoical resignation, but the patient achievement of deliberate perspective was to be cultivated. Thus Confucius could say that in his early years he had made a small beginning, in middle age he had begun to realize how little he knew, and old age he had acquired a little wisdom which was not really his own but which had been used for the sake of humanity.

Zoroaster, though perhaps chronologically previous to the others, still belongs to the same period of the transition of man out of tribal and crudely sacrificial and merely mythological ways. The triumph of the Good in its struggle with Evil is the best known aspect of message, but his so-called dualism is exaggerated in most interpretations. The triumph of the Good will come about through altruistic love, thus we already have a vision of all mankind living in concord and coming out on top of the struggles between opposing forces. The best interpretations stress not this triumph but Zoroaster's supreme monotheism transcending all dualities.

Zoroaster's is a way of revelation, but a revelation to a quest that is all consuming and which is expressed in a sense of prayer rather than of declamation Rather than being sublated by rational inquiry or ethical primacy, Zoroaster's prophetic spirit pervades his whole message. There is something of promise of future good, in contrast with Confucius and Socrates to whom the present is supremely in extent, although Confucius perhaps had greater reverence for the past than did Socrates or Zoroaster. Fire and the sun remain the chief symbols in the cult that followed Zoroaster, but the texts attributed to him have less of this than an emphasis on reverence and purity in thought, word, and deed.

For Second Isaiah, on the other hand, it is the Lord who speaks, and not like the oracle of Delphi—mantically, ecstatically—but, at least to the believer, authentically. His message is not of self-knowledge and personal wisdom, nor a system of morals nor even a promise of immortality, not the exaltation of a golden age, nor consolation for troubles past and/or present, but a proclamation of justice, righteousness, retribution, and universal benediction because of the appearance of the Glory of the Lord, who is high and exalted even above being named (as in the previous Israelite tradition) but also supremely personal and, heresy of heresies to the rigorous Mosaic code, merciful. The author completely disappears behind the work and it becomes difficult to shift to a completely objective appraisal of the 'word' thus spoken. There is still too much of an undertone of expectation that the Israelites will be avenged and brought into glorious liberation. Beneath the proclamations of the wondrous appearance of the Lord there is a sense of persecution which is not found in the other 'revelations' of this period. But at least if one asks, "Who is this Lord ?", the answer will be that it is no longer a merely tribal deity—though perhaps still a little more anthropomorphic than Socrates or Confucius would have liked. This Deity declares that human goodness and the light of salvation for humanity may not come from mere ritual burning of incense or seasonal sacrifices nor from rational speculation (this is not even thought of), but only from on high. Many of the metaphors are still all too vividly biological, but they are only poetic fictions; the consciousness is not limited by them. The Spirit of the Lord speaks in a way that is not to be questioned. Completely unsystematic, however, this 'speaking' is still primarily emotional and oscillates even more than the Zoroastrian canon between violent denunciations of evil and a marvellous promise—not an affirmation in the logical sense, for all is *hope* rather than present possibility—that all evil will be banished and God as Redeemer will reign.

The *redeemer* concept is the characteristic contribution of the Semitic heritage and at first appears to be unique. But we must not generalize too hastily. The *avatār* of Hindu tradition is also a redeemer in a definite sense, coming to restore *dharma* not only among men but in the cosmic order also, banishing demons and bringing Light and mediating the Unattainable to the finite condition of mankind. The usual notion that all of Hindu tradition is a cosmic and at best stoical is absolutely mistaken. In India the theistic tradition is established as clearly and as rationally as an emergent out of the gods of nature as in any other culture. Also, the establishment of a doctrine of salvation *ab extra* is as clear as the parallel tradition of the practice of ascetic extremes as a means of attaining merit to escape from the eternal round of metempsychosis. It may well be that the idea of heaven and hell here precedes its appearance in other parts of the world.

But the chief point to be noted is that even before the Buddha there was already a movement away from the merely mythological mentality that, nevertheless, still prevails in most of the village cultures of India. In India, as elsewhere, the concept of sacrifice was in some instances sublated by a more radical discipline of self-knowledge—the self (*ātman*) being sharply distinguished from the ego (*ahaṃkāra*) in a way that even Socrates seems not quite to have been clear about—and, in other instances, refined from offerings of animals slaughtered in honor of the deities to the offering of even the 'life breaths' (*prāṇas*) in complete surrender to the supremely personal Deity (*paramapuruṣa*).

The Śaiva forms of Hinduism also undergo a radical revision between the age of the Vedas and the age of the Six Systems (a time span comparable to the period of the Pre-Socratic speculations; the Six Systems are Sāṃkhya-Yoga, Nyāya-Vaiśeṣika, and Mīmāṁsā-Vedānta). Through Śaiva's theological reinterpretations of the older myths, Śiva becomes a supremely personal God, although there is still a remnant of henotheism rather than strict monotheism. The chief Śaiva contribution is the emphasis on involution and the exaltation of the destructive aspect of God over His attributes of creativity and preservation.

These reformations within Hinduism were not enough, however, and Mahāvīra and the Buddha should be seen as initiators emerging against this background. The tendency within the Hindu context was too speculative. Mahāvīra reacted in the direction of more rigorous moral precepts, emphasizing nonviolence (*ahiṃsā*) and spiritual purification by ascetic practice. The Buddha's reaction was more towards the exercise of simple moral precepts and the practical solution of the problem of suffering without extremes of asceticism. Whereas before them ascetics had tended to live separately, exalting the ideal of *kaivalya* (isolation) above the social virtues, both founded a distinctly monastic order upon which the lay-folk were to be dependent.

The basic outline of the Buddha's life is well known: his birth, his boyhood, the search among ascetics for an adequate teacher who could resolve for him the problem of suffering, the enlightenment at Bodh Gaya, the first sermon at Sarnath, the gathering of disciples, his difficulties in keeping his renunciation against the demands of his princely heritage, his annual retreats, his great psychic attainments, his great compassion, and his final *nirvāṇa*. But to uncover the historic person and his actual teachings has not been easy; tradition has covered him over with legends and attributed teachings even more than Jesus, Socrates or almost any other Great Soul that has appeared on this planet. Some texts written more than 1000 years after his death were still put into his mouth.

It is difficult to ascertain what method he used in teaching. Largely by his silent presence he seems to have dissolved all misgivings in those he met, having, through his great psychic aptitude, anticipated each event in advance. He was able to perform miracles as much as anyone in history ever was, but he emphatically taught his disciples not to use such extraordinary means except in the most extreme cases.

In some ways the Buddha's teaching may best be compared to that of Heraclitus, in other ways, to Christ and to Socrates, and in still other ways, he remains unique. From the standpoint of philosophy, he is unique in that he unites religious consciousness with philosophic method rather than dividing them. Capable of refuting even the most astute intellectuals of his age, he nevertheless refrained from unnecessary disputation, simply answering enquiries by enlightening questions rather than by opening discussions with unanswerable dialectics.

The *pratītyasamutpāda* is perhaps his most distinctive contribution. This is the strict causal law governing the endless temporal sequence of events in which men are caught. For the unenlightened, existence in the realm of endless causation is "just one thing after another", not to mention one rebirth after another. One cannot overcome suffering and get beyond the wheel of causation until one realizes that the source of suffering is clinging. That all suffering follows from attachment in a strictly determined way is the *pratītyasamutpāda*. The *pratītyasamutpāda* and the emphasis on the development of the capacity to *absorb* suffering by adequate contemplation, rather than combating it and thereby risking the setting-up of counterforces that also might bring sorrow, fit together as the foundation of his middle path (*madhyamā pratipat*) between extreme asceticism and careless indulgence as well as between metaphysical speculation of the purely intellectualistic sort and the complete neglect of meta-empirical reality altogether.

His method was chiefly that of detached observation, equally of oneself and of all things and processes. Closely linked with this are the doctrines of *kṣaṇavāda* (momentariness) and *anatta* (no soul). According to the first, each passing moment is considered (by all Buddhists, Mahāyāna and Hīnayāna, but more emphatically by the Hīnayāna) not so much a part of a flux or flow but a perspective from which each event can be considered as a passing phenomenon outside the real nexus of Consciousness or Awareness. Whether we consider the time it takes to experience a single flash of insight or the evolution of the whole of the spatio-temporal universe, we are still only dealing with a *kṣaṇa*, a moment. This is *māyā* according to the Buddhist interpretation of what is so erroneously, considered 'illusion' on the part of most of the Hindu systems. *Māyā* for the Buddhist is not just an appearance or the mistake of taking nonpermanent things for real. Its understanding requires the realization that even the notion of permanence is also only a concept and, as such, is less real than the fundamental increment of consciousness that undergirds all possible conceptualization. Thus, all that is not completely undifferentiated, beyond all possible contrariety, is to be considered as a mere passing show, like the katherine-wheel which appears to be a complete circle of light but is only a rotating pattern of sparks. The universe is like this, and we have not begun to get at reality until we realize it. What is 'real' about the universe is the Awareness which links the ideational nexus whereby it takes on name-and-form (*nāma-rūpa*) with our own awareness that it is only *nāmarūpa* that we are dealing with all the time.

There is a continuity of the stream of consciousness somewhat analogous to the Scholastic interpretation of the eternal and perfect knowledge that God has and, in a sense, *is*, including without division the knowledge which he has of Himself and of the world. This continuity of consciousness can be discerned on different levels as the psychic and spiritual realms open up to the soul under Buddhist ascetic discipline. The stages of attainments—winning the stream, the once-returning, the no-returning, and the completely liberated—are all as distinctly mapped out in Saint Bernard's schematization of the stages in the way of obedience according to the Holy Rule of Saint Benedict. Since the Buddhists have known that schematizing is only that and is not to be taken so seriously as valid metaphysical structure, they have been past masters at setting up schemes of meditation and stages of psychic and/or spiritual progress.

The doctrine of *anatta* (no soul) likewise sharply distinguishes the Buddhist systems from the Hindu, Aristotelian, and Confucian systems. The Buddha questioned whether there is any *thing* that we can really call a soul or substantial self. This is also only a passing process and is subject, moreover, to the deluding bondage of ego (*ahaṃkāra*). 'I' (what this psycho-physical organism is stupid enough to point to when it speaks of itself) am only a nexus or process of influences and counter-influences which accumulate as the years go on—or, in some cases, as the ages go on, for beings in such a state of delusion will continue to come back into the world until they learn the proper method of liberation from this dynamic chain of causation.

The desirelessness—the extinction of desire, craving, clinging (*kleśa*)—for which the Buddha has become famous follows from the *anatta* doctrine and is not, therefore, the mere stoic self-denial or world-negating attitude with which he is often credited. For once one realizes that even his own ego is really not his but simply a delusory notion to which he clings lest his precious 'identity' be lost in the associations in which he finds himself, then there is freedom to go ahead into and through any possible situation in complete detachment, recollectedness, compassion, equanimity, and, where it is proper, even obscurity; speaking or remaining silent, eating or not eating, sleeping or not sleeping, even, to a great extent, breathing or not breathing, and, ultimately, dying or not dying, with complete detachment except as concerns the promotion of good that will not have any counterevil possible. Even this is done or undone as though it were not done or undone. One only *observes*, unperturbed, the things going on in oneself, in others, and in the world. This cultivation of Awareness, therefore, is almost synonymous with enlightenment and is the key to the Buddha's 'middle way' (*mādhyamika*) in distinction from the Greek *meden agan* (nothing too much) or the Confucianist Doctrine of the Mean which we shall discuss later.

Once the transitoriness of all things is completely realized, a great upsurge of genuine, deep-seated altruism will arise of its own momentum, not calculated to promote any particular program, but closely integrated with an expansive compassion for all beings who are subject to this surging sea of suffering and sorrow. Then, like a Saint Catherine of Sienna, a Saint Anthony the Hermit, or a Mahatma Gandhi, one realizes what the true need of the world at that particular time is and one is enabled to supply that need, whether it be a better socio-political system, the simple personalistic evangelization of a few souls, or, for that matter, the simple doing of one's appointed daily task, without any consideration that "I" am "doing" something for someone else (who is different or unequal to myself). One sees, immediately and intuitively, "Well, this much can be done without any injury to any creature and without any negative reaction".

Needless to say, out of this also comes the Buddhist interpretation of *ahiṃsā* (non-injury or nonviolence). It is by no means a mere negative restriction against killing or injuring any living creature, but it is also a positive realization that if injury —even at the mental or psychical level, not to mention the physical level—is done, there will be the likelihood of counteraction, of non-liberation, of an increase of sorrow and suffering in the world. Not merely the 'golden rule' is involved, but the inherent and immediate concern for the maximum possible mitigation of unpleasantness, suffering, injury, and bondage to the world.

Finally, *nirvāṇa* is, therefore, not just a negative extinction of 'living in the world' but the cessation of the endlessness of nonsense that goes on in the world. Instead of combatting or trying to overcome evil by the questionable method of opposing 'good', one must understand *nirvāṇa* as release from *all* opposition.

The Jaina *Tīrthaṅkara* Vardhamāna Mahāvīra is perhaps the purest of the ascetic type of men the world has ever known. He is by no means without predecessors, although there is still some controversy about the nature of the era before him. Some still claim that it was only a variety of Hindu asceticism that preceded him, while others, mostly Jainas themselves, claim that the Jaina tradition itself precedes the Hindu considerably. He is acknowledged as the chief of the *Tīrthaṅkaras* just as Buddhology claimed that Gautama was only the chief, not necessarily the first, Buddha and just as the doctrine of the prototype in Christianity puts Melchizedek, Moses, and David as predecessors extraordinary of Jesus.

Renunciation of the world, the flesh, and of all involvement in finite affairs was the first principle of the Jaina Tīrthaṅkaras. The discipline, which is based primarily on the famous "three jewels" (*triratna*) of faith (*śraddhā*), knowledge (*jñāna*), and good conduct (*cāritra*), leads to attainments of a supernatural order, the chief of which is a certain omniscience. Extremes of nonviolence (*ahiṁsā*) are observed, not so much out of compassion as with the Buddha, but to avoid the accumulation of *karma*. The Jainas view *karma* in a material manner. Each act or thought has a psycho-physical component which must be purged out. Impure thoughts or deeds cause the soul to attract karmic particles (*karmans*) which weigh it down.

Through ascetic discipline the soul may be cleansed and thus 'float to the top' of the universe to liberation. The Jainas are not idealists, either in this respect or in any other, but realists who consider even spiritual things as components of reality subject to constant purification.

True liberation (*mokṣa*) is the entrance into a purely transcendental plane wherein the Jaina yogi knows everything that needs to be known through immediate mystical insight. There is nothing like the Bodhisattva ideal of the Mahāyāna but only a straight, continuous path of ascetic discipline based primarily on fasting and breath control whereby the extreme of 'isolation' (*kaivalya*) is considered, as with the Patañjali Yoga, the final end. As soon as all the *kleśas*, the subconscious tendencies, are purged away, the body may be discarded like a snake shedding its skin. The Jaina considers the Buddhist a compromiser who stops unnecessarily at a half-way house on the way to final liberation from all bondage to finite existence.

Mahāvīra stands like a spiritual giant by comparison with most of the Old Testament prophets, and his example as well as his way of victory over everything that binds us to the finite may yet be fruitful in all the world. When it came to problems of conduct and knowledge, he did not stop with a Socratic 'ignorance'. He found an answer to Socrates' questioning and left a light that will never be extinguished. Although there may not be many who are willing to pay the price, his challenge is still with us.

THREE

The Classical Age : The Context

In cosmology, Hesiod (8th century B.C.) tried to make a rational 'theology' out of the welter of early Greek polytheism and came out with a basic scheme of Chaos, Eros, and Zeus who thereby was elevated from his earlier position as a not too secure chief member of the mischief-making immortals dwelling on Mount Olympus to a position of the One and Supreme Orderer of all things. Sāṃkhya, on the other hand, more comparable to Plato than Hesiod, later pushes the Hindu pantheon correspondingly into the background, allowing *Īśvara* an abstract quasi-monotheistic position in a philosophical rather than a mythological mode. In China, the Tao remains the primordial Chaos, while *yin* and *yang* take care of the fluctuations between active and passive, light and dark, male and female, heaven and earth, embracing, in fact, virtually all of the dualities. In Israel, Yawhe emerges as the Creator and Lawgiver whose 'Spirit' brings the world into order out of Chaos and whose existence is more or less unexplained (in spite of more recent overlays of dogmatism) though he does take on the role of deliverer from bondage and darkness.

In India, China, and Greece virtually the same problems were dealt with almost simultaneously : the nature of the world, soul, and God; the distinction of matter and mind and/or spirit; the faculties of the soul and the pressing questions of salvation and immortality; the paradoxes; the beginnings of mathematics; the distinction of Being, Becoming, and non-Being; the importance of self-knowledge; the necessity of greater precision in discussing the nature of God or ultimate reality; and the setting up of rules of conduct. And the answers in all areas were varied. It will be found that the full range from crass empirical materialism to transcendental idealism and uncompromising monotheism was developed in all three cultures of this period. All the possibilities were opened up, necessitating the later dialectical juxtapositions in order to attempt some synthesis.

We shall take each of these topics and examine their variations, although we must remember that in each, and therefore in the total *weltgeist* of this period, the basic effort was the discovery of a Single Principle whereby to explain everything. We will attempt to view comprehensively the discernment of the basic components of what will later become the great metaphysical systems of the traditions.

A. The Elements

The elements earth, fire, and water are common in all traditions. It remains to be explained why the Chinese postulated wood and metal, why the Indian systems added *ākāśa* (the ether, sometimes also translated as "space" or "the void"), and why the Buddhists sometimes posited consciousness (*vijñāna*).

Tsou Yen (c. 350-270 B.C.) is attributed with the first systematic combining of the two previously independent doctrines of *yin-yang* and the Five Agents (Elements). Both concepts go back to antiquity, but we know nothing of the early propounders or their works. Nothing very definitive about these doctrines can be found in ancient Chinese literature. The Five Agents are more like powers or principles of a cosmological order than mere material elements as the early Greeks thought of them. The varying degrees of domination of these Agents were used as the basis of a virtual theory of cultural dynamics. Thus the *Tsou Tzu Ching Shih* records :

> 'When some new dynasty is going to arise, Heaven exhibits suspicious signs to the people. During the rise of Huang Ti (The Yellow Emperor) large earth-worms and large ants appeared. He said, 'This indicates that the element Earth is in the ascendent, so our color must be yellow, and our affairs must be placed under the sign of Earth'.[1]

Needham goes on to record the remaining colors, elements, signs of this ancient text. Since the Agents were thought to succeed each other, overcome each other, and/or produce each other, a theory of cycles developed which was applied to nearly everything and was especially influential in form—the Chinese concept of history as cyclical.

A theory of correspondences apparently developed very early in Chinese thought. From the Five Agents and *yin-yang* doctrines there developed one of the most important and most characteristic of Chinese views : the unity of man and nature. In the *Huai-nan-tzu* (2nd century B.C.) we have the following correlations (to which, by the way, nothing comparable is found in India and Greece) :

wood	east	green	*chih*,	wisdom
fire	south	red	*chung*,	faithfulness
metal	west	white	*wen*,	refinement
water	north	black	*chih*,	simplicity
earth	center	yellow	*ching*,	respectfulness

Not only these correlations, however, but almost any set of five things was correlated with the Five Agents.

In early Indian systems (*darśanas*) the doctrine of elements (*dravyas*) as the ultimate principles is found most explicitly in Lokāyata (Cārvāka). Mādhava says in his *Sarvasiddhānta Saṁgraha*: "According to the Lokāyatika doctrine the four elements alone are the ultimate principles—earth, water, fire and air; there is none other".[2] All things, including consciousness, were considered to be the result of a combination of these four elements.

The Jainas divide the universe into two independent but interrelated and co-existing groups: living (*jīva*) and non-living (*ajīva*). The elements are part of the non-living group only. The elements are reducible since they, like all material things, are composed of atoms. The lowliest evolved *jīvas* (souls) live in the atoms of earth, air, water, and fire, and have only one sense—touch. More highly evolved *jīvas* live in other material things.

The Theravāda Buddhists mentioned the elements but they certainly did not offer them as a metaphysical explanation of the world. Occasionally in addition to earth, air, fire, and water, they added space and consciousness as elements. They were used, however, only as a basis for meditation. If one meditates on himself as only a conglomeration of elements, then one may be able to root out attachment, for beyond these groups of elements there is no substance, self, spirit, or soul.

> But apart from moral reflections of this kind the Buddhists show no interest at all in these physical elements, and are not particularly concerned about what they actually are and do.[3]

According to Sāṃkhya, the multiplicity of the world gradually evolved from *prakrti* (primordial matter). The subtle elements (sight, smell, taste, touch, and sound) do not evolve until mind (*manas*), ego-consciousness (*ahaṃkāra*), and intellect (*buddhi*) have evolved; and it is from the subtle elements that the gross, material elements evolve—ether, fire, water, earth, and air. But also, *prakṛti* is actually nothing but the three *guṇas*: *sattva*, *tamas*, *rajas*. "They themselves possess qualities like lightness, activity, heaviness, etc. They are extremely fine and ever-changing elements. They make up *prakṛti* which is nothing apart from them."[4] Thus in Sāṃkhya, one may see the 'elements' at both ends of the evolutionary hierarchy.

For Vaiśeṣika, all material objects are reducible to atoms of earth, air, water, and fire. Ether, rather than being a kind of atom, is the all-pervading medium in which atoms combine. Vaiśeṣika and Empedocles both posited two principles of motion: merit (*dharma*)/demerit (*adharma*) and love/strife respectively. Since there are spiritual as well as material substances—time (*kāla*), space (*dik*), spirit (*ātman*), mind (*manas* also considered to be atomic)—Vaiśeṣika is not materialistic like Empedocles and Lokāyata.

B. Mind.

It is difficult on the larger scale to separate the Greek and the Indian atomic theories from the theories constructed about mind. The great question for this period remains: is mind a composite of atoms, or separate from them, or is it by mind that the atoms themselves come into relation with each other, forming the composites of nature?

As a generalization, we may risk the hypothesis that not only in Anaxagoras but also in the Indian and Chinese traditions of this period (specifically Sāṃkhya, Vaiśeṣika, Mīmāṁsā, the Lieh Tzu, Kao Tzu and the Neo-Mohists) there was a progression from the notion that mind (*manas*, *hsin*) and knowing are a function and/or faculty of the individual knower through the notion that mind (*buddhi, chih*) is *that by which* all else is known, even though it itself remains unknown, to the speculation that mind (here no longer *manas* or *hsin* or simply *chih*, but *chih chih*, 'extension of knowledge', and *citta*) is a panpsychic if not indeed a cosmogenetic or a theogenetic principle such that it becomes the key to wisdom (*sophia, chih, gnosis, jñāna*, or at least *vijñāna*, conjunction of knowledge and spiritual will) or *vidyā*, the immediate 'seeing' of the Supreme Truth and all beneath and/or within it.

To trace out the correlates to these in the Old Testament (which more resembles the Hindu *Purāṇas* than the schools of philosophy of India, China, and Greece) and other Semitic literature, however, is not so easy. The exaggerated moralism, a type quite different from the Chinese will-to-harmony in that the "thou shalt" becomes inexorable as directly from God the all-Terrible, tends to side-step or eliminate the possibilities of philosophical and/ or scientific theorizing. There are, nevertheless, weak echoes in phrases like the "Mind of the Lord", where "mind" is really quite synonymous with will. Essentially the Hebrews in type remained in the mythological mode much longer than their contemporaries; but instead of graduating out of the mythological into a speculative mode, they developed the mythological to a degree of refinement which compensates, perhaps, for their defaulting in metaphysics.

The concept of revelation is a relatively recently constructed apologetic and is possibly over-developed in contrast with the Hellenic *geist*. It still seems odd of God to have chosen the Jews ; but every civilization, as Toynbee has brought out very vividly, has had its sense of superiority over its neighbors. Barbarian, heathen, non-Aryan, and such terms also are paralleled in China; and in spite of the Buddha and Socrates and Mo Tzu, the genuinely ecumenical perspective was not achieved in this period—but then neither have we achieved it with all our 'progress' 2,500 years later !

C. *Soul, Spirit, and Self*

Within this period is the gradual discernment of the distinction of, and hierarchical relation between, individual soul, spirit, or self. In the Greek tradition, *psyche* ceases to be a mythological figure and becomes a definite immortal being of the individual person. *Pneuma* does not yet figure so prominently as in Hellenistic times, but there begins to be a more rational, less superstitious attitude towards the 'spirits' of the departed and the demi-gods and heroes.

In the Indian tradition there is not only in Sāṃkhya the all-important distinction between *jīva* and *ātman*, as well as between *puruṣa* and *prakṛti*, but the sharp contrast which stems all the way back to the Upaniṣads between these and *ahaṃkāra* (ego or personality). *Ahaṃkāra* is also classified according to Sāṃkhya's three *guṇas* : *sattva* (pure, intelligent, subtle), *rajas* (active, animal, irascible), and *tamas* (heavy, gross, vegetative). These correlate with the three levels of the soul according to Plato and Aristotle, although, of course, these levels may have been derived from Pythagoras who probably was influenced from 'further east'.

There is endless discussion and disagreement as to the substantiality of the *jīva*, *ātman*, and *ahaṃkāra*. Later Mīmāṁsā somewhat anticipates Śaṅkara in proposing that nothing less than Brahman is really substantial, permanent, and indestructible. In the Vaiśeṣika, soul (*jīva*), it is claimed, is as observable as any possible object of knowledge and therefore 'real'. The soul's immortality was, of course, assumed.

For the Chinese thinkers in general the question of the relationship between soul and body did not arise as a philosophical question for the simple reason that they did not make such a clear distinction between them but rather considered man to be an organic whole. However, the immortality of ancestors seems seldom if ever to have been questioned. Confucius is reported to have said, "One should respect the spirits, but keep them at a distance". The cult of ancestors, once prominent in India also (the so-called *pitṛyāna*, which was considered inferior to the *devayāna*, the path of the gods), dominated the scene until very recent times indeed.

The Chinese word generally translated as "spirit" is *shen*, but *shen* has various meanings and in some sense it was thought that only sages and rulers had a *shen*. Concerning the Confucian concept of soul, Munro says :

> In early Chinese works, too, there are terms that were associated with mental activity and are translated today as "soul" : *p'o*, "sentient soul"; *hun*, "spiritual soul"; and *shen*, "soul". However, they also did not refer to any eternal entity having special metaphysical status, as did the Greek term *psyche* in works reflecting Orphic, Pythagorean, and Platonic doctrines.[5]

At death, the *hun* rose to Heaven and joined the ancestors while the *p'o* sank down to earth.

The micro-macrocosm notion of the nature of man and his relation to the universe came into formulation very early in Greece, India, and China. In Taoism, the Tao as manifested in each particular thing is called *teh*; thus, each man has "his Tao", that is, his *teh*. There is a sense in which a man's *teh* may be looked upon as his soul, spirit, or self. At death the *teh* 'returns' to the primordial Tao although, of course, since all is Tao, it never really left. Munro says :

> In its new meaning among the Taoists, *teh* continued to be a link between man and "deity"; but Tao had taken the place of the deity . . . In the Taoist writings "rewards" come to the person who takes care of his *teh*, that is, he who obeys the dictates of his internal life principle.[6]

In the *Huai-nan-tzu* we find the following summary of the soul's relation to reality :

> If we look back to antiquity, to the Great Beginning, man was there born out of non-Being to assume form in Being. Having form, he was regulated by things. But he who is able to revert to that state out of which he was born, so as to be as if he had never had physical form, is called the True Man (*chen jen*). The True Man is he who is as if he had not yet separated from the Great Oneness.[7]

Here we have something suggestive of Parmenides as well as the *ātman*-Brahman 'Supreme Identity' of the Vedāntins. Soul, 'reduced' to its own pristine component and foundation, turns out to be Reality itself, even to some extent bridging the difference between God and individual. Later in the Christian heritage, something like this will be found in the doctrine of the restoration of the image of God in man as a result of the Redemption. The other Indian schools (Nyāya in particular) did not go quite so far.

The Buddhists, of course, denied the existence of an unchanging soul or self. Just as the things of experience are complexes of elements, so the things we call individuals are complexes of physical and psychical elements which are ultimately liable to dissolution.

D. The Concept of Number

It is important that, equally with soul theories, the nature of number began to take its place in this period as a basis of speculation in all three cultures. Needham has traced this out in detail and we shall only make a few general observations.

In Pythagoras and in the Chinese commentaries on the *I Ching* there was by no means the sense of opposition between mathematics and spiritual matters that post-Renaissance Europeans have. Although mathematics had a very early development in India, it did not figure so prominently in classical philosophizing as it did in Plato and Aristotle. Nevertheless, in the Vaiśeṣika school in particular, considerable importance was given to number as a basis of distinguishing between eternal and non-eternal reality. The eternal must perforce be one, and the question arises quite cogently concerning the relation of numerable things to this unity. The designation of dyads, triads, etc., was also the basis of theorizing about the difference in composition of different kinds of atoms. Whether number constituted a distinct *dravya* (element) was also debated.

With Pythagoras, number was not only the basis of mathematical theory and geometry, but also of 'scientific' musical theory and thus was closely linked with the Pythagorean method of soul-purification. It must not be forgotten, by the way, that the Pythagorean community was a definitely monastic institution, and that the Indian philosophers were also *munis* (wise men) observing rules of ascetic discipline. Some, though not all, of the Chinese sages were also of this type.

To undertake a complete exposition of the *I Ching* would constitute a separate work in itself. The student must study it carefully, nevertheless, for no education is complete without a thorough grounding in its mode of modulated thinking. It contains all the dialectics of Plato's philosophizing about the 'odd' (*yin*) and the 'even' (*yang*), and its application is still quite universal. Karl Jung's more recent use of it is only one possible case in point. The tables in Needham in particular may be consulted to show how universal its application may be, embracing as it does most, if not all, possible theories of time, space and motion, dissolution and creation and involution, cyclic return, action and repose, etc.[8] True enough, from time to time its use has degenerated into superstition and fortune telling but this is due to the ignorance of the users and not to the system itself.

E. Matter

The Buddhists were not concerned with matter, but they did recognize it as one of the *dharmas* (basic components of reality). They were much more concerned with the non-material *dharmas* however. In realizing that consciousness was not simply an epiphenomenon, they were certainly more sophisticated than their Pre-Socratic Greek contemporaries.

In the Greek tradition it was assumed that everything was made out of 'something' and the search was to find what that 'something' was. Suggestive of the Ionic philosophers' attempts to discern the "world stuff" (*Urstoff*) which is the basis of the entire process of nature is the Chinese treatment of *ch'i* :

> It was believed that the universe was made up of *ch'i* but this *ch'i* varied in consistency. The grosser *ch'i*, being heavy, settled to become the earth, while the refined *ch'i*, being light, rose to become the sky. Man, being half-way between the two, is a hormonious mixture of the two kinds of *ch'i*.[9]

When we realize that one translation for *ch'i* is "vital breath", the comparison with Anaximenes becomes obvious.

In general, the Chinese had more a sense of modulation than of sharply contrasting distinction. Matter was thought to be a component of universal nature in concretions of varying degrees. The elements we have already discussed were considered to be varying degrees of condensation rather than discrete components in combination and commixture. There were schools (Tsou Yen and Hsun Tzu) of a more frankly materialist nature in China than is generally supposed, as well as in Greece where there were also the extreme idealists (Parmenides) as well as the materialists (Democritus, Empedocles). The generalized concept of matter as such thus played a varying role in both traditions.

In the Hindu tradition the same generalization holds almost equally true. *Prakṛti* in the Sāmkhya school, though sometimes almost personalized or at least metaphorically treated as 'dancing' for the sake of *puruṣa* (soul or 'person'), is radically the matter of which all things are individualizations according to the combinations of the *guṇas* (threads, strands, components). This is as non-mythological a concept as may be found in Greece right up to the time of Aristotle and perhaps more explicit than anything found in the same period in China, Iran, or the Old Testament. In the other schools, the Jaina and Vaiśeṣika in particular, there was a sharp distinction drawn between living and nonliving matter, and there was considerable argument about the eternality of material reality. According to Sāṃkhya, at the time of *pralaya* (the general dissolution of the world) the imbalance of the *guṇas* is restored and, with *sattva* prevailing, the tendency toward concretion is stopped. As the imbalance comes again into play in the cyclic turn of the ages, *tamas* again prevails and the tendency towards grossness brings reality into material manifestation. In the later Nyāya-Vaiśeṣika, however, this is done by *Īśvara* (God) rather than by an inherent self-operative principle, and in some interpretations the idea that this is done as a play (*līlā*) of *Īśvara* already begins to take shape.

The relation of matter and motion thus comes prominently into focus, as it also does in China and Greece, but perhaps with greater emphasis. According to some Hindu schools, when motion ceases matter returns to mind, and mind to transcendental reality according to the principle of involution. In the Greek tradition this does not figure so prominently, the emphasis being almost entirely on evolution. In Chinese tradition the sense of the cyclic nature of all things is almost always present, but in the Hindu Schools the pattern of the full cycle (*pralaya*) seems to be most clearly and explicitly developed.

In all three, however, there is no *ex nihilo* concept of creation like that which the Scholastics later derived from the Old Testament and the Koran. As a matter of fact, it is difficult to find in the Old Testament texts themselves anything quite so definitive. The metaphor of the clay and the potter which figures in the literature of this period is also found in Indian tradition and is not unique. The metaphor of Heaven as the throne of the Lord and the Earth as His footstool yields very little. There are other texts where the Lord is credited with the power to destroy as well as to create, but the question about what He makes things out of and the corollary question of the relative materiality of nature seems not to have arisen in sharp focus. It is true that all things are considered 'like grass, withering before they are plucked up',—creation is extremly *impermanent*—but there seems to be very little systematic, non-metaphorical, non-mythological theorizing about its naure. We may partially conclude that the Israelites were so hectically situated between Babylon and Assyria that they had little leisure for metaphysical speculation; the moral and economic considerations were all-encompassing. Nevertheless, there was again a wide range of views, from the almost crass hedonistic and skeptical materialism of the book of Ecclesiastes to the lofty vision of second Isaiah. The intensity of the question of the relation of man and nature to their Creator seems to increase in this period, as we may see in the book of Job.

Thus, in spite of the variations in the answers, we may risk the general conclusion that in this period the 'problem of matter' was recognized, as it was not in the purely mythological era preceding, and that this applies for mankind as a whole. Again the division between East and West breaks down. *Somehow* there was a unity in the movement of thought throughout Eurasia. Mankind as a whole began to "look behind the scenes" and seek out the underlying nature of all things.

F. Logic and Paradoxes

The classical paradoxes also came into focus during this period. In Greece, Zeno the Eleatic (not to be confused with Zeno the Stoic) illustrated these with stories of Achilles and the tortoise and of the flying arrow which will never meet its mark because of the infinite regress of the interstices through which it must travel. There is also the paradox of the grain and the heap, illustrating the problem of the one and the many (there will never be a heap because there will only be a multitude of individual grains), and the paradox of the infinitely small and the infinitely large. These, of course, illustrate the difficulty in making the progression from the empirically observed 'fact' to the logically constructed universal, and perhaps the inherent difficulty in the relation between the finite and infinite as such.

In China the same problems are discerned although they were usually stated in more quipsical and cryptic terms. Hui Shih was one of the more prominent Chinese logicians. In the *Chuang Tzu*, which discusses the various philosophical schools, we find:

> The sun at noon is the sun declining, the creature born in the creature dying.
> Going to the State of Yüeh today, one arrives there yesterday.
> An egg has feathers.
> A fowl has three legs.
> Horses have eggs.
> Frogs have tails.
> Fire is not hot.
> Wheels do not touch the ground.
> Eyes do not see.
> Tortoises are longer than snakes.
> Carpenters' squares are not square; compasses cannot make circles.
> The shadow of a flying bird has never yet moved.

> There are times when a flying arrow is neither in motion nor at rest.
>
> A brown horse and dark ox make three.
>
> A white dog is black.
>
> An orphan colt has never had a mother.
>
> If a stick one foot long is cut in half every day, it will still have something left after ten thousand generations.[10]

These need a lot of explanation, of course; the Chinese language lends itself to different semantical configurations than Indo-European phonetic languages, but the student can consult the texts for further puzzling. In general, the difficulty is quite the same as that with the paradoxes of Zeno: universals and attributes do not easily combine, and it is often difficult to determine whether a universal is exclusively the 'thing' or whether the attribute is not also a separate universal somehow hooked on to the universal 'thing'. Hence, for example, we have the question of whether there is always a *nescio quid* left over after all characteristics are discerned.

The Greek Sophists had their counterpart in ancient China. These Chinese Sophists were masters at using the basic ambiguity of language to further their own ends. Just as Socrates responded to the Greek Sophists by seeking clear definitions, so Confucius responded to the Chinese Sophists by insisting on his Rectification of Names.

The Chinese were good logicians in that they were good debaters, but there is nothing in Chinese logic comparable to Aristotle's *Organon* or the Nyāya *Sūtras*. The most common method of argument was that of argument by analogy. If, for example, we wish to clarify something that is obscure, we may make an analogy with something that is familiar. We can then try to see if the analogy in fact contains a valid comparison. D.C. Lau says: "...an analogy is at least as instructive, if not more, when it breaks down as when it holds".[11] Also he points out that analogy is often the only possible tool for probing subject matter that is obscure, intangible, or elusive. Analogical argumentation shows an interest in the form of propositions, but the ancient Chinese did not carry this interest in form far enough to arrive at what we know as Aristotelian formal logic.

As for India, Dasgupta notes that the distinction between vicious and harmless infinite regresses was known as early as the sixth or seventh century B.C.[12] and probably much earlier. Many statements similar to those of Zeno and the Chinese sages cited above are found in the Upaniṣads, in particular the seeing of the infinitely small and the infinitely great as one and the concept that all is contained in *that by which* all else is known. In the Six Systems one finds very close reasonings about these things in the logic of negation, as Ingals has shown very vividly in his translation of Nyāya texts into modern symbolic notation. The chief problem is whether 'absence' (*abhāva*) is a positive or negative or non-existent category. The logical fallacies (five in number) were discerned quite early, and types of argumentation were listed, although not all the schools were agreed as to the relative validity of each. In particular, arguments which were constructed merely for the sake of winning a dispute were suspect. But more problematic is the distinction between arguments whereby one may reason about a non-existent object (e.g., sky flower, son of a barren woman), and arguments which, though formally the same, must be taken as validly designating nonobservable reality.

In general, then, we may conclude that in this period the discernment of the paradoxes led towards the logic of negation long before Hegel ever came on the scene and towards the delimitation of the function of universals in validating human knowledge long before Abelard wrote his *Sic et Non* which caused such a stir in medieval Europe. These problems are still with us. Common-sense rebels against logical expertise and sophisticated dialectic, realizing that mere expertise does not necessarily give truth but is only one tool for arriving at metalogical principles. Still, a return to the naivete of mere common-sense is not the answer.

G. *The Flux*

The universality of the doctrine of the flux is somewhat more controversial because all of the Hindu systems stressed permanence instead. The basic insight of Heraclitus (*panta hrei* everything flows) was known in China not only in the commentaries and expositions of the *I Ching* but also in the pre-

Confucian Classics. According to the *I Ching* there is constant change, cyclic and regulated. There is movement from one extreme to another and then back again: the sun at noon, the sun at midnight, the sun at noon again. The basic insight of the *I Ching* is that since change is regular, one may understand, and order one's affairs according to the principles of change. After the *I Ching*, the concept of flux is found in Chuang Tzu who said: "The existence of things is like a galloping horse. There is no movement through which they do not become modified, no time when they are not changed".[13] The similarities between Heraclitus and Chuang Tzu have often been noted. Also, qualified doctrines of flux comparable to that in Sāṃkhya may be found in Hui Shih and Kung Sung Lung.

The doctrine of momentariness (*kṣaṇavāda*) no doubt had its earliest beginning soon after the Buddha, and perhaps in his own teaching, so that there was argumentation between his followers and the Sāṃkhya school from a rather early date. Dasgupta notes:

> The Buddhists also believed in change, as much as Sāṃkhya did, but with them there was no background to the change; every change was thus absolutely a new one, and when it was past, the next moment the change was lost absolutely. There were only the passing *dharmas* or manifestations of forms and qualities, but there was no permanent underlying *dharma* or substance. Sāṃkhya also holds in the continual change of *dharmas*, but it also holds that these *dharmas* represent only the conditions of the permanent reals. The conditions and collocations of the reals change constantly, but the reals themselves are unchangeable."[14]

Heraclitus' greatness can by no means be lessened in the total perspective, but his uniqueness can no longer be maintained.

As examples of qualified flux, one could bring to the fore passages from the *Mahābhārata* or the Patañjali *Sūtras* or the Old Testament where often there is the sentiment that although the whole of the finite world is like grass, fading and failing, the Word of the Lord endures forever. The refuge in transcendence in this period is, therefore, not a matter of 'escape' but of a faith that there is, in spite of the flux, in spite of all change, a way that is changeless, to which, whether from God directly or through human ascetic discipline, man may and must become the heir. Whether the Chinese achieved this without the terrifying sense of guilt that plagued both Hebrew and Greek, and without the bondage to *karma* from which the Jaina, Buddhist, and Hindu struggled so hard to get deliverance, may be a good question for the student to investigate quite thoroughly and thoughtfully.

H. Causation

The real beginnings of philosophizing about causation can be found in Democritus, who was a contemporary of Mo Tzu. According to Democritus, it will be remembered, the atoms are combined and put into operation by *nous* (mind) in an almost mechanical way. The distinction of minor and major causes, and the various intergrades as well, can be easily read into if not directly derived out of the *I Ching*; and later Chinese philosophers, e.g., Hsün Tzu and the Neo-Mohists, did derive doctrines of causation from the *I Ching*. The chief point of departure in the *I Ching* and Greek theories of causation was in handling the polarities. As Democritus discerned them, agent and patient, like and unlike, *eros* and *eris* ('love' and 'hatred'), combine not so much in harmonious inter-reciprocation but in a more mechanical pattern of attraction and repulsion, whereas Chinese thought". . . developed their organic aspect, visualizing the universe as a hierarchy of parts and wholes suffused by a harmony of wills".[15] Also, the emphasis in China during this period was more on the cyclic and not the catenarian. One need not unravel a network in order to observe its structure and function: the knots may be almost infinite in number and one might not finish one's task; but if one simply proceeds according to Tao, one comprehends the total *gestalt* in all of its particularities without destroying it.

In the Indian context of this period, however, there is a third position in regard to the problem of change and/or causation. Instead of the emphasis on external forces or total harmony, the basic problem is that of internal relations. Is the cause inherent in the effect, or does the effect take the cause into itself so that it 'disappears' in the effect, or is there simply a complete transformation of cause into effect ? The difficulty later encountered in European medieval philosophy in regard to the *creatio ex nihilo* was already encountered by the Buddhists whose theory of causation is termed *asatkāryavāda* in contrast to the Sāṃkhyan theory of *satkāryavāda*. The latter simply means that the effect is really only a rearrangement of what has already (and, perforce, eternally) existed : the oil already exists in the seed, the statue in the stone, and curd in milk. The causal operation only manifests that which was formerly unmanifested.[16] The theory of *asatkāryavāda* denies this and insists that the effect does not pre-exist in the cause but is a completely new creation. There was also some argument about the immediate or indirect causal operation of *Īśvara*. To some, God only observes contemplatively what is caused and active; to others, He operates directly; to others, He does not exist in the strict sense but is only a symbolic function of Brahman.

I. Pramāṇas

It is extremely difficult in all schools to make a strict separation of epistemology and ontology. Ultimately, the identity or qualified identity of knowledge (*jñāna, gnosis, chih*) and Being (*sat, ousia, Tao*) will be traced out as the basic reality, although the modes of demonstrating this will vary considerably. Even at this early date the problem of the knower emerges as more important than the problem of the known for some of the schools; also, there is a growing tendency in some schools (Taoist, Mohist, Mīmāṁsā, Parmenides, Sophists) to recognize an identity or qualified identity of knower and known.

In the Indian schools the means of gaining knowledge are called *pramāṇas* and they are generally listed as six : *pratyakṣa* (perception), *anumāna* (inference), *śabda* (testimony, authority, revelation), *upamāna* (analogy), *arthāpatti* (implication), and *anupalabdhi* (nonperception). We append a table of these *pramāṇas* classified according to the means of gaining valid knowledge and of discerning invalid, erroneous, or fallacious knowledge'. Although it may readily be acknowledged that epistemology was developed to a greater degree in India earlier than elsewhere, still, we do not have a very clear picture of these developments chronologically. One must view this chart with the understanding that these *pramāṇas* were no doubt developments and have not been given an absolute date historically.

Inference and perception are the only *pramāṇas* discussed in early Greek philosophy. Empedocles made no distinction between seeing and thinking, between perception and thought. It is not until Parmenides that an explicit distinction is made between inference and perception. Heraclitus, Parmenides, and Anaxagoras not only distinguished inference and perception but gave the preference to inference where the two conflict. Most of the Pre-Socratics did believe that knowledge and certainty were possible, whether through inference, perception, or both. Protagoras, however, considered the only source of knowledge, perception, to give only relative knowledge —knowledge valid only for the perceiver and valid only at the time of the perceiving. The Sophists in general arrived at the conclusion that universal truth was unattainable. Democritus agrees that knowledge gained by perception is relative, but he insists with Plato that absolute knowledge can be attained through thought.

In China, only the Mohists discussed *pramāṇas* explicitly, but *śabda* (authority) and perception are assumed as valid means of knowing by most of the Chinese thinkers, especially the Confucianists. The Taoists, as exemplified in Chuang Tzu, did not, however, consider ordinary perception as conducive to profound knowledge but advocated a 'nonconceptual' perception :

> Ordinarily, we know things through concepts and names. When the concepts and names are applied to the things coming to our attention, we meet the things halfway. Here the mind is not purely receptive. The only remedy for such ordinary thinking is to transcend and withdraw our ordinary concepts and names and let the vacuity of mind be realized. Then the mind becomes purely

> receptive, and is willing to welcome things wholeheartedly, and all the things are thus transparent to us.[17]

Mo Tzu discusses *pramāṇas* when he considers the three tests for determining the validity of any theory. First, we must discern its origin and whether or not it is compatible with the views of the sage-kings of antiquity (*śabda*). Secondly, we must be able to verify it through perception (*pratyakṣa*). Thirdly, we must determine its utilitarian value : will it benefit the people and the state if put into practice ? This, of course, is not strictly a *pramāṇa* except that it does, according to Mo Tzu, allow us to distinguish truth from falsehood in the broadest sense. The Neo-Mohists dropped the criterion of utilitarian value and introduced inference as a *pramāṇa*. What the Neo-Mohists called inference, i.e., going from the known to the unknown and thus gaining knowledge of the unknown, is comparable to Mencius' concept of analogy and the Indian *upamāna*. Though "hearing" (*śabda*) is also a *pramāṇa*, the empiricist perspective that all knowledge ultimately depends on perception dominates.

In the old Testament there seems to be no 'problem' of knowledge. God tries to teach man wisdom and to give him understanding, but as a sinner, man is slow to learn. Again the moral and prophetic emphases drown out all epistemological speculation and the mythopoetic prevails.

Table of *Pramāṇas* (Means of valid Knowledge)

	pratyakṣa (sense perception)	anumāna (inference)	śabda (verbal testimony)	anupalabadhi (non-perception non-cognition)	upamāna analogy)	arthāpatti (implication)
1	2	3	4	5	6	7
Cārvāka	**	o	o	o	o	o
Jaina	*	*	*	+	+	(confuse, see Tatia
Śūnyavāda Mādhyamika)	*	*(+)	o	o	o	o
Yogācāra (Vijñānavāda)	*	+	o	o	o	o
Sautrāntika	*	+	o	o	o	o
Vaibhāṣika	*	+	o	o	o	o
Nyāya	*	**	*	o	*(+)	+
Vaiśeṣika	*	+	+	+	+	o

1	2	3	4	5	6	7
Sāṃkhya	*	*	*	o	o	o
Prabhākara	*	o	**	o	*	*
Kumārila Bhaṭṭa	*	*	**	*	*	**
Śaṅkara	*	o	*	+	+	+

Key: *—Yes, + — Qualified, O — No

*Tatia, Nathmal, *Studies in Jain Philosophy*, Banaras, Jain Cultural Research Society, 1951.

FOUR

Ethical Speculation : Man

It seems that in the Axial Age the basic standards were set and the ethical problems that still vex mankind as a whole were distinguished. We shall treat in this and the next chapter several themes which should give a fairly representative and at the same time comprehensive picture of the situation of the world of gods and men at this stage in the development of human civilization : a comparison of the concepts of *karma*, *moira*, and *ming*; the range of theories of the goodness or evil of human nature; the norm of the Golden Mean, with comparison and contrast between Greek, Confucian, and Buddhist sources; some further observations on self-knowledge and enlightenment; the beginnings and early development of the concept of law—divine, natural, and human; a consideration of the various treatments of the polarity of freedom and necessity. Of course, each of these topics is worthy of an entire volume in itself.

A. *The Concept of Fate*

Much misconception about the classical meaning of the term *karma* must be cleared away. Basically, it comes from a root which indicates "doing"; secondly, it connotes ritual observances; and thirdly, it designates merit, good and bad, accumulated by the individual soul both in the present and in past lives. As merit, it is usually subdivided into that which has been accumulated in the past and that which is being accumulated in the present. In the case of ordinary mortals, *karma* has the power to cause, automatically and inevitably, a future course of action and spiritual progress or regress. It controls the *vāsanās* or subconscious habituations into which the unliberated soul falls unawares; even the emancipated soul (*mukta*) learns to control these only with difficulty. In the case of the *mukta*, *karma* still remains but with no causal effect on the future course of life. *Karma* is basically individual, but it may readily be seen that social consequences follow from it, such as the caste system and the four *āśramas* : the *brahmacharya* or student, the *gṛhastha* or householder, the *vānaprastha* or 'retired' older person completing his social duties, and the *sannyāsa* or one who has renounced all worldly ties. *Karma* has a slightly different connotation in the Buddhistic systems, however, since it does not accrue to an individual soul.

In all schools *karma* is considered as beginningless, and in most schools the ethical systems are geared toward deliverance from its bondage. *Karma* is inherently linked with the almost ineradicable ignorance of man-in-the-world. The net result is that usually good conduct alone does not result in liberation; it is rather the lifting of the veil of ignorance; (*ajñāna*) that brings man into the realm of the absolutely Permanent (Hindu Schools) or absolutely Empty (Buddhist Schools) and constitutes salvation. In the theistic developments there is debate as to whether *Īśvara* (God) governs this law of merit and demerit and whether He can alleviate it even if He so wishes.

Though for the Hindu and the Jaina *karma* is rather strictly individual, for the Buddhist (Mahāyāna) Bodhisattva the vicarious level is opened up; he can absorb and eliminate the sorrows and sufferings of others by his contemplation. To a certain extent this is also true of the Hindu *jīvanmukta*. The true yogi can operate even from a distance in coming to the relief of a devotee and is obliged to set up patterns of determination in the devotee which will lead him automatically to emancipation.

It is admittedly true that to a certain extent the concept of *karma* leads to a rather fatalistic world-view. But by no means is this altogether true. Every soul is obliged to seek every means of attaining deliverance from the 'fatalism', whether he responds to this obligation or not.

For the Greeks, according to such authorities as William Chase Greene, the key to the whole ethical as well as political system was *moira* (fate). This is not to be found explicitly so much in the philosophers themselves as in the Greek literary tradition. It is linked with *ananke*, the necessity which governs all things (the adage is there that "even the gods bow to necessity") and which man struggles to overcome. If he goes too far, if he infringes upon the law (*nomos*) that governs his situation in the world, he suffers *nemesis* (retribution) for this *hybris* (pride). Icarus may not fly too high, and Prometheus is chained upon the rock in eternal punishment for stealing fire from the gods and giving it to men. Tragedy, then, is inevitable for the man who would rise above nature; but by tragedy he is purified (experiences *katharsis*), ennobled, and made wise. Virtue (*arete*) is cultivated as the exercise of nobility and right measure in the face of this struggle. Justice (*dike*), mythologically the right of the gods, is thereby brought into the operation of the human *polis*, the city-state, by the exercise of reason. Reason here is the operation of mind (*nous*), the autogenous principle governing all things. Thus, as in the other aspects of the Greek tradition, the triumph of inherent principle over the mythological gives man a large measure of freedom (*eleutheria*). But this comes only with a certain presupposition of conflict, so that nothing is gained without a considerable price.

For the Greeks as for the Hindus, but in sharp distinction from the Israelites, the shift from merely traditional morality to the quest for salvation and wisdom constituted a basis of philosophizing about man's possibilities of deliverance from bondage to nature and causation. But the Greeks tended to leave a certain hiatus between the metaphysical foundation of their ethics and their metaphysics of Being so that salvation *from* the 'world' was not the end, as it was with the Hindus, Buddhists, and Jainas, but rather freedom *in* the world. *Sophrosune* (wisdom) thus became the crowning virtue and moderation rather than ascetic discipline became the basic norm. Not that this was always adhered to; the Dionysian spirit still prevailed in spite of great clarity and excellence in art and philosophy. Above all, the Greeks remained devoted to form. The conceptless ground of *nirguṇa* Brahman and the ideal of *nirvāṇa*, which entails the total extinction of desire, remain at the antipodes of the Greek tradition.

In spite of the popular tendency to lump Chinese and Indian traditions together, in the ethical realm in particular we have many differences although essentially the same problems are discovered and designated. One generalization which might be risked, however, is that the Chinese tradition is basically ethical, and ethical in a mode that has nothing to do with the prophetic tradition of Israel, but ethical in a more or less humanist mode which still might leaven our twentieth century international scene even after almost 2,500 years. And yet this humanism is far removed from our Renaissance 'rationalistic' humanism in which, in a Pelagian way, as Toynbee points out, man has become the measure of all things. For Chinese humanism is grounded in the harmony of man with *ming*, the Decree of Heaven. This concept is pre-Confucian, appearing in the classical Odes where it is most closely allied with ShangTi, perhaps the closest Chinese correlate to the Judeo-Christian concept of God. Confucius considered himself to be merely interpreting and applying these classics and made no essential enlargement upon *ming*, always simply pointing out that if the ways of men were in accordance with *ming* things would prosper, and if not, they would fail and chaos would ensue. Mencius said of *ming* : "The Superior Man simply follows the law (of right) and then waits for his Fate (*ming*)".[18] Again : "That which is done without man's doing it, is from Heaven. That which happens without man's causing it to happen, is from Fate".[19]

The Mohist School, in opposition to the Confucian/Mencian Schools, strongly objected to the concept of fate.[20] The Taoist School, on the other hand, rather than expecting a harmonious relation, counselled complete and even quiescent submission to *ming* :

> All things, howsoever they flourish, return to their root. This return to their root is called quiescence (*ching*), which is called submission to Fate (*ming*). Submission to Fate is called the Invariable. To know this Invariable is called enlightenment.[21]

The Taoists were inclined to teach that government should be minimized so that *ming* and Tao could prevail most completely. Mencius, however, was a little more practical : "The Emperor can present a man to Heaven, but he cannot cause Heaven to give that man the empire".[22] Mo Tzu went even farther :

> Now those who hold that there is a Fate say : 'Whoever is rewarded by his superior was destined by Fate to be rewarded, and it is not because of his virtue that he is rewarded'. If this were the case, the people would not be filial . . . They would not observe propriety in conduct, moderation in going out and coming in, or decency between men and women.[23]

Hsün Tzu, however, prefers to remain focused on the concrete particulars at hand as a counterbalance to the excessive emphasis on supramundane forces :

> Instead of exalting Heaven and thinking about it, why not heap up wealth and use it advantageously? Instead of obeying Heaven and praising it, why not adapt Heaven's Fate (*T'ien Ming*) and make use of it? Instead of looking toward the propitious time and waiting for it, why not seize the opportunity and utilize it? Instead of relying on things to increase of themselves, why not put forth one's ability and develop them? . . . Thus if a person neglects what man can do and thinks about Heaven, he fails to understand the nature of things.[24]

According to Hsün Tzu, "It is only the Sage who does not seek to know Heaven"[25]; but Han Fei Tzu the Legalist found in *ming*, the basis for establishing and regulating everything according to law :

> There are the rules of action, propriety, righteousness and awe-inspiring majesty for securing the (Heavenly) Decree. Men of ability nourish these rules and so secure blessing, while those devoid of ability violate them and so bring on themselves calamity. Therefore superior men diligently attend to the rules of propriety (*li*), and men in an inferior position do their labor.[26]

In the Ten Commandments of Moses we find, quite similar to the concept of *karma*, the notion that God visits the sins of the fathers upon the succeeding generations. The Israelites seem to have been pastmasters of what Hegel rather aptly called the contrite consciousness. The sense of sin plagued them all through their exiles and returns from Egypt and Babylon, and of course the psalms of penitence are still very much with us, perhaps even more than the psalms of praise and exaltation. Whether or not this can be explained in naturalistic terms is not easy to judge. True enough, in the light of their persecutions they can scarcely be blamed for the recurrent motif of vengeance over enemies which the Lord is supposed to give in protection to His 'chosen people'; but the punishment and wrath of the Lord against them when they rebel or prove unfaithful is also there in a very unphilosophical mode. The Old Testament allows of little objectification indeed; one does not *rationalize* there but rather subjects oneself to total commitment.

It seems to be fairly universal in this period that most of humanity was in a struggle to achieve, under Divine Command, societal loyalty, although hardly with the completely universal perspective which was projected into the future. Family, tribe, and nation or city-state were still the basic units, although there were some suggestions of a future dawn of universal peace and brotherhood. But only gradually was this wider perspective realized as a possibility, and, of course, it still remains to be actualized. The fate or destiny of man under God (or 'Heaven') was variously conceived and realized; but it did tend toward something beyond the merely economic well-being of all and toward the achievement of a harmonious transcendence of nature. Shall we say that here was something of a universal 'revelation'?

B. *The Nature of Man*

Perhaps the most controversial issue of this period, as indeed throughout the history of most cultures, is that concerning the relative goodness or evil of human nature. Even though there is the Israelites' strange sense of superiority over the gentiles, there is little to indicate that the true Israelite ever asked whether man was good or evil. He asked instead whether or to what extent he himself and/or his nation had sinned against the Will of the Lord : "All our righteousness is like filthy rags before Thee, the All-holy, the Almighty, the all-terrible; yet art Thou merciful to those who fear Thee". Such is the basic motif, and one finds few variants indeed.

The typical Hindu finds this "wholly Thou" orientation difficult to understand. To him the self (*ātman*) above the ego transcends all possible thou's, even though in the popular cults of the *bhakti* (devotion) type—not so prominent, perhaps, in this period as in the medieval—devotional ardor sometimes rises to such a state of exhaustion that even threats of suicide are made to God if He does not reveal Himself to the devotee. To gain the *darśana* ('vision') of one's chosen deity, even though one knows this to be only a symbolic form, one will make any and every sacrifice. The asceticism that characterizes much of the tradition is thus motivated, and not, as is commonly thought, by the mere desire to 'escape' or by masochism or world denial. One does penance (*tapas*) not merely to mortify the flesh, but either to gain some special favor from God (although this is not considered the highest motive) or to purify the soul of all defilements and attachments to the extent that, rising above concern for both good and evil, unassailable spiritual stability and equanimity may be attained and the supernatural realm may become one's commonplace Impurity and ignorance are emphasized more than ordinary moral good and evil, although the latter are elementary pre-requisite fields of self-conquest. Man, then is always more or less good or evil according to his *saṃskāras* (dispositions) inherited from previous births. The innumerable prescriptions against further defilement must be followed throughout life until the mind and will are brought under complete control and one achieves liberation from all bondage to world, body, senses, intellect, ego, and passions.

As with the Hindus and probably with any view which includes reincarnation, man's 'nature' for the Jainas is dependent on past lives. Since *karma* is beginningless, there is no need for reference to a fallen Adam or original sin. For the Jainas, 'sin' is action which incurs bad *karma*, but there is nothing of the incurring the wrath of the Lord. Sin is simply what one *does*; it is not one's inherent sinfulness that is of importance. As the Jainas are atheists, they cannot sin against God, nor can they expect help from a Deity in attempting to overcome *karma*. The Jaina monk, by his own individual efforts, seeks enlightenment (omniscience) and the attainment of the ten *dharmas*: self-control (*saṃyama*), truthfulness (*sūnṛta*), purity (*śauca*), chastity (*brahma*), absolute want of greed (*akiñcanatā*), asceticism (*tapas*), patience (*kṣānti*), mildness (*mārdava*), sincerity (*ṛjutā*), emancipation (*mukti*).

It should be realized that, in general, for the Hindus, Jainas, Buddhists, and Taoists good and evil were considered as only one of the dualities to be transcended, and *ahaṃkāra* (egoity) was the last hurdle to be surmounted. There were some variations, although rather slight, as to how this was to be done; but the basic goal was always the same, and engagement in the attainment of that goal—the Unchanging Reality beyond all possible corruptibility—subordinates speculation about the inherent goodness or evil of man's nature. *Nirvāṇa* is a positive extinction of all craving, the solution to the problem of suffering by going beyond all possible dichotomies, and an establishment in the "peace that passeth understanding". However, virtue remains the *sine qua non* for even the most elementary realizations.

In the Chinese schools the relative goodness or evil of human nature constitutes almost the principle theme for argumentation. Confucius himself seems to have taken a middle position, holding a rather neutral opinion as to the inherent goodness of human nature (*hsing*). He saw human capacities more in terms of education than presupposed doctrines: "In their original natures (*hsing*) men closely resemble each other. In their acquired practices (*hsi*) they grow wide apart".[27] Though men may begin with similar natures, Confucius was not hesitant to acknowledge the differences between men at later times :

> There are some with whom one can associate in study, but who are not yet able to make common advance toward the Way (*Tao*). There are others with whom one can make common advance toward the Way, but who are not yet able to take with you a like firm stand; and there are others with whom one can take such a firm stand but with whom one cannot make emergency decisions.[28]

The emphasis is constantly on the cultivation of filial piety and the correlative virtues: respectfulness (*ching*), faithfulness (*chung*) refinement (*wen*), simplicity (*chih*), wisdom (*chih*). The cultivation of the rules of propriety (*li*) and the conduct of life according to human-heartedness (*jen*) cement these virtues into an integral whole that cannot be praised enough nor followed too assiduously:

> Be correct in righteousness without considering the profitableness (of the result of action); be pure in one's principles without considering whether they bring material return . . . The Superior Man is informed in what is right (*i*). The inferior man is informed in what is profitable (*li*).[29]

Mo Tzu even more pointedly believed in a certain neutrality of human nature, comparing it to raw silk which varies considerable according to the dye used on it. Perhaps more than Confucius, Mo Tzu stressed rewards and punishments in accordance with the Will of Heaven in moulding human nature. He is sometimes treated as an outright utilitarian although this may be exaggerated since his ideal of justice seems to have an almost theocratic justification. His was a "social gospel" long before modernist ecclesiastics began to wake up to the Marxist challenge, and he expected the Golden Rule to be applied quite universally:

> Whoever criticizes others must have something to put in the place of (what he criticizes)...Therefore Mo Tzu said: 'Partiality is to be replaced by universality ?' But how is partiality to be replaced by universality. I say that when everyone regards the states of others as he regards his own, who would attack the others' states ? Others should be regarded like self. . .[30]

Mencius had a great concern for the application of the virtues of *jen* (genuineness, human-heartedness), *chung* (conscientiousness to others), and *shu* (altruism toward society and not only toward the individual). Like Confucius, he suffered much from his attempts, both successful and unsuccessful, to reform the empire and unite the separated states. He taught (and practised) that this could not be done except by personal example, which, of course, is not possible without internal purification and rectification. Mencius seems to have discussed the issue of the goodness of human nature at greater length than most of the others. He taught that human nature is inherently good:

> All men have a mind which cannot bear (to see the sufferings) of others. . . .If today men suddenly see a child about to fall into a well, they will without exception experience a feeling of alarm and distress...
> From this case we may perceive that he who lacks the feeling of commiseration (*ts'e yin*) is not a man;. . . and that he who lacks a sense of right and wrong (*shih fei*) is not a man. The feeling of commiseration is the beginning of human-heartedness (*jen*). The feeling of shame and dislike is the beginning of righteousness (*i*). The feeling of modesty and yielding is the beginning of propriety (*li*). The sense of right and wrong is the beginning of wisdom (*chih*). Man has these four beginnings just as he has his four limbs.[31]

Kao Tzu, however, disagreed. Holding a middle position between Mencius and Hsūn Tzu, he said that original human nature is neutral and that later goodness or evil is the result of experience.

> The nature is like whirling water. Open a passage for it to the east, and it will flow to the east; open a passage for it to the west, and it will flow to the west. Man's nature makes no distinction between what is good and what is not good, just as the water makes no distinction between east and west.[32]

Mencius commits himself to what might be called an ethical naturalism, but he does not commit himself to anything like a modern superficial humanism. His metaphysics of human possibility is at least as great as that of Aristotle. In addition to the doctrine that man sometimes becomes evil simply by neglecting to develop his best faculties, Mencius insists that above the 'natural' faculties there is the *ta t'i* (the part of man which is great) which is the endowment of Heaven and which distinguishes man from the beasts. If this is cultivated with sufficient interiorization, a Superior Man will result.

Hsün Tzu argued in direct contradiction to Mencius. In plain language he said : "The nature (*hsing*) of man is evil ; his goodness is only acquired training (*wei*) . . ."[33] Nevertheless, every man may become good :

> Suppose this man on the street directs his capacities to learning, concentrating his mind on one object, thinking and studying and investigating thoroughly, adding daily to his knowledge and long retaining it. If he accumulates goodness and does not stop, he will reach to spiritual clairvoyance, and will form a trinity with Heaven and Earth. Thus the Sage is a man who has attained to that state by cumulative effort.[34]

This doctrine of becoming "a trinity with Heaven and Earth" resembles rather astonishingly what the Greek fathers of the Church will later include under the doctrine of *theosis* : in spite of the Fall, man, any man, through adequate identification with Christ the perfect God-man, can attain to a certain god-like condition. But more of that in its proper place, for it has strange roots and very far reaching implications indeed. In Hsün Tzu, however, it is not quite so advanced. Although man's capacities are virtually unlimited if his spiritualization is complete, his cultivation of humility and the similar Chinese virtues protect him from any Faustian ambition. Man, with his governmental systems, rules of proper conduct, and capacity for culture, simply follows the pattern of Heaven in making use of the natural resources of the earth. But this should be done according to *wu wei* (acting without acting), not with a will to conquest as is the case in too much modern technology. In classic proportions Hsün Tzu demarcates the three realms of philosophizing with a clarity and distinctness that is rare even in Greece. Indeed, to a certain extent it might be said that the Indian systems neglected earth, the Greek systems (at least until Plato) neglected 'Heaven', and the Semitic heritage neglected man, but the Chinese sages had to a remarkable degree a more nearly complete picture.

Han Fei Tzu even more than Hsün Tzu (who was his teacher) gives a sharp retort to those who would lump all of "Asiatic" or "Eastern" thought into a vague amorphous mysticism. A hard-headed legalist, he had not much more confidence in human nature than Hobbes, although he did not fall into the same trap of despondency and disgruntledness. He immediately sought for and supplied remedial measures with a system of rewards and punishments that was much more rigorous than that of Mo Tzu and perhaps as complete as those of the Platonic *Republic* and *Laws* or of Kauṭilya's *Arthaśāstra* :

> All ruling of the empire must be done by utilizing human nature. In human nature there are the feelings of like and dislike, and hence rewards and punishments may be employed. When rewards and punishments may be employed, interdicts and commands may be established, and the way of government is completed. The ruler holds on to these handles so as to rest in his power (*shih*), and hence his orders operate and his interdicts serve to prevent. These handles consist in the control over death and life ; power (*shih*) is the means of maintaining supremacy over the masses.[35]

Characteristically, and contrary to Confucius who wanted equal distribution of land, Han Fei Tzu advocated free competition. He did not believe in democratic 'equality' but recognized the obvious fact that men vary in degrees of excellence as well as in kinds of aptitude. He felt that any sort of nonregulated production for the common good would only lead to laziness.

> If we had to depend upon an arrow being perfectly straight of itself, there would be no arrows in a hundred generations. If we had to depend upon a piece of wood being perfectly round of itself, there would be no wheels in a thousand generations . . . How is it then that everyone in the world rides carriages and shoots birds? It is the result of applying the art of stretching and bending . . . Therefore the ruler who possesses methods of government, does not follow the good that happens by chance, but practices according to necessary principles.[36]

Taoist teachings on original human nature may remind one of the concepts of the "noble savage". Lao Tzu discusses the

Age of Perfect Virtue, a time very much like the Garden of Eden period in the Old Testament :

> . . . the world had been in a state of paradisiacal innocence and simplicity, under the guidance of the Tao, untroubled by any consideration of what was right and what was wrong, men passively allowing their nature to have its quiet development, and happy in that condition.[37]

Man's original nature is free from hostility and aggression, but men become competitive when society attempts to force them into its mold. In order to return to "the uncarved block" of their original nature (*p'u*), men must rid themselves of their unnatural desires for power and importance which society has inculcated in them. Man's original nature (microcosm) is a reflection of the nature of the universe (macrocosm). Thus man should take as a model for his actions the universe which spontaneously accomplishes everything without struggling and straining. Thus follows the doctrine of *wu wei* (accomplishment without effort). The equation between man and nature was common in the Axial Age, but the Taoists, instead of anthropomorphizing nature, naturalize man.

Since *wu wei* is completely natural, it has more power than that which goes into our reformations and counter-reformations. The Taoists were charged with being poor politicians, but at least they realized that much—far too much—of 'politics' is really unnecessary, for if all men lived in pure simplicity there would be no need of wrangling and dissention. The Taoist sage, in absolute freedom, indifferent even to life and death because he has already attained a measure of immortality, assumes a spiritual responsibility—even without being active—that is almost coterminous with the basic metaphysical roots of existence. He has transcended all contention about trivial 'right' and 'wrong' and therefore is able to direct man toward the highest good because his *teh* has become *Hsüan Teh*, the Mysterious Power that remains unseparated from the Beginning. It is out of this resource, and not merely out of a Kantian moral obligation as such, that he is able to treat all men as ends and not as means while remaining untrammelled by any dichotomizing of ends and means.

His identity is complete because his identification is unaggressively universal.

What then may we conclude from these various views? Is there a Single Principle even within the ethical sphere that we may fall back on? Or must we wait for Aristotle to try to answer this question? Perhaps the only safe answer is that there is no answer; the question is really not a question but an ever more widely opening quest. But at least we may conclude that during this period the quest was raised to the level of the employment of intelligence over superstition and the deliberate and conscious cultivation of virtue was universally advocated. It would seem that whatever human nature may be, it became clear what it *should* be or become.

C. The Mean

The first and almost universal way of realizing the ethical ideal was the doctrine of the Mean, a doctrine closely connected with the Golden Rule (which, it should be remembered, was not original with Jesus but had its roots in the Deuteronomic reform). However, in the Semitic code, the Mean seems not to have been so closely related to the exercise of moderation and the avoidance of extremes as in the Confucian, Buddhist, and Greek versions. The Chinese term is *chung*. To Confucius especially, and to Mencius after him supremely, this was the secret of all successful enterprises and efforts at reform and as such was almost synonymous with the virtue of *jen*. Thus Confucius said:

> When the 'basic stuff' (*chih*) exceeds training (*wen*), you have the rustic. When the training exceeds the 'basic stuff', you have the clerk. It is only when the 'basic stuff' and training are proportionately blended that you have the Superior Man.[38]

As linked with *jen*, Confucius said:

> When abroad, behave as if interviewing an honored guest; in directing the people, act as if officiating at a great sacrifice; do not do to others what you do not like yourself. Then neither in your state nor in private home will there be any resentment against you.[39]

It has been suggested that this, at least as interpreted by the Confucianists of the Ch'in and Han Dynasties, is almost identical with the Mean of Aristotle.[40] It seems to us that the Greeks in general and Aristotle in particular did not quite have the Tao of this ideal and applied it rather as a rational calculus to be used in any particular situation instead of seeing it as a matter of interior spiritual cultivation in a timeless context which encompasses all things.

The term *chung* is also found in the interpretive use of the hexagrams of the *I Ching* where it is the right balancing of the *yin* and *yang*. The metaphysical implications are rather far-reaching. There is no possible invariability as long as the universe continues, but it is possible for man to conduct himself harmoniously in accordance with the variations. Like the pendulum, everything that reaches one extreme must swing back to the other. The Appendix to the *I Ching* says:

> He who keeps danger in mind will rest safe in his seat; he who keeps ruin in mind will preserve his interests secure; he who sets the danger of disorder before him will maintain good order. Therefore the Superior Man, resting in safety, does not forget danger; resting in security, he does not forget disaster; and when having good government, does not forget disorder. Thus his person is kept safe and his country is preserved.[41]

The Chinese version of the Middle Way or the Mean is a rather direct expression of the oscillation and the inherent rhythm of the universe itself, and as such it is a dynamic mode that keeps a subtle balance between extremes that are never constant. Typically, there is no sharp division between the moral and the metaphysical aspects of this Middle Way; the harmony of man with nature as well as with Heaven includes all possible conflicts as only temporary tensions which will be rectified in due course. What effort is needed, therefore, is simply that of conforming to this Primordial Harmony, observing the seasons and the festivals and fasts with appropriate ceremonies, and adequately dedicating everything in human affairs toward the reflection of the Supreme Unity out of which and returning to which all things have their reasons and existence. Thus, humility is itself almost synonymous with the Mean. Beyond this man cannot easily discern any true possibility.

The Buddhist mode of the Middle Path also developed radical metaphysical implications. The Middle Way is not a calculus of right and wrong but rather the infinite inaccessibility of the theoretical 'center of the circle' from which all things and possibilities radiate. To what degree and in what manner the metaphysical implications of the Middle Way may be found in the doctrines of the Buddha himself is not easy to discern because there is yet a lot of higher criticism to be done on the vast canon (or canons, for the texts were variously fixed at different councils) of Buddhist literature to winnow out the authentic grain from the chaff of traditional accumulation; but at least we may safely point to the Noble Eight-Fold Path. According to Kashyap, this scheme of spiritual progress should be divided into three groups. The first two, right understanding and rightmindedness, constitute the basic beginning in wisdom (*prajñā*). The next three steps constitute the ethical discipline: right speech, right action, right livelihood. The final three steps are known as the mental discipline: right effort, right mindfulness, right-concentration.[42] The adjectives in each case indicate the avoidance of extremes as appropriate to proper tranquillity and desirelessness. Here there is no essential metaphysical commitment, for the Buddha himself seems to have been impatient with metaphysical speculation as a source of wrangling disputation. The nonclinging to any dogma is also characteristically central: the Middle Path simply avoids any and all possible commitments to what may in the end (and probably sooner than that, for it is vividly realized that all is changing constantly) prove to be nonpermanent.

This also applies to the moral and ascetic disciplines. The Buddha, after a pampered and over-protected youth, had gone through the full range of ascetic penances, including fasting until he could not even drag his bones to get water. Like Saint Benedict and Saint Ignatius Loyola, he could not ask his followers to go through the hells of mortifications he had been through. We may also think of Jesus and the distance that remained, in spite of his great spiritual generosity, between him and his disciples. The paradox always seems to be there that without the extremes, even though afterwards they were believed to have been relatively inadvisable, the Great Soul, the Avatar, would not have come forth. And yet it may well be that in, or rather through, his (their) own extremes he (they) discovered the valid Middle Path which all could follow, not as a matter of compromise with valid rigors of discipline, but as a spiritual shift from gross forms of mortification to more subtle forms that pierce the will more than the body and the intellect. The shift, especially with the Buddha, is away from violent efforts at control towards detached awareness of what is going on. Thus ignorance, the ignorance of sinking into subjective involvement, as well as the ignorance of fanatically forcing everything into foolproof schemes of objectivity, is more important than 'sin' against the habituated patterns of conscience.

The commentaries on the Noble Eight-Fold Path are endless, of course, and the student will do well to examine at least a few of them and to try to put them into practice. The Buddhist discipline, however, was given primarily as a rule of life for monks and only secondarily for laymen and for secular affairs. Like the Holy Rule of Saint Benedict, it was a guide for the conduct of a community as a reform over the old pattern of free-lance hermit existence. And yet by the application of these principles Aśoka instituted a reign of peace such as the world has seldom seen.

The original Chinese spirit seems to have been inherently moderate, whereas the original Hindu spirit—especially among the early Śaivas with all their gods and goddesses, both terrible and benign—seems to have reveled in the extremes or even to have stretched them further than any other cultural imagination. And yet the net advice seems to be rather universal. Humanity in this period underwent a spiritual shift toward a new level of civility which still in many quarters has not been equalled.

For the Buddhists and the Chinese, the strictly rational aspect of the Mean was subordinated to the deeper intuitive dynamic of all-inclusiveness. In the Greek version the *meden agan* (Middle Way) was not so much a counsel against ascetic and aesthetic extremes as a counter-balance to the urge towards transcendence and the almost unavoidable *hybris* that involves. Man remains a child of the gods in spite of his mischievous attempts at taking their place or ousting them from Olympus, and he must pay for this mischief. The application of the *meden agan* was as equally enjoined in relation to the passions of grief and anger as to the pursuit of pleasure, and the net result is the introduction of intelligence in the calculated control of all things. Although it preserves due proportion in actuality between the possible extremes, it is not a humble harmonization within the whole, but a situating of the soul in such a relation with all things that reason may prevail.

D. *Self-Knowledge and Enlightenment*

In Israel there is very little emphasis on either self-knowledge or enlightenment. Revelation takes its place and "know that I am the Lord your God" is about all we find. In Greece, the Delphic Oracle had given self-knowledge as the basic counsel long before Socrates. The *gnothi seauton* (know thyself) was closely associated with the *meden agan*, and its long history, as Wilkins has shown, can be traced through the literary as well as the philosophical tradition.[43] The *gnothi seauton* was considered a prerequisite to any virtue and a divine command, not in the sense of a " thou shalt" from a monotheistic transcendental Deity, but a sort of oracular upsurge from the hidden depths of the Greek psyche, dimly discerning the Unknown Infinity that guided and governed the paths of human destiny, but giving sufficient form to this Unknown to allow the individual some definite beginning and orientation in his combat with Chaos.

In Socrates it becomes somewhat more sophisticated : to know oneself involves knowledge of what knowledge as such is and must be, and thus it becomes the implicit goal of any dialectical enquiry. In order to know anything one must first know the knower. The Socratic 'ignorance', grounded though it was in wonder, was the humility of an enquirer, not that of a pious devotee, much less the humility of a disciplined ascetic committed to self-purgation by self-abnegation according to a Rule or through obedience to a guru. Self-knowledge, nevertheless, entails knowledge of the soul in the sense of an understanding of the nature of that which one is as distinct from the nature of what one has or does. But there seems to be nothing here yet like the intimate relation between self-knowledge and the knowledge of God which we shall find later in Saint Augustine or adumbrated loosely and vaguely in the Stoics.

This *gnothi seauton* lacks the supremely ethical implications that we find in the Confucian context. The *Ta Hsüeh* (one of the Confucian *Four Books* which constitute the basis of Chinese classical learning) insists on self-knowledge in the sense of that which is necessary for self-rectification before one can successfully go on to other reforms. As the *Ta Hsueh* says, "What sincerely is within will be manifested without."[44] In considering self-knowledge, the Confucianists understand the word "self" in the sense of "person". The Confucianist "self" is very much human and social. To know who you really are is to know where you really belong in the social realms: family, community, state, and even history. Unlike some Hindu Schools, Sāṃkhya and Vaiśeṣika for example, there was not the distinction in early Confucianism between mundane, temporary, and even false identity on the one hand and transcendental, permanent, and absolute identity on the other. According to Sāṃkhya, when the *puruṣa* (self, soul) is identified with mind, body, memory, social position and duties, this is a false identity. But for the Confucianists, to know oneself in terms of roles and categories is to know oneself in a real and important way.

According to the Confucianists, all men have a mind as part of their human nature.

> Once the mind decides that something is right or proper, it commands action in accordance with its judgment. So the mind both *evaluates* the requirements of a situation and *commands* proper action; these are its two primary functions.[45]

But the mind does not turn upon itself in order to discover some hidden transcendental self-nature of which the person is ignorant. Mencius posited the human 'heart' as a given in human nature. This may be considered as a certain benevolent potential in all men which, when developed, makes one human rather than merely animal. Mencius exemplifies the Confucian orientation toward self-cultivation rather than self-discovery. One develops his "humanity" (*jen*) rather than discovers his 'divinity' (*ātman*).

In short, the concept of a social person dominates over any concept of a cosmic-self. Cosmic-self concepts usually tend to entail abstraction and isolation, and the Confucianists were too much humanists, too much concerned with duties and "humanity", to become distracted into such nebulous queries. After all, what does *ātman* have to do with filial piety and insuring the (*mundane*) welfare of the people ? We express the same attitude toward identity and self-knowledge as these early Confucianists when we say of a person who oversteps his social position, "Who does he think he is anyway?, or when we ignore our social position and are told, "Remember who you *are*".

It might be said of the *Tao Teh Ching* that the 'problem' of self-knowledge does not even arise because it presupposes the cultivation of selflessness, even to the point of encouraging 'ignorance' in the sense of remaining in innocence and harmony. For the Taoists, the nearest equivalent to a concept of "self" would be the concept of *teh*. How does one come 'to know the *teh* ? The answer is two-fold: by naturalness (*wu wei*) and emptiness (*hsü*). In cultivating these two virtues one is virtually emulating the Tao, for these are the characteristics of the Tao. It may be said that here also one arrives at self-knowledge through self-cultivation, but this self-cultivation and the resulting self-knowledge are quite different from those of the Confucianists.

Teh is referred to as the link between man and Tao, the internal Tao, the life principle, the embodied principle, and as that which is found in "recovering *hsing*" (human nature). *Teh* definitely has an impersonal quality; it is more a principle than a "self". Is not the Vedantic *ātman* like this also? Rather than bliss (*ānanda*), the Taoist attains tranquillity (*ching*). Also, although the Taoist does not emphasize *māyā* or illusion, there is *avidyā* (ignorance) in the sense that one, once enlightened, ceases to make such judgments as good, bad, right, wrong. This is stated in the negative as "no knowledge" (*wu chih*), but in its positive aspect does it not resemble *jñāna* ('knowledge')? Taoist self-knowledge does not mean knowledge of the self as distinct from all other transformations of the Tao (contrast Sāṃkhya which advocates knowledge of *puruṣa* as distinct from all transformations of *prakṛti*); rather, the mind of the enlightened man is like a mirror which reflects whatever comes before it but does not cling to anything. And this 'reflection' is more like identity; in Chuang Tzu's story, there was not Chuang Tzu *and* the butterfly but only the butterfly which was Chuang Tzu.

According to the Taoists, the unenlightened man lives in an imperfect, non-tranquil condition, even an unnatural condition. In order to attain enlightenment one must seek, know, cultivate his *teh* which is the same as Tao. In Vedānta, one seeks the *ātman* which is the same as Brahman. One difference between *ātman* and *teh* is that *ātman* is totally transcendent while *teh* seems to have a large degree of immanence. Also, Tao and the world seem to be less distinct than Brahman and the world. For the Taoists, all things have their *teh*, not man only.

Nyāya-Vaiśeṣika, Sāṃkhya-Yoga, Mīmāṃsā-Vedānta, and Jainism all admit some concept of an eternal self (*ātman*) while Cārvāka and Buddhism do not admit the existence of "self" in any eternal or transcendental sense. Self-knowledge is knowledge of this eternal self as distinct from the changing individual personality with its ego (*ahaṃkāra*) and all of its impulses, drives, desires, and delusions. The general view of the *ātman*, which almost invariably has come to be the Vedāntic view of the *ātman*, is that it is the speculative *suppositum* (to use the Scholastic term) or Ground, the immortal and indestructible core of the human soul, although it is somewhat controversial whether it is in complete identity with the soul (*jīva*), or in qualified identity, or quite different. At least it may be identified as a *that by which* all else is known, but only in the context of the rigorous *neti neti* (not this, not that). As such its identity with Brahman also becomes somewhat problematic. The *ātman*-Brahman equation, however, is less disputed than the *jīva-ātman* equation (the transcendental soul and the embodied soul respectively). It follows that he who is a knower of *ātman* knows himself as a relative non-entity, but he also knows himself as basically and authentically that identity which remains after all of the superfluous surfaces are peeled off. The 'surfaces' are all the *karmas* and the false notions of permanence and relationality. *Ātman* is that to which all else is related, not the relations themselves. For in itself, *ātman* is relationless, qualityless, unqualifiable, unlimitable, infinite, the unembodied (even though it undergoes a quasi-embodiment the reason for which is again the subject of endless dispute). The relation of *ātman* to *Īśvara* is not always perfectly clear, although the consensus seems to be that *Īśvara* is more the symbolic form of the *ātman*-Brahman equation.

It should not be forgotten that the Vedāntic view of the *ātman* with its doctrines of bliss, consciousness, and mystical identity with Brahman was a view which developed from and in opposition to some other views. In all of the major Hindu Schools which posit the *ātman* (with the possible exception of Mīmāṁsā) self-knowledge is the cause of liberation. That self-knowledge may be achieved is the *raison detre* of all particular creations; however, before Vedānta the realist view dominates and thus 'matter' is not considered to 'disappear' upon the achievement of this self-knowledge. Thus in Sāṃkhya-Yoga and Nyāya-Vaiśeṣika we find a spirit-matter dualism which was taken to be eternal, a dualism which Vedānta later discarded by making Brahman the only reality and by positing *māyā* and *avidyā* as the causes of any apparent dualities.

In the Axial Age the Sāṃkhya-Yoga concept of *ātman* most resembles the later Vedāntic concept, but even here, and especially in Nyāya-Vaiśeṣika, there were major differences. Sāṃkhya and Vaiśeṣika teach that there are an innumerable number of *puruṣas* or *ātmans* and these are not identical with God. Indeed, they originally saw no need to posit the God-concept at all, and the God of Yoga is only a slightly superior *puruṣa* which can help the others when requested. For Vaiśeṣika the *ātman* is considered to be a substance without any essential attributes whatsoever; thus in a state of liberation, there is no bliss or consciousness—a view which Vedānta later 'corrected'. Mīmāṁsā, which may be considered the forerunner of Vedānta, also did not like this concept of a neutral liberation, though it admitted such a state to be an available option for those people who had had enough of ceaseless activity; however, instead of introducing the ideas of consciousness and bliss into this liberation, Mīmāṁsā simply preferred the cultivation of good *karma* in the state of embodiment.

In short, the central concept in most Hindu thought may be taken to be that of self-knowledge. The methods for attaining this self-knowledge—study under the guidance of a teacher, reflection on the study, and meditation—are more or less similar in all the schools, but the self which is to be known is variously conceived and the view of *ātman* was not by any means always the Vedāntic view.

We should note that Nyāya made considerable contributions to the logical explanation of the mode in which *ātman*, although itself of the nature of the knower, can still be an object of knowledge. Indeed the theory of negation developed out of this far exceeds Hegel's, whose relatively simple negation of negation leaves many loopholes of distinction between negation opposition, negation-absence, negation-non existence, etc. Also, Nyāya theories of classes and varieties of inferences and identities—all of them subsumed under the effort at knowing the knower—at least equal those of Aristotle.

Whereas in the Greek context self-knowledge is only a basic exercise in the proper conduct of life, in the Hindu it is almost a complete way of liberation. As Dasgupta says :

> Emancipation is the natural and only goal of man simply because it represents the true nature and essence of man. It is the realization of our own nature that is called emancipation. Since we are all already and always in our own true nature as such emancipated, the only thing necessary for us is to know that we are so. Self-knowledge is therefore the only desideratum which can wipe all false knowledge, all illusions of death and rebirth.[46]

The Buddhist Schools, especially the Hīnayāna sects of this earlier period, resolutely followed the Buddha himself in rejecting any *ātman* concept. As we have already observed, this is the basic and ineradicable distinction between Hinduism and Buddhism. There is no substantial self (*anātman*) to be known. This is the bedrock foundation of all things Buddhist. What, then, follows from this as far as 'self-knowledge' is concerned? The answer may be, in a word, meditation. Indeed, one may distinguish rather sharply between Buddhist meditation and Patañjali yoga, although much of the latter is more or less presupposed by the Buddhist meditation and almost all of it comes in later. Patañjali seeks to liberate the self from its fetters ; Buddhist meditation seeks to expand the psychic aptitude of the meditator until his spiritual influence becomes a benefit to mankind corporately. This, of course, is truer of the Mahāyāna than of Hīnayāna which remains more realistic and individual, but the basic distinction still applies to a great extent. The Buddhist is concerned with Becoming, the Hindu with Being. The Hindu is concerned with ways of knowing; the Buddhist simply cultivates recollectedness and Awareness until they become constant with equal tranquillity and detachment what is going on in himself, in others, and in the world, mindful that this, too, is non substantial, a process, a passing-away.

We cannot go into detail about the prescribed meditations and stages attainable by this method; the student so inclined may spend the rest of his life at this for the field is inexhaustible. It is sufficient here to mention some typical themes of meditation : the body, the Buddha, the Dharma, the saṅgha ; impermanence, suffering, non ego ; past, future, present (note the order for the future is even more illusory than the past ; the present 'moment' is always the focus for a well-recollected monk) ; the senses, the passions, the 'breaths'; and consciousness as such (so that detachment is gained not only from passing thoughts and the stream of consciousness but cognitiveness itself, this last coming close to a good definition of *nirvāṇa*.

Self-knowledge in some mode or other remains a necessity and we still have much to learn from the great sages of this era. But perhaps we should leave the question open as to whether there is a possible point of convergence of the varieties of self-knowledge or whether it may be necessary to make some leap out of the impasse of realizing that whatever 'I' encounter is related to 'me', that there is a process of ever-increasing encountering, and that no matter how much is encountered is still the Great Remainder. Above all, the question is still with us : By what is self-knowledge 'known' ? Is transcendence possible by some flight of lyric ecstasy or by some as yet undiscovered 'logic' whereby the veil of *māyā* may be lifted ? Is such a realization even possible for more than a few individuals ? Or is a new revelation needed, a message from on high, a prophecy of deliverance even from this ?

FIVE

Ethical Speculation : Law

The concept of law, conduct according to it, and the ordering of all things within human enterprises, are almost synonymous with civilization itself. Our very language suggests this, at least in the European heritage : "civilization" is a word derived from *civis*, the city-state. The city-state was the unit within which and for which legislation, the making of laws, began.

The development of the law (*nomos*) should be considered in relation to the development of the Word (*logos*). It is an open question whether or not the first shift of these terms from common parlance to terms of primary metaphysical weight had their almost exact parallels in the Hindu-Buddhist pair *Om* (*Aum*) and *karma*, which are very much misunderstood as being exotically mystical. *Om* is really a metaphysical expression of the fundamental undivided Unity behind all manifested reality (or embracing comprehensively all finite existence, depending on the interpretations of different Schools), and *karma* is its activation and/or operation, primarily in the human moral realm but also at the cosmogenetic level (for even the gods were conceived of as being subject to *karma*, and only at the end of the *kalpas* will all *karma* be exhausted and the finite world return to the infinite and differenceless). The Tao and its empowering *teh* (in the Taoist school) or *li* (in the Confucianist School) also parallel this shifting of terms from ordinary language to philosophical expressions of the basic Unity and its operation. The consideration of the relation between these word pairs is only one aspect of the attempts to answer the basic question for the whole world today of whether there is or is not a 'That Beyond the Rational' (*logos*, *Om*, Tao) of which the 'rational' (*nomos*, *karma*, *teh*, or *li*) is an instrument.

Nomos to the Greek mind is an expression of man's freedom *from* Nature, not his harmonious conformity to Nature (as in the Chinese tradition) nor transcendence over *māyā* (as in the

Hindu tradition). Much less is *nomos* the revealed command from the Almighty (*Torah*). *Nomos*, like Prometheus' gift of fire, is man's liberation, his declaration of independence from the bondage to tribal mores and mythological image-thinking. But there is still a tragic limitation set on this freedom, or rather, paradoxically (as perhaps the Greeks did not realize themselves or they might have been able to find the *wu wei* through the tragedy), *nomos* is also the expression of this limitation. Thus Plato constitutes his laws as the deliberate "second best", the maximum possible sheering off of the edges of *ananke* (necessity).

It is not without significance that the concept of *nomos* had its greatest development among the Sophists, to whom wisdom was a matter of man's self-assertion of centrality; man was the 'measure of all things', as Protagoras in particular epithetized his doctrine. Under this positivism, *logos* began to lose its metaphysical import and tended to take on the semantical weight of 'meaning' : *logon didonai* comes to mean "to give a rational account of" rather than "to search for the hidden metaphysical meaning of". Socrates, nevertheless, softens this somewhat by associating *nomos* with the inner *daemon*, and acknowledges again some sense in which *nomos* is associated with things divine as well as human. But it is no longer the primordially established law of the gods; rather, it is what man must do in order to please the 'god' within who demands that man must be consistent and establish nothing until it is thoroughly examined and proven to be true and good. Law, then, becomes the guardian of justice (*dike*), not so much as a guarantee of punishment from the gods as man's own deliberate codification of the principles whereby the *polis* may become a community of rational men living according to that which is divine within them, and whereby they are distinguished from the beasts. The significance of the Sophists and Socrates here is that nothing is to be held superstitiously sacrosanct; everything must come under rational investigation and be logically integrated into a nature that can be taught and established for man's own well-being.

The lawlessness of the Greek gods put them into disrepute; therefore, a higher concept of God as First Principle had to be developed by Plato and Aristotle. But this was the *result* of, not the *prelude* to, the manner of proceeding according to law. Thus Antiphon theorizes that the chief function of law is the restraint of nature so that desire may be overcome and corruption in society may be curbed.[47] The important thing here is not the concept of nature or the law made in opposition to it, but the fact that Antiphon has begun to theorize about it. In short, law for the Greeks is theory-making.

Some mention should be made of the Persian system of laws which, according to Dhalla, reflected the concept of the struggle between good and evil in which the ultimate good, the Divine Ahura Mazda, will eventually triumph.[48] The legal system of the Achaemenian period (558-350 B.C.) was extremely rigorous, and the punishments were quite severe. The power of the king was absolute, although he was bound to be right and just by divine obligation.

> Though the king was thus above all human law, he felt himself bound to recognize the higher or divine law of Ahura Mazda. However great and unequalled his status among mankind, the king was himself the minister of God upon earth to dispense his goodness to mankind, and was, therefore, in duty bound to carry out the behests of the heavenly king. We are informed that a chamberlain was ordered to approach his royal master every morning to remind him of the duty which God had imposed upon him.[49]

It will be remembered also that even in the Bible it is mentioned that the laws of the Medes and Persians do not change. However, this period was followed by a period of stagnation from 330 B.C. to A.D. 225, and the Hellenic influence almost wiped out the original Zoroastrian concepts in Persia, although, of course, those in turn had spread far and wide. The available evidence indicates that there was not much strictly philosophical development. The legal system was positive and strictly enforced, and the teachings of Zoroaster himself seem to have been perpetuated by a well-ensconced ecclesiastical hierarchy which emphasized ritual and astrology more than speculation. Here there is no fixed law nor legislation in the Greek sense but the absolute moral obligation of choice between good and evil. Man is in a completely subordinate position in the world, and the question of his relation to nature does not forcibly arise. But this much is vividly clear: the identification of Truth with the Good is quite complete. The question of the origin of Truth does not come to the fore; it is presupposed that it is of God, and man must conform accordingly or suffer the consequences.

In Israel there was much influence from this Zoroastrian source, although the concept of a covenant can be found in Egypt. It is perhaps not absolutely certain that here uniquely is a concept of law as a covenant (*berith*) with God, but certainly it is uppermost in most of the Old Testament in a manner that is difficult to find in other texts of the same period. Again the concept of reward and punishment figures prominently, but it is reward and punishment to be visited directly on the people by God Himself. It is not merely the automatic force of the operation of *karma* that we find in most Indian Schools nor the inevitable working of *moira* in relation to *hybris* such as we have in the Greek tradition. In the Israelites' view, man certainly is not free to *make* the legislation; nor is there anything like the Chinese concept of enforcing rewards and punishments merely *in accordance with* the Will of Heaven or to gain the blessing of Heaven, i.e., the impersonality of the Chinese concept of Heaven is actually more suggestive of the law of *karma* in many ways than of the Hebrew concept of Yahwe. The law is absolute, revealed through the prophets it is true, but *from* God who is Almighty and who will broach no compromise. Leviticus and Deuteronomy alike carry this perspective, and the prophets only remind the people of their infidelity. This is to be distinguished from the Greek view where man is equally open to delusion and skepticism as well as to the possibility of a positive establishment of his own position in the universe.

The concept of nature does not figure prominently, although there is the motif, 'Thou has given them (the stars and the seasons) (also) a law which shall not be broken'. The concept in the Old Testament of a God who enters history is probably over-stressed by apologists and theologians. Yahwe is the Lord of Hosts, the God of Battle, not of Good and Evil in the absolute sense but in the sense of promising victory to His people, a small minority, over *their* enemies. This is a rather smaller concept than the Zoroastrian, Chinese, or Hindu concepts. It is true that in the *Mahābhārata* Kṛṣṇa engages in battle in person as the Avatar of Viṣṇu in order to guarantee that *dharma* shall be restored, but at the same time he teaches that the Absolute Deity, the Undivided Brahman, is above partisanship and really wants all men to do their *sādhanā* (spiritual duty), which can include fighting. In other words, Kṛṣṇa is really no more on Arjuna's side than on the others' but is rather impersonally concerned for the *ultimate* welfare of the whole.

It is difficult for most of those who have been conditioned since childhood to get an objective perspective on this. Such a perspective does not entail a berating of either the high quality of the moral challenge in the Old Testament or the vision of man entering societally into an intimate relation with Deity. But it does mean that we must be cautious in cultivating the concept of the enemy, which is difficult to extricate from the concept of the Covenant.

We must turn primarily to China to find the concept of law as the agent which unites what otherwise remains diverse and at odds. The Greeks failed even in their little federations of city-states; the Israelites had enough difficulty preserving themselves as a minority; the Hindus under the Guptas and the earlier Dravidian states in the south enjoyed some measure of unification, and under Aśoka India enjoyed a reign of peace that remains unique, but his success was not a venture in legality. For this we turn to China. Han Fei Tzu says :

> The intelligent ruler bases his regulations on laws and standards, and therefore his multitude of ministers govern squarely and uprightly, without daring to be wicked. The people know that the ruler conducts affairs according to law, and so when the officials have law for what they enforce, the people obey them, and when they lack law, the people stop (obeying them). By means of law the people can check the officials, and superiors can conduct business together.[50]

There is really only one essential principle involved in Han

Fei Tzu's concept of law, but it is one of the most basic principles yet known to man—the conduct of affairs according to the natural tendencies of humanity, i.e., government based on a system of strict rewards and punishments in accordance with well-defined laws.

According to the Confucianists, however, the ruler must rectify himself; he must gain supremacy simply by gaining open recognition for his integrity. If his spiritual qualities are sufficient, society will be transformed ; if not, all systems are useless, for without the man, the person, no system will work. Law, then, is not divine command or the revolutionary effort on the part of man to assert his freedom from God or nature, but the instrument for promoting right order according to principles of virtue.

There is one other means of promoting this order which should still be extremely practical. That is the Rectification of Names.

> . . . when subjects have made great claims, while their actual accomplishment is small, they are punished. This is not punishment because of the smallness of the accomplishment, but because the accomplishment is not equal to its name. And when subjects have made small claims while the actual accomplishment is great, they are also punished. This is not because no pleasure is taken in the larger accomplishment, but because it is not in accord with the name given to it. The injury done is greater than if the larger accomplishment had not been performed, and therefore they are punished.[51]

If you talk of peace, do not prepare for war; if you legislate for social reform, do not befuddle the people with euphemisms; if you employ a clerk, do not give him the title of an executive; if you give out a message of goodwill, be prepared to conduct your affairs according to your promises; if you speak of equality, be prepared to break down racial, economic, and cultural barriers. Deceit, in other words, *malgré* Machiavelli and Kauṭilya, can have no place in sound polity. Again, the principle is devastatingly simple; there can be no sustained discrepancy between law and truth (as Gandhi knew from wide experience). The man or government that is purged of all untruth can disarm anyone or any nation (and now the whole world ?) who has not come up to that standard.

The concept of law of the Confucianists of the Ch'in and Han Dynasties includes the idea that *li* and *i* must be harmonized. The semantical weight of these two terms is greater than any possible translations in any European language. *Li* is, practically speaking, rights and regulations, ritual prescriptions, and rules of propriety; but its extension reaches far into the metaphysical concept of "principle" as such. *I* actually means justice, but if it is in accord with the *yin* and *yang* it is virtually identical with the Will of Heaven. Law, then, is the right accord of the 'vertical' with the 'horizontal'.

Among the Taoists there is not such a definitive conception of law in this positive sense, but there is considerable discussion concerning the relation of *shih* (power) and *teh*. There is always some danger in the exercise of power, but the Taoists seem to have concluded that power does not corrupt if it is exercised in accordance with the Tao. If those exercising the power have arrived at sufficient humility in accordance with the Will of Heaven—which they can do by a maximum of the practice of 'emptiness'—then the exercise of the whole gamut of legal functions can go on selflessly and with a minimum of effort. Simplicity again is the key to everything.

There is in the Taoists a more organic conception of the relation between human nature and cosmic nature than one finds in the Greek conception as well as a lack—for good or ill—of the positivistic note found in the Greek concept of law. Reversal is the way of the Tao; there is constant change from one extreme to another. But this way ('law') of Tao is not the absolutely binding concept we find in the Old Testament, for to know the law of reversal is to know one's own nature and attain a positive harmony with Tao rather than to gain facility within a scheme of rewards and punishments. In a sense, the Taoist becomes the/his law whereas the Israelite can only strive to obey a law imposed on him from above. The sage and the prophet, nevertheless, have this common denominator : they declare the necessity of self-purification on the part of ruler and ruled alike.

We shall turn now to the concept of *dharma* in Hindu,

Jaina, and Buddhist traditions, and then we shall try to come to some tentative comprehensive synthesis of what humanity achieved in this period concerning the topic law.

Although *dharma* sometimes has the meaning of a basic element in any compound, whether material, mental, or metaphysical, its discussion in Hindu writings as one of the four *puruṣārthas* (ends of human life) should first be considered in this context. In this sense it has been defined as ". . . duty based on physico-psychological development of the individual; mechanism of special interaction; principle of integration underlying different segments of social reality."[52] The pursuit of *dharma* (virtue) in this sense receives its classic (Hindu) exposition in Manu's *Dharma Śāstra* (c. 1000 B.C.) which explains the nature of *dharma* and the means of its attainment. Motwani has rightly reinterpreted Manu's work as a "science of social forces". According to Manu, there are different types of human beings, different levels of society, and different duties (*dharma*) according to the different periods of life. There are, therefore, different manifestations of Law governing these in cosmic harmony. *Dharma* in this sense is certainly closer to the Chinese *li* than to the Greek *nomos* or the Hebrew *mishpat*. Here too there is not the sharp separation of the divine, the natural, and the human, but a metaphysical dynamic universal uniting them. Practice and theory are not disjunctive, although such is often erroneously thought to be the case with Hinduism.

Parenthetically, Manu's influence spread throughout Southeast Asia—the 'Greater India'. It remains to be seen whether there may be a renaissance of these cultural roots, or whether other strange fruits must be transplanted into that rich soil in the quest for global unity. But no matter what the eventual outcome, there is in Manu at least the minimum of comprehensiveness necessary for integration into a World Order latent here no less than in Greece or Israel. Such traditions must be taken into account, for rectification of the World Order must be, as Northrup intimates, not so much according to a constitutional blueprint, but according to inherent tendencies already alive, even though they sleep. And, it must be noted, these tendencies have cosmic roots.

The various Indian philosophical schools differ considerably on the specific meaning of *dharma* and its importance. We can observe the following variations : (1) in the Upanisads, *dharma* is virtually the equivalent of essence—all that is latent in a thing, but especially in the transmigrating soul—*adharma* being the opposite, that which is expended. (2) In Sāmkhya, there is considerable discussion about the relation of *dharma* and the phenomenon of change, i.e., which causes which? Even atoms are thought to behave according to *dharma*; but is it *dharma* which causes them to change their combinations or do they change in spite of *dharma*, which tends to keep everything constant? (3) In Nyāya and Vaiśeṣika *dharma* (merit) is viewed as a quality of the soul. Its presence produces the knowledge which leads to salvation. It is not, however, the absence of *dharma* but the presence of *adharma* (demerit) which produces suffering. *Dharma* and *adharma*, according to this theory, are more properly distinguished by the respective *adṛṣṭa* produced by each. Whenever an effect is not directly or immediately produced by a cause, the existence of an *adrṣta* (unseen potency) is to be inferred. Many phenomena, including the combinations of atoms, were explained with the use of this concept by the Vaiśeṣikas. Acts of *adharma* produce an *adṛṣṭa* which brings about the union of soul and body and, therefore, the tendency to be reborn. Works of *dharma* (the performance of Vedic injunctions) produce an *adṛṣṭa* which has the opposite effect. The annihilation of the tendency to be reborn has as its natural result salvation or emancipation. *Adrṣta* is sometimes translated as destiny and spoken of as bringing about the cosmic order according to the *dharma* and *adharma* of sentient beings. At the time of *pralaya*, *Īśvara* 'turns off' the *adrṣta* and all atomic combination ceases. At the same time all existing atomic configurations disintegrate and a state of maximum entropy is reached. When this 'cosmic siesta' is over, *Īśv ra* turns on the *adṛṣṭa* again and the universe re-evolves. (4) Mīmāṁsā agrees with Vaiśeṣika that *dharma* is to be closely associated with the ritual prescriptions of the Vedas (the *arthavādas*, literally "straight paths", or ways leading to the spiritual end or goal). For according to Mīmāṁsā, only the Vedic sacrifices can produce the *apūrva* (force or potency produced by the hidden storehouse of personal and corporate spiritual merit held in latency—more or less consciously and deliberately—until the time of fruition) necessary for salvation. Thus for the Mīmāṁsakas, *dharma* is a 'something' which is acquired by following the injunctions of the Vedas. Mīmāṁsā seems to be most comparable to the Mosaic code as found in Leviticus.

Those who might claim that Hindu philosophy lacks ethics in the strict sense should take note. Instead of an ethics 'drowned' in an ontology, it may well be claimed that quite the contrary is true : the ontology is the direct outgrowth of the metaphysical roots of Hindu ethics.

Typical of the Jaina view is the *Tattvārthādhigama Sūtra* in which it is argued that *dharma* and *adharma* are eternal and imperceptible substances coterminous with and entirely pervading the mundane universe (as opposed to the supramundane universe, the abode of the liberated souls). Interestingly enough, in contrast to the Hindu Schools in which *dharma* is that which must be acquired in order to achieve liberation, *dharma* is listed by the Jainas as one of the elements which must be purged from the soul (in an astonishingly 'scientific' program the stages of which are marked out with remarkable precision) before *mokṣa* is reached. *Dharma*, according to this view, is the 'passive' cause of motion and *adharma* is the 'passive' cause of rest, i.e., that without which motion and rest are impossible but which alone cannot cause them. The basic analogy here is that of water which, though it does not cause a fish to move, is necessary for the fish's motion. The lack of *dharma* in the supramundane world is the cause of the perfect rest attained by liberated souls, for as long as there is *dharma* souls must 'move'. Final liberation entails an acosmic condition in which there is no movement, neither of the mind nor of the soul.

As Conze remarks, what we call Buddhism the Buddhists call the *Dharma*.[53] As such, the term *dharma* (Pāli, *dhamma*), especially in the Pāli canon, is almost synonymous with the teachings of the Buddha—the Noble Eight-Fold Path, the Four Noble Truths, the *pratītyasamutpāda* (scheme of dependent origination)—and these, of course, are almost purely moral.

The heart of Buddhist teachings is always the solution of the problem of suffering, and central here is the teaching in which the Buddha in his first sermon at Sarnath set the *Dharma-cakra* (the Wheel of Righteousness) in motion for all time to come, opening the way to *nirvāṇa* (Pāli, *nibbāna*) for all men. *Dharma*, then, is more the way or the path (Greek, *hodos*) than the law (Greek, *nomos*), and again the stages are quite well-defined.

The Dharma is one of the four major fields for meditation, along with the body, the Buddha, and the *saṅgha* (the Buddhist priesthood). As such it would be foolish merely to try to come to an academic definition of it, for the *Dharma* must be learned by precept and interior discipline as well as, or even before, being put into practice. This discipline, so exhaustively discussed in the *Vinaya-Piṭaka*, was basically for the monks, but, not unlike Saint Thomas Aquinas' interpretation of the Evangelical Councils, it applies in essentials—though not necessarily in all details—to the laity also.

In addition to its use as 'Law' of 'Teaching', *dharma* is used by the Buddhists in a more technical sense. *Dharmas* are the ultimately real constituents of reality and form the conceptual basis of attempts to explain reality without reference to a 'self' or to 'substance'. A description of a thing in terms of these momentary, impersonal, nonsubstantial elements (*dharmas*) is much closer to reality than a description in ordinary terms. Apparent units such as persons are actually conglomerates of *dharmas* and meditation on this fact is recommended as quite conducive to ridding oneself of all attachments to such conglomerations.

Although Hīnayāna Buddhism is a philosophy of Becoming and not of Being, and therefore primarily moral and not metaphysical, it is through a process of total transformation through such meditation, and not simply by observing rules of ethical behavior, that the realm of *dharma* is passed through and liberation is achieved. Its majestic simplicity recommends it to all. Above all, it is not a way of conflict such as has been inherited from both Greek and Hebrew sources. It is a vision of humanity totally free from the ancient bonds of selfishness, narrowness, and all the other hindrances to Peace. And is that not the implicit end of all Law ? And does it not always begin from within ? If there be but one soul in the world who completely measures up to these requirements, the whole world is benefited. In society, legislation can only give negative safeguards; already Saint Paul's "be ye transformed by the renewing of your minds" is anticipated. Law should be like music : for one composer there may be a thousand performers; but the spirit of composer and performer must be the same, and that spirit is the divine within, essentially one though manifesting itself in untold variations. Anything else is falsely done.

It is indeed strange that humanity seems to have progressed so little since this period. But perhaps 'progress' is the wrong criterion. As we see in Plato, the Good is eternal, and perhaps eternally the need is only for an awakening. In this period man became aware of the necessity of codifying patterns of conduct beyond the merely political sphere. Some sort of universalization was the great burden, whether it was found in the transcendent Yahwe and mediated by the prophets, or in the harmony of Nature and Heaven and Man, or in the attempt at completely freeing Man from both of these roots, as in the Greek developments. What is the universal to these divergences ? Surely it is the common aim of attaining peace. And again the challenge is still with us.

A. *Freedom, Necessity, Salvation*

Ananke (necessity) for the Greeks was closely allied with *moira* (fate), and man's tragic unwillingness to accede to necessity leaves him in constant tension. *Eleutheria* (freedom) was the desideratum, nevertheless, and the striving for it must be unceasing. Within the global context one is led to ask, were the Greeks not striving for freedom from the wrong thing? Were they striving for freedom for themselves, with all the *hybris* that that involves, and for unhindered investigation of everything without clearly realizing what it was that was thus to be freed or freed from what ? In the Chinese context the problem of freedom does not arise with the same urgency because a basic harmony is presupposed even though the operations of *ming* (often best translated as destiny), and the only effort needed is that necessary in attempting to resolve the discords that enter that harmony as a result of the variations of the *yin* and *yang*. In both the Greek and Chinese (especially Confucian) contexts, freedom from the bonds of animality and freedom for culture and civilization are of the highest value.

To the Hebrews, however, only Yahwe could be free, and freedom could come to man only when He willed. Only His mercy would bring the final deliverance. As for the concept of salvation, even the Israelites did not quite have it yet. The Christian concept is allegorized 'over' the Israelites' deliverances from their enemies in battles and their 'deliverance' (not salvation, for their only plea to God was for mercy and forgiveness; they could not conceive of the possibility of escape from their lot in this world or their meted reward or punishment in the hereafter, concerning which they had only a very vague idea) from bondage in Egypt or from the Babylonian captivity.

It is true that in Greece Pythagoras did have a purgative way (*hodos*) which entailed a withdrawal from the world into intentional community, but even he did not dare to dream of any deliverance from the lot assigned to man (or to the gods either) by the inevitable *ananke*. Protagoras, although he insisted on a certain *ascesis* (spiritual discipline), had no thought of surmounting the *nomos* that governed man's position in the universe. Gorgias, adept though he was at teaching cleverness through which a man—any man if he is only properly taught—could learn to conduct himself *as if* he were free, would have qualified his teaching as dealing only with surfaces, only further involving his pupils in *māyā*. Much less would he have conceived his eristical and stylistic devices as having any effect in cutting the Gordian knot with the *gnosis* whereby the soul itself, and not the mind only, could be delivered from the ignorance that separates Being from non-Being. The radical individualism of the Greeks betrayed itself : one could improve his excellence in the *polis* and even outwit his opponent in the courts of law; one could declare his freedom if he were willing to risk ostracism and the wrath of the gods in whom one might still have a secret safety-first qualified belief but concerning whom one could also be completely indifferent for they did not conduct themselves in accordance with reason.

But sooner or later drama drowns him like a flood even when he builds his ships according to the best of craftsmanship. The very' nature which he believed to establish him in his clarity and brilliance sooner or later devoured him in her greater obscurity. The *mythos* prevailed. The *ethos* proved to be only a fragile construction. Tragedy crowned his most valiant assertions of victory. At best, tragedy could give *katharsis* but not salvation.

Among the Chinese sages the ideal of salvation was also relatively foreign, for their concern was rather with rectification and proper adjustment of the relations of individual and society. Mencius in particular stressed the cultivation of liberty in the individual, allowing that if the customs were not right the individual had the right not to follow them but to improve them by setting an example of the better pattern. Herein he differed somewhat from Confucius who stressed the proper moulding of the individual in conformity to custom. As for necessity, there was nothing like the inexorability of the Greek *ananke*, for the Will of Heaven could be appeased by proper rites and ceremonies and was always expected to reward true virtue. The sage sought only the blessing of Heaven on his efforts at reform, and he was unconstrained by any limitation if he gained that blessing. Indeed, in the Taoist School it was conceivably quite possible for the sage to attain absolute freedom. The perfect man, having become spirit-like (*shen*), had a psychic range of operation coterminous with the universe itself, and he need depend on nothing other than his own cultivation of the Tao.

The Chinese stabilized an empire that still endures; because of a lack of voluntary subordination, the Greeks burned themselves out in internecine strife and rivalry. Alas, indeed, that the city-states of Greece had no Confucius to unite. them and fuse them merely by the exercise of virtue into an enduring empire. But somehow it was not to be. The Greeks paid a very high price for liberty.

In the Hindu context it is difficult to say that there was any strict concept of necessity. The nearest to this is found in the inevitable working of the law of *karma*. One simply reaps what one has sown, and that is that. In all schools there was general agreement that salvation involves a hierachical progression from sense experience and pleasure of the merely human sort to the completely transcendent and attributeless. Nyāya tried to work out in detail the extent to which and manner in which one level in the hierarchy was dependent on or inherent in the others, but the order was conceived as unalterable and fixed. Freedom, therefore, in almost all schools was taken as a matter of deliverance from bondage to the lower levels. But from whence comes the freedom to undertake the quest for enlightement (*mokṣa sādhanā nivṛtti mārga*)? The answer seems generally to be that it is simply presupposed, or that it is a part of the original 'necessity', the beginningless *karma*, governing the whole pattern. In spite of the popular notion that all 'oriental' philosophy is fatalistic, only one philosopher, Madhva, who comes in a later period, argued for predestination.

The chief point of disagreement between the different schools as far as our present context is concerned was over the nature of *mokṣa* (liberation) itself. All agreed that it entails deliverance from the bonds of *karma*, but there was considerable argument as to the 'positive' versus the 'negative' condition of this liberation, i.e., whether it entails only the removal of hindrances, or complete cessation, or complete transposition to a different condition including such qualities as pure consciousness, omniscience, and bliss. There was also the question of the liberated soul's relation to, or even identification with, 'reality'. Early Mīmāṁsakas questioned the very desirability of liberation since, to their understanding, it entails total cessation. The Jainas, and to a great extent Patañjali, associated *mokṣa* with *kaivalya*, supreme 'isolation', a severance from all connections with things of this world including the senses and lower empirical functions of the mind, carrying with it some degree of, if not actual, omniscience.

In spite of the variations, it is safe to generalize that the Hindu doctrine of freedom is not to be confused with the superficial notion that freedom is simply the liberty to do as one pleases (although the *jīvanmukta* may have this privilege to a certain extent, for he has risen above all possible evil); freedom at the minimum is instead the deliverance from all things that bind the soul. There are spiritual states which most modern psychologists still doubt because they do not have an adequate method of entering into them—at least not yet. But they are still available to one who searches far enough for a guru, although they can be dangerous to anyone who experiments without a guru. This is especially true of attempts to reach the *jīvanmukti* state—liberation while the body still lingers, a certain enjoyment of immortality while still in this world—which Patañjali yoga is designed to make possible.

In the Buddhist tradition as distinct from the Hindu—and we must never confuse the two as some neo-orthodox Hindus are trying to do—there is not just a suffering of the consequences of the law of causation (*pratītyasamutpāda*) or a cancelling of the consequences of the law by adequate *tapas* (ascetic discipline), but a *stopping* of the operation of this law and the beginnings of a new *dharma* to replace it. Concerning the nature of *nirvāṇa* (Pāli, *nibbāna*) we offer the definition from the glossary of Morgan's book though it is weighted with Mahāyāna terms:

> ...the cessation of selfish desires (or of ignorance) which leaves a man free from the bonds of this life of suffering; freedom from the delusions of ego; Enlightenment; the state of him who is worthy; freedom from all suffering and sorrow; the state of an Arhat after his passing away, a state which is indescribable but is by no means annihilation. The spontaneous attainment of the pure and peaceful realm of mind;...[54]

Unambiguous definitions of *nibbāna* have been as difficult to arrive at for the Buddhists as unambiguous definitions of the Tao have been for the Taoists. Even in the earliest Buddhist writings a variety of descriptions of *nibbāna* can be found. One of the traditional differences between Mahāyāna and Hīnayāna is that the latter stresses the 'cessation' aspect of *nibbāna* while the former speaks of *nibbāna* as a state of bliss. But the Hīnayāna view has tended to become more 'positive, historically, so that a modern Theravādin, Maha Thera U Thittila, points out that in the *Piṭakas* ("baskets" of doctrine) "...we find many positive definitions of *nibbāna*, such as Highest Refuge, Safety,

Unique, Absolute Purity, Supramundane, Security, Emancipation, Peace, and the like . . ."[55] However, the negative tone of original Hīnayāna's concept of *nibbāna* is conveyed in their metaphor which says that the attainment of *nibbāna* is analogous to the extinction of a candle flame.

The societal implications of attempts to attain *nibbāna* should not be difficult to discern in spite of many popular criticisms that Hinduism and Buddhism, at least the Hīnayāna schools, have been too individualistic. The path is equally applicable to whole societies as well as to individuals, for if craving and ego are uprooted, how can there be any hindrances to good order in society ? The superficial notion that the uprooting of craving and ego leaves no motivation for action can easily be countered by arguments that: (1) one must always question the necessity and value of 'action' anyway since it is too often associated with aggressiveness; (2) right action—egoless remedial measures of a definitely positive nature—is always possible as the alternative to "fighting evil", which always invites counter-attack. *Nibbāna* lies beyond the dualism of 'tough' and 'tender'. Another reply which should be fairly obvious is that if one individual truly attains the goal, his society will be purified by his vicarious identification with the world, both in time and in hodological spread.

There is some vagueness about the sense in which *nibbāna* refers to a state attained while still in the body on this earth. The attainment is normally accompanied by supernormal powers—miraculous healing, levitation, telepathic aptitude, ability to be in more than one place at a time, etc.—but according to the repeated advice of all the best texts these are stringently to be avoided. But it is primarily understood that *nibbāna* is attained after the final departure from the body in a holy death.

Whereas the Mahāyānists strongly emphasized the altruistic aspect of meditation, it is debatable whether the Theravādins considered meditation which benefits more than the individual to be necessary in order to attain *nibbāna*. It is possible to find such passages as the following in Hīnayāna literature, however : the monk". . . dwells having suffused the whole world everywhere, in every way, with a mind of friendliness that is far-reaching, wide-spread, immeasurable, without enmity, without malevolence."[56] And compassion is one of the stages in the monk's progress toward *nibbāna* :

(1) Aloofness from sense impressions and pleasures, but a joyful and rapturous aloofness, not detached from discursive thought,
(2) Detachment from discursive thought,
(3) Realization of impermanence, even of the meditation,
(4) Joy and anguish left behind,
(5) Cultivation of friendliness for the whole world,
(6) Compassion,
(7) Transcendence of material shapes,
(8) Infinite consciousness entered,
(9) From infinite consciousness to 'no thing' [57]

The Buddhist doctrines of necessity and freedom and of deliverance can scarcely be called an 'opiate' even from a Marxist point of view. The Buddhist has left the Marxist behind at the third level. It is difficult indeed to account for the beginnings of such a doctrine and practice by any materialist dialectic.

In all traditions the Golden Rule was formulated in some form or other, although it may be conditionally admitted that the Hindu Schools did not emphasize it so strenuously, but for a reason much misunderstood. An altruistic ethics is really presupposed as a prerequisite for the higher spiritual attainments.

Perhaps the greatest ethical contribution to this era and, for that matter, to the world for much time to come—he was criticized even by his contemporaries for being too advanced in the matter—was Mo Tzu's doctrine of universal love. Rather puritanical (he discouraged even music and wanted a radical reduction of expensive ceremonies), like Gandhi he lived in radical simplicity and expected the people and the government to follow suit. Although he is generally regarded by modern interpreters as a utilitarian, perhaps he was more than that. He merely wanted to deliver the world from the calamities due to the lack of altruism and insisted that the means should be harmonious with the end. We close this section on ethics with the following passage from Mo Tzu :

> Whoever criticizes others must have something to put in place of (what he criticizes) . . . Therefore Mo Tzu said: 'Partiality is to be replaced by universality.' But how is partiality to be replaced by universality ? I say that when everyone regards the states of others as he regards his own, who would attack the others' states ? Others would be regarded like self . . . When we come to consider the origins of the various benefits, how have they arisen ? Have they arisen out of hate of others and injuring others ? We must say not so. We should say that they have arisen out of love of others. If we should classify all those who love others and benefit others, should we find them to be partial or universal? We must say that they are universal. Now since universality is really the cause of the major benefits of the world, therefore Mo Tzu proclaims universality to be right.[58]

It is true that Mo Tzu was not successful in putting his doctrines into effect throughout the Chinese empire, and his influence died out before many centuries. But this does not compromise the quality of his ideas; the balance of the blame is rather on the empire than on him. And so with history generally—if indeed we may speak of blame or 'ought to' in strict historical terms. Had Thucydides, for example, known of Mo Tzu, he would no doubt have been not only curious but almost envious and would have used him as a foil for still further rebuke to the Greeks who destroyed themselves by lack of the universality that Mo Tzu taught. In the record of history, even the history of ideas and ideals, it is perhaps wrong to moralize; but there is scarcely any valid reason for reinvestigating history except in the search for an adequate basis for an ethics in one's own era.

Perhaps in the near future the social scientists will give us more adequate means of carrying out these ancient—perhaps eternal ? that is the question—ideals, but it remains patent that they were as clearly enunciated in the first five centuries B.C. as in any period since then: peace, altruism, humility, and the proper use of power; harmony with nature; submission to and/or rising up to cope with destiny; obedience to and/or entrance into the 'Will' of the One God. The list could easily be expanded and one might prefer to make the list in the reverse order; but ultimately, according to the insights—or shall we call them revelations ?—already available in this period, the order of exposition does not matter so long as one sees the items as manifestations or embracings of one Tao, Brahman, *Dharma*, *Shekinah*, *logos*—in short, one Mystery.

SIX

Deity

The accounts of the prophets, sages, and *avatars*, not to mention the philosophers who try to make sense out of them even in this period, all bespeak, as one inadequate concept of Deity falls before and is replaced by another, of Something that is impinging upon man from beyond himself—a Something, to put it minimally, that is more than Nature or any force of Nature, challenging both heart and head to seek that which is not subject to death.

True enough, there were already in this period systematic skeptics and open atheists, e.g., the atomists of Greece, the Cārvākas of India, the author of the book of Ecclesiastes. Then too, Mahāvīra, Gautama the Buddha, and Confucius are by no means strict theists. But with only a few exceptions there is still the attempt to put into rational formulations problems concerning man's origin, destiny, and latent possibilities in terms of the universe and its origin and sustenance, and/or at least in terms of the meaning behind the fact of force and counter-force in all observable phenomena and moral involvement.

Every student—and, in spite of all notions of progress, we are still largely students of these classics—must come to his own conclusion; and out of the 'conclusions' there may yet come a more comprehensive vision, for certainly nothing less than vision is necessary. But even after that, as a Socrates will remind us, we shall have much to do if we are going to develop a comprehensive explication. For this we shall turn to Plato and Aristotle, but for the present we shall note humanity's struggle to emerge from its childhood to the point of breaking with ancestral ties. In some cases this was an evolution, in others, an evocation, response, or revolution.

In considering the pluralist conceptions of deity we do not necessarily mean frank polytheism nor the non-theological theory of a plurality of basic factors governing all things, but rather the introduction of varying degrees of mediating spirits, demons, angels, or subordinate deities. Thus, in the Zoroastrian tradition, whether according to Zoroaster's own revelation or as the result of a gradual return to the polytheism which prevailed before his reform, we have the *Yazatas*, the Angels, which, according to Williams Jackson, number into the hundreds and thousands.[59] They are subdivided into spiritual and material, and Fire, Water, Sun, Moon, *Sraosha* (Obedience), *Rashnu* (Justice), *Verethraghna* (Victory), Heaven and Earth are the chief. But there are also the *Amesha Spenta*, which are almost hypostases (in the sense of later Christian theology) or at least emanations or existentialized Attributes of Ahura Mazda. These are six in number and they are usually arranged according to the points of the Star of David, the double triangle, which, incidentally, also figures prominently in Hindu symbology.

The emphasis on the dualism of the Zoroastrians has been much exaggerated. The Parsi apologists stress much more the monotheism, which is really of a very high order. It is true that Zoroaster and his followers conceived the role of human existence as one of struggle between right and wrong, light and darkness, ignorance and knowledge, but this is by no means final and does not extend into the nature of the Deity. The concept of "satan" probably had its beginnings either in Mesopotamia or in Persia, but he is not admitted to be a 'negative deity' so much as a sort of unexplainable antipodes to the Ultimate Good over which God will eventually triumph completely. As Dhalla says :

> The Prophet (Zarathustra) proclaimed one supreme God whom man could address with the warmth of his heart as person to person, or as friend to friend. Ahura Mazda is the name of this incomparable and matchless being.
>
> Ahura Mazda has destined man to the high honor of being his co-worker for the furtherance of goodness, and his fellow-soldier in the war against the forces of evil. Humanity is in arms for the cause of goodness. This warfare is as old as man, and will go on uninterruptedly until, at last, mankind will inflict a crushing defeat upon the forces of evil, and bind the Sovereign of Evil

himself to impotence. Truth will ultimately gain over falsehood, goodness will be all-pervading, and evil will vanish.[60]

In Israel we do not, except in the later prophets, have such a pure monotheism as is generally supposed. Whether from Zoroastrian or other influences, there are mediating angels, although they do not have such an immediately intimate role with the Deity as in the Zoroastrian scheme. There is also the concept of the *Elohim*, which, according to Voegelin, ". . . were not false gods, nor no-gods, but were believed to be real gods, even though of minor status", although in many cases these were only the spirits of dead humans. Voegelin feels too that if Genesis 3 : 22—24 is rightly translated, Yahwe Himself is to be taken as a sort of super-*Elohim*, jealous lest man should become like Him or, literally, "one of us" [61] In later Hebrew (especially Hassid) tradition, the *Elohim* were conceived of as illuminating presences like the cherubim and seraphim surrounding the Person of the Most High, and were closely related to His *ruach*, His Presence, and to the *Shekinah*, His protecting presence over His people. Thus we have a strange anomaly : although Yahwe is taken as the God revealed by Moses and the prophets, high and exalted so that no man is worthy even of naming Him, He is, from the strictly objective historical standpoint (as Deussen best shows), really a henotheistic deity who does not deny the existence of rivalling *false* gods but triumphs over them and demands more rigorous standards of ethical and cultic practice. Thus, although it is relatively weak, and in the later prophets almost completely disappears, the pluralistic element is by no means lacking in the Old Testament conception.

In the Chinese tradition there is also considerable variation. In addition to Ta T'ien and/or Shang Ti there are the 'spirits' (*shen*), variously interpreted as related to, independent of, or controlled by Shang Ti. Confucius did not disbelieve in them, although he would not have the people become addicted to their cultivation or appeasement. Hsün Tzu virtually discredited them altogether. The other philosophers ranged variously between these extremes. The interpreters of the *I Ching* seem to have preferred the concept of a dynamic, variable range of spirituality emanating from and returning to the Tao.

According to Fung we may distinguish five basic meanings of *T'ien*, usually translated as "Heaven".

(1) A material or physical *T'ien* or sky, that is, the *T'ien* often spoken of in apposition to earth, as in the common phrase which refers to the physical universe as 'Heaven and Earth' (*T'ien Ti*).

(2) A ruling or presiding *T'ien*, that is, one such as is meant in the phrase, 'Imperial Heaven Supreme Emperor' (*Huang T'ien Shang Ti*), in which anthropomorphic *T'ien* and *Ti* are signified.

(3) A Fatalistic *T'ien*, equivalent to the concept of Fate (*ming*), a term applied to all those events in human life over which man himself has no control. This is the *T'ien* Mencius refers to when he says : "As to the accomplishment of a great deed, that is with *T'ien*".

(4) A naturalistic *T'ien*, that is one equivalent to the English word Nature. This is the sort of *T'ien* described in the 'Discussion on *T'ien*' in the *Hsün-tzü*.

(5) An ethical *T'ien*, that is, one having a moral principle and which is the highest primordial principle of the universe. This is the sort of *T'ien* which the *Chung Yung* (Doctrine of the Mean) refers to in its opening sentence when it says : "What *T'ien* confers (on man) is called his nature".[62]

But it must not be thought that there is more than one *T'ien*.

In Hinduism, at least in this period, the picture is extremely complex, and this complexity, as in the Jaina parable of the elephant and the blind men, has led to many misunderstandings. The polytheism of the popular cults continues, although even today when the villager speaks of *Bhagavān* or *Īśvara* he has some rather definite conception of a Single Deity beyond the powers of Nature. In the stricter philosophical formulation, however, the relation between *saguṇa* and *nirguṇa* Brahman remains for the most part problematical, although the distinction between the *pravṛtti* and *nivṛtti mārga* is already found in the *Mahābhārata*. In Sāmkhya there is considerable discussion concerning the relation of the Supreme Person (*paramapuruṣa*) to the soul of the world and the souls of those dwelling in it. And not only in Sāṃkhya but eventually in other schools as well (Vaiśeṣika in particular), the relation of the Supreme Person to *Īśvara* is thoroughly debated.

Against this background from the *Mahābhārata* and the *Bhagavadgītā* one is advised to 'choose one's *iṣṭa-devatā*', that is to say, the form according to which one feels most inclined to worship God until the time when he is ready to embrace the formless conception of Deity (Brahman) with all that that entails. This is not because the *devatās*, the gods, are mere inventions of the human imagination, but because God allows, out of His great generosity, and even encourages, because of their weaknesses, men to worship Him under the guise of these forms which both reveal and conceal Him. Thus the pluralistic element is not denied, but it is not seen in contradiction to the monistic; and it takes on both a systematic and symbolic aspect. This may seem strange to those accustomed to think in terms of either or dichotomies and absolute choices. It may seem to result in confusion, but the Nyāya school of logic has reasoned out the degrees of variation, distinction, and conjunction that make this picture possible. Moreover, the Vaiśeṣika School, in refutation of the Jaina, Sāṃkhya, and Buddhist Schools, constructed definite rational proofs for the existence of *Īśvara*.

Strictly speaking, the Jainas are atheists. However, we may still note a strong degree of pluralism in them because, in spite of their atheism, they were able to 'deify' their *Tīrthaṅkaras* without committing themselves to any absolutistic monism or theism. So to this extent God does exist : man by yoga may become god-like. Such seems to be their basic attitude.

Much more so than in later Mahāyāna where a rather elaborate Buddhology developed, the Hīnayāna Buddhism of this period was virtually as atheistic as Jainism but for a different reason. It is fairly evident that the Buddha himself did not cultivate the rituals of the *devas*, although he did not absolutely forbid his followers to do so. He only reasoned with them, arguing that these *devas* were only creations of consciousness, and since they also are subject to change they are not really real. Moreover, insofar as they do not help in alleviating human suffering, they are not worthy of consideration. The pluralistic element, in other words, is quite weak. Perhaps the chief characteristic here is best seen in the picture of the Buddha's enlightenment. Both above him and below are *devatās* and demons. But rather than being on top, as in a Germanic Valhalla, he sits unperturbed in the center, knowing that all these are only fictions of the mind.

What is taken as God in the higher sense in other traditions is replaced by the formless *Tathatā*, 'Thusness'. The extent, however, to which this *Tathatā* in its original formulations corresponds to such later views as the Vijñānavāda idealistic interpretation is not easy to determine. This Viñjānavāda interpretation does not deny all pluralism but inclusively regards it as only a passing show. The *devatās* and demons are regarded as symbolic particularizations. At certain stages of Buddhist meditation these are penetrated and the pure *nirvāṇa* is achieved when it is realized that there is the possibility of 'emptying out' even these. This way of emptying is certainly in the Buddha's own teaching, but the controversies as to what is really nearer the Buddha's own teaching began at least by the time of Aśoka.

The accusation that the followers of the Buddha deified him in spite of his own view of deity is not strictly true. The worship of the images and the admission of ancillary deities into the temples is solely a symbolic matter for the sake of the masses as an aid to meditation in the earlier stages. All the Hīnayāna Schools, regardless of their metaphysical or anti-metaphysical bias, replaced both metaphysical speculation and supplicatory prayer with methods of meditation. It is within these schemes of meditation that the pluralistic elements in reality are considered. The Theravādins considered them as having actual reality but capable of being surpassed; the Mahāyāna considered them as unreal altogether and mere fictions.

The purer Buddhist tradition is not strictly theistic or atheistic in the modern Western sense of those terms. The Theravāda only teaches that self-effort—according to the Buddha's saying, "be ye lights unto yourselves"—is more important than dependence on grace from a Godhead. Thus the pluralism is operative in each individual until he surmounts it along the path of emancipation. In the Mahāyāna of later periods there is a doctrine of grace in which the individual depends on the psychic powers of Bodhisattvas. Here the pluralism is admitted in the interceding roles of the Bodhisattvas; nevertheless, it must be remembered that this is only transitory. Ultimately, in all the schools, the pluralism is to be either obliterated, transcended, or simply disregarded as illusory.

In short, it might well be said that according to the Buddhist scheme of things the realm of the gods, the whole of the 'theological' range, is really within the psychic range and therefore must be regarded as inherently pluralistic. The spiritual realm, though delivered from plurality, is still not necessarily God for the strict Buddhist. It is, as it were, beyond 'God', in a continuum of awareness (or of substantial consciousness, according to some schools) which is beyond even the distinction of finite and infinite.

In other words, as far as theology is concerned, the typical Buddhist seems to hold the view that as long as you are going to have an existent Deity who can be designated, it might as well be acknowledged that one can have several deities, since the very nature of designation involves one in plurality. As Kashyap writes :

> Buddhism differs from Hinduism concerning belief in a creator God. Buddhism, based on the principle of the dependent origination of all existence, cannot accept a first cause, a creator. Some Hindus say that God dwells in Heaven—a deistic conception; others say that God pervades each atom of existence—a pantheistic conception; still others believe in a personal God, such as Rāma, Kṛṣṇa, or Śiva. These different conceptions of God are unacceptable to the Buddhist. In Buddhism, the gods are celestial beings on different subtle planes of existence where they are born, live, and die at the end of their span of life. Human beings are also born on these planes at certain stages of mystic realization in the course of their religious practices.
>
> . . . the saints in the Holy Order of the Buddha are regarded as spiritually higher than these gods. The Buddha

> taught his disciples to preach the Dhamma to men and gods alike.[63]

It is better not to try to speak about God so much and to admit that almost all that we worship, all our local loyalties and fixations of piety, are *devatās*, concrescences not less multifarious than ourselves and only slightly more subtle.

It is not easy to get a complete picture of the religious life of the Greeks before Socrates. As we have already pointed out, there seems to have been considerable friction between the clinging to the mythological consciousness and the development of the monistic trends of metaphysical speculation. The latter is so emphasized that it is generally supposed—largely due to the influence of Saint Augustine—that the Greeks were not a religious people. This is far from true. Piety still prevailed, almost fanatically, not only among the masses, but also among the aristocracy. The mystery cults of Dionysius and Aphrodite, for example, suffered no decrease until long after the time of Saint Paul, and the hymns addressed to the gods were of high spiritual fervor, rivaling in many ways those of the *Mahābhārata* and the Old Testament and of Zoroaster himself. The symbolic role was not so clear as in Hinduism; the gods were more definitely personal, even though there was the vague sense that behind their manifoldness there was a single *Ho Theos* closely allied with *moira*. Usually, nevertheless, in a way that is not quite henotheistic, the metaphysical speculation was focused on Zeus as the personification (if we may distinguish this from symbolization) of the thinking of the philosophers. One may again point equally to Hesiod, the Homeric Hymns, and to Parmenides.

We must follow the consequences of an acknowledgement that the One God has had a hand in all of this or else find some other explanation for the will to unity and aspirations toward transcendence that had their beginnings long before the advent of the Christ. We have a long way to go if we are going to meet the religious and theo-philosophical challenges of the past. Those in each tradition still have considerable adjustments to make, and it remains to be seen whether the result will be a comprehensive synthesis or whether syntheses will have to be made as was the case, as we shall see, in the medieval period.

Our attempt to come to a composite picture of the mind of man in this period has encompassed much that is still living in the world today. How many of us, in spite of our predilections to monotheism of some sort or other, are still tainted with devotion to a single god or goddess, whether Lakṣmī, Sarasvati, Kālī, Kuan-yin, the Blessed Theotokos, or Mary ever-Virgin? Few indeed are prepared to embrace the Formless and what that entails without falling over backwards into gross atheism/skepticism, the two being separated only, as it were, by a razor's edge although they are poles apart.

Few even today have come into a truly comprehensive perspective. But then, one must not play favorites nor play one side against the other too vigorously; theology is not a game of chess but an entrance and an Abiding. We must make an effort to make sense out of the composite of the past that still lives, wanes, and is reborn constantly. Somehow, truth, though eternal, flows. Man does not know what realm he belongs to until the throes of the enquiry into God engage him completely. Not Socrates alone but mankind as a whole is "full of gods". The *theia mania* remains.

Revelation, in some sense, cannot be denied. But there must be criteria for discerning primary and secondary revelations, and there must be a master-criterion for authenticating what is supremely of the revelational order. We simply suggest that, whether in a person or in a scripture, that is of the revelational order which inspires man toward a higher and more comprehensive, all-encompassing *darśana* (visionary apperception in immediacy) of God and at the same time conduces towards the unification of humanity. In this perspective it is not possible any longer for any one tradition to lay claim to a pipeline to God, competitively owned and operated; but neither does this entail default of the category of revelational truth.

During these centuries something was impinging on the psyche, the total being, of man that was not of Nature nor from his own sense of inadequacy. It took somewhat different forms, but the substance remains essentially the same. Each tradition must make its own adjustments until amity is possible, not compromising the greatness of its vision nor mitigating the ethical and dialectical demands that it makes on the world. Tradition, in short, although it must constantly be pruned in order to bear good fruit, cannot be discarded as the supplement to revelation. And the dialectic between revelation and tradition necessitates systems, even though systems remain only ancillary to the Tao that transmerges them back to their primal source while at the same time giving them vitality and charismatic authority.

PART TWO

SEVEN

Introduction

A. Plato

If we see Plato in the perspective of the total development of world history up until his time, he takes a position as if at a fulcrum in the history of ideas. Indeed, it is tempting to think of the history of man thus far in an organic manner with the over-soul of the species flowering especially in this figure of fifth century Athens. He was roughly contemporary with Mo Tzu, the Buddha, Mahāvīra, and Confucius. The Buddhist Council of Rajagṛha (483 B.C.) had taken place not too many years before his birth and the Council of Vaiśāli (383 B.C.) would take place not many years after his death. The empire of Magadha was at the zenith of its glory, and Aśoka was ready for his great conversion. Persia was also in the height of its splendor having made some inroads into India; Egypt was by no means in decline; Rome and Carthage were beginning their upward incline; Israel, settled down again after the exile, was producing the best of Second Isaiah. Human culture was being developed and the basic ideas that have shaped human destiny ever since were being formulated. It was, almost as much as at the birth of Jesus, a "fullness of time".

Although we have been accustomed to study all these things in isolation, we must shift to the one-world perspective and see Plato as a one-world philosopher. Is there anything in any of the schools, Chinese, Indian, and Semitic, in addition to the Greek background which he deals with so artfully, which is not in his dialogues?

He had been a poet dependent on inspiration before meeting Socrates. *Eros* was his vehicle, the soul (*psyche*) and its immortality his theme, and harmony his goal. But these proved inadequate without being supplemented with sincere and not merely disputatious argumentation. From this comes the dialogue form of writing in which he still remains unexcelled. This form had already been used to some extent in some of the Upaniṣads and was not unknown in the argument and counterargument of the Six Systems of Indian philosophy; also, in early Chinese philosophy this use of dialectical disputation was known and even became the uppermost method of discourse among the early followers of Mo Tzu. Thus, in all three civilizations not only dialogue but dialectic as such emerged about the time of Plato. No longer was merely single-point inspiration adequate as philosophy ; counterposing these 'points' against each other to reveal contradictions and thus evoking open-endedness became the norm from henceforth for the rest of the history of mankind.

Plato devotes much effort to the problem of knowledge and the difficulty of arriving at absolute certainty. The "as if" of *māyā*, the utilitarian practicality of Mo Tzu, the importance of deep-seated self-knowledge in "remembering" as a means of uncovering falsehood, the reintegration of all these in a higher concept of Deity—such are some of the recurrent themes in Plato's works. They are by no means original with him but are convergent in him in a way that is rather unique in the history of human culture.

A few still think that Plato has been overrated. He was not able to put his political vision into actuality, and Aristotle supposedly refuted his theory of Ideas. He remained too much of an aristocrat for many, even among his fellow Greeks. Except for truth *about* God, there is scarcely anything categorically demanding *from* God, no "Thus says the Lord". His soul lapses back into allegory after the most brilliant sorties of logical formulations. He understands the problem of *hybris*, adulates the Good, which is known to be eternal, but his personal *ascesis* (spiritual discipline) is inadequate so that he does not transcend *ahaṃkāra* directly, and *nirguṇa* Brahman remains only a desideratum, not a realization. He established an academy, but did not come into the full charisma of "turning the Wheel of the Dharma" and instituting a new cosmic order as the Buddha did.

Perhaps, in spite of his supposed "puritanism" evidenced by his censuring of Homer, he remained too aesthetic, too mythologically oriented ; and although he could treat all phenomena as copies of their Ideal types, he could not quite surrender the work of his Demiurge as only *māyā* after all. Or, in Chinese terms, although he knew *li* and *jen*, did he really cultivate the Tao? That is to say, although Plato had an appreciation of the importance of abstract principles and some knowledge of natural laws (*li*), and although this was put into a thoroughly humanist frame of reference which values cultivation of those qualities that distinguish man from the beasts yet without wild speculations about super-essential spirits and other objects of superstition (*jen*), nevertheless, did Plato really get a complete intuitive grasp of the Way (Tao)?

To Plato philosophy is not a doctrine or even a "method" in the modern sense of the word, but a mode of life, a perspective from which to view the world, or at least the search for such a perspective. The most assailable point in his 'way' is that of the desirability of the Good as over against the way of desirelessness of the Buddha and the Taoists. It is indeed doubtful whether Plato knew anything like *nirvāṇa*, which is imageless as well as a state of desirelessness. Had he been able to attain this, he would have found an alternative to his remythologizing in the *Timaeus*.

Plato's concept of "the Holy" is sometimes attacked, especially from the perspective of the Old Testament. And correspondingly, he may not have had sufficient place for *mokṣa* in his hierarchy of values; he did not preach a doctrine of salvation. However, the philosopher does finally emerge from the cave. After his 'enlightenment', Plato's philosopher, like the *jīvan mukta*, dutifully returns to deal with, or even to rule in, the "second best", the world; in contrast, the Bodhisattva willingly and even *lovingly* returns to serve in the world. Besides his teachings of metempsychosis and his keen interest in the problem of immortality, Plato treated the things concerned with human destiny almost as sacred mysteries not to be approached without purification, preferably the purgation by Socratic dialectic.

Education is to be rationally geared to the bringing of youth and the populace into a state, not of saintly blessedness, but of psycho-physical well-being. For this, the integral small community of the city-state—not the sacred Empire of the Confucianists, nor yet the World State governed by the unopposed *cakravartin* ('world ruler') in accordance with the almost Machiavellian polity of Kauṭilya—is the instrument, the means toward the end, that end remaining, in spite of all the striving of *Eros* toward it, ultimately unattainable. The Idea of Perfection forever inspires us or even entraps us, as well as the universe, in a sort of inevitable entelechy. *Eros* is to be worshipped devoutly as the Inspirer-toward-the-Good rather than as the Absolute Legislator of ethical and natural laws as seems to be the case with the Old Testament tradition.

The query may well be made as to whether any of the Greeks really had or honored humility. Of course, the Hindus did not have it so much either; their rigorous asceticism indicates that their struggles to get beyond *ahaṃkāra* may have been partially misguided. The *Aham Brahma asmi* of the Upaniṣads was often misconstrued; instead of finding the Tao, they expanded their ego to cosmic proportions—at least this may have been the case before the Buddha.

Perhaps Plato almost bridges Being and Becoming, but there remains, according to him, "bastard reasoning" (*logismos nothos*) which is the opposite of true rationality even though it appears to be rational. It is the rationalizing we do after the wrong thing has been done in order to try to make it right when it really is not. There is an unaccountable factor of brute discord inherent in the universe which always obstructs perfection and reason in every human and cosmic enterprise. Rationalizing and irrationality are the human manifestations of this basic imperfection of the universe. For man, it is this bastard reasoning which makes Becoming necessary as an effort to overcome imperfection and to return to the perfection of Being or Pure Idea. For Plato, faith (*pistis*) as the response to *Eros* fulfils this function. Although this faith cannot eliminate or harmonize imperfection, it does lead to striving and thus to expansion.

When the Demiurge created the world he had only imperfect matter with which to make the "copies". This idea of an inherent deficiency in matter is the basis of the early Upaniṣadic concept of *māyā*; thus, Plato's Becoming is very much like this *māyā*. The Taoist concept of *teh* is also comparable to Plato's Becoming and to the Upaniṣadic *māyā*. It is *teh* which gives the dynamism, the manifestation, without which Tao would simply remain undifferentiated and unknown, even though perfect indeed. Being/Becoming, Brahman/*māyā*, Tao/*teh*--it is doubtful that Plato reduced the antinomy these represent any better than his contemporaries.

For Plato, the Myth rather than the imageless Tao triumphs. Man remains a child of the gods in spite of his capacity for reason. Because of his strong mythopoetical strain, Plato never comes to complete clarity about the relation between God and the gods. What the nature of the Highest Deity must be is left for Aristotle to attempt to define with greater precision, whether that precision is existentially more acceptable or not. Plato's explanation of the Demiurge is vague even by comparison with Nyāya's relatively weak analogizing. Nyāya and Vaiśeṣika are actually more definitely theistic than Plato. Much that is theistic can be *derived*, nevertheless, from Plato, as was done later by Ficino, for example, who finds a firm foundation for the Christian theology of the Trinity in Plato's metaphysics, and others insisted that there is a presage of the concept of the incarnation of the *logos* as well.

Herein may be Plato's greatness rather than his weakness: he remains *open* at all turns. The critical, the speculative, the analogical and the analytical, the contemplative and the approximative all take their place without jarring. Plato remains even more inexhaustible in our perspective than in the usual perspective of the Greek tradition only. Perhaps his greatest achievement was the capacity to think multidimensionally.

B. Aristotle

Plato penetrates the inherent nature; Aristotle classifies according to attributes. Plato, like the Taoists, was concerned with the eternal and unchanging; Aristotle, like the Theravādins, was concerned with causation and motion and change. Plato's dialectic sought to eliminate the false; Aristotle's, to establish an organon whereby truth could be reliably stated and related to actuality. Aristotle is concerned with valid distinctions, with difference; Plato with likeness. Plato begins and ends with openness and harmony; Aristotle, with totality and order. It seems that in every era there is the *yin* and *yang* among philosophies also. Plato and Aristotle, Sāṃkhya and Buddhist, Confucian and Taoist—they must be seen together to get some notion of the whole truth.

We have essentially the same problem in interpreting Aristotle at every turn: we read into him more than we read out of him. Our predispositions, based very largely on interpretations of from 500 to 2000 or more years, condition our search in the text for things that sometimes are not there and make it too easy to gloss over what is already and actually spelled out. There is a spiritual Aristotle, and there is the Aristotle who is entirely too materialistic, and everything in between.

Too many interpreters through the centuries, astounded by the precision and wholeness of his system, have been impressed by that without noting the actual nonfinality of his results. He ends in *aporia* ('openness'), with difficulty at every turn, even though he has been more thorough, more systematic in his exposition or explication and refutations and counter-refutations of the views which he juxtaposes one against the other, occasionally adding something new or distinctively his own but more typically letting the others knock each other down, as it were, until the board is cleared and we are ready to start another game.

In a very definite sense Aristotle is the first philosopher to build a system of philosophy, striving not only to refute others, but to achieve both internal consistency and designed coherence so that no one aspect of his system could show discrepancy with any other. And yet, perhaps Aristotle did not intend to construct a system. Even in the *Metaphysics* he is still only making an "inquiry" whether a science of first principles is possible; but in most of the other works he seems quite sure of himself, proceeding with a type of certainty that the Sophists falsely thought they had and that Socrates knew he did not have.

It appears that Aristotle finds a Single Principle in each

field that he investigates: Being *qua* Being in metaphysics, the Unmoved Mover in theology, the Golden Mean in ethics, Democratic-Oligarchic polity in politics, noncontradiction in logic. But Aristotle never explicitly picks one as a crowning point to his whole system. We may even doubt that he conceived of his philosophizing as a system in the same sense that, say, German philosophers of the 18th and 19th centuries began to think of systems. As in his reviews of his predecessors' works, so also when he incorporates new information from any source whatsoever, there seems to be a sort of process of 'reduction' to some Single Principle or other. This does not mean that he is a monist, however, since even the monism in Parmenides is also subject to the same reduction in comparison with other "isms". Scarcely can we find any explicit attempt to create a 'pyramidal' system until Plotinus at least, or perhaps some of the Byzantines many centuries later, or Avicenna, Averroes, and the Thomists.

We sometimes wonder whether even the attempt at system as distinct from Socratic Openness or Buddhist noncraving or Taoist Change (living in-and-through the Becoming; trying to 'unwind' it all instead of winding it up even tighter, as it were)—whether the attempt at systematic rigor itself has not been the great mistake after all.

It might be that we are still indulging in a prejudice in putting Aristotle at the core of future comparisons. Others may have been equally great with Plato and Aristotle; that is yet for students of some coming generation to judge. The important thing is not to make judgments about the relative greatness of our sages but rather to seek some comprehensive understanding of their wisdoms by putting them together as consistently and coherently as possible.

In Aristotle humanity reached a level of systematic integration that is rare in the history of culture and civilization. He was undoubtedly the most all-inclusive philosopher of his period, but can the parts of his system stand against the positions advocated by his global contemporaries? In other words, although Aristotle talked about "more" than anyone else, did he necessarily do it "better"? One of our intentions in this section is to test him out against his global contemporaries (necessarily being liberal with dates) on different fields within his system. However, to the extent that system as such is a value, Aristotle for now must remain unassailable.

EIGHT

Logic

For Aristotle, as not for Socrates, and not for Plato for the most part, questions necessarily have answers. Aristotle was to a very great extent an empiricist, proceeding from particular to universal by abstraction long before formulating syllogisms based on the universals so derived. His genius is shown by his balance and proportion between inductive and deductive logic. For Aristotle, science, and therefore logic, included both necessary *a priori* forms of statements and observational investigation. In other words, finding significant premises and playing with logical forms as such was not for him the point. Aristotle considered logic to be a method for arriving at truth, obviously not just because the conclusion necessarily follows from the premises in a deductive syllogism, but because discovering and testing the truth (not validity) of the premises was also part of the 'logic'. For Aristotle, logic deals both with discovery and testing of truth and with explication of valid forms of argumentation.

In regard to the syllogism, it is generally considered that this is a sort of 'scientific' precising of Socratic dialectical investigation. But is it really a hardening or even a closing of the Openness of the Socratic method of questioning ? There are not many particulars in Aristotle's logic that are distinctly original with him. Nyāya logic also combined induction and deduction, in fact, in the same syllogism, for which the model is as follows :

(1) Theory (*pratijñā*) : (The) mountain possesses fire
(2) Cause (*hetu*) : because of smoke
(3) Example (*udāharaṇa*) : Where (there is) smoke there (is) fire, as in a kitchen, etc.
(4) Application (*upanaya*) : This (mountain is) similar (i.e., possesses smoke).
(5) Conclusion (*nigamana*) : Therefore (it is) similar (i.e., possesses fire).[1]

It might appear that the Nyāya form could easily be reduced to the Aristotelian form; and some might even argue that steps three and four are nonessential. But this is the way by which Nyāya unifies inductive and deductive logic. Insistence upon an existential referent forces one to talk about the actual world. As a matter of fact, instead of reducing the Nyāya formula, some of the Jainas later expanded it to as many as ten steps.

It is all too easy to pass over the logical aspect of classical Chinese philosophy unless one is looking for it. Logic begins in Greece essentially with Socrates asking for clear and precise definitions, and so in ancient China we find similar concerns under the Rectification of Names discipline. But it is curious that (as far as we can tell) this did not lead to the development of a formal logic in China. The Rectification of Names is one of the principal bases of Confucius' reforms. It became a central part of the Chinese (especially Confucianist) theories of government. Basically this discipline attempts to unify theory and practice by removing all discrepancies between actualities and names. Instead of allowing stereotypes and euphemisms to crystallize into dogmas, it is better simply to call everything by its proper name. If the Rectification of Names discipline were employed, what would happen, for example, to the advertising industry, or to the exaggerated propaganda in political elections, or even in international relations ? But the application of this discipline extends much farther than this and really constitutes the basic principle behind the whole science of semantics. Also, it tends to involve a realistic epistemology and therefore realism in metaphysics and a domination of denotation over connotation. From the later Mohist Canon we may note this interesting statement of the Rectification of Names :

> That and this: 'That' and 'this' agree with 'that' and 'this'. The reason is given under 'difference'.
>
> That (i.e., the above statement) refers to the Rectification of Names, 'that' and 'this'. 'That' and 'this' are correct when the that-ness of 'that' stops at 'that', and the this-ness of 'this' stops at 'this'. 'That' and 'this' are not correct when 'that' is moreover 'this', and 'this' is moreover 'that'. (To say) that 'that' is 'this' is also

> correct, if that 'that' is 'this' stops at 'that' being 'this' If in this way they are 'that' and 'this' then 'that' may also be 'this', and 'this' may also be 'that'.[2]

Considering Pāṇini's attempts in India and Aristotle's in Greece as well as these thinkers in China, we may query whether at the high points in the developments of civilizations one will find not only the emergence of systematic thinking over mythologizing and a high degree of development in the fine arts, but also an attempt at refinement and regularization of language, for folk language in every culture, although colorful and emotionally satisfying, is notably poor in precision and clear denotation.

We should also note Kung-sung Lung whom we find struggling with the problem of universals no less than Aristotle. He is especially noted for his discourse about "a white horse is not a horse" which may be taken as the first attempt in China to deal explicitly with questions of universals. Kung-sun Lung is also concerned with the nature of attribution—a matter that was pivotal in Aristotle's refutation of Plato's theory of Ideas and a matter which Nyāya logic considers in some detail. He deals with the problem of whether we can have things without attributes or have attributes without the things of which they are attributes. Kung-sun Lung's logic is not that of the syllogism as found in Aristotle and Nyāya. At the maximum it is the logic of classes and at the minimum something close to the paradoxes of Zeno.

Perhaps most distinctively different from Aristotle is the Jaina logic of *syādvāda*, the theory of the relativity of all knowledge. Reality, insist the Jainas, is infinite and we can only know some of its aspects. All of our judgments, therefore, are relative. To simply state the proposition "Socrates is wise" is misleading. All propositions should be prefixed by *syāt*, "perhaps" or "relatively speaking", to remind us that no statement is absolutely true or absolutely false. The Jainas distinguish seven propositional forms expressing this relativity: (1) relatively speaking, P true; (2) relatively speaking, Pi is not true; (3) relatively speaking, P is true and P is not true; (4) relatively speaking, P is indescribable; (5) relatively speaking, P is true and P is indescribable; (6)relatively speaking, P is not true and P is indescribable; (7) relatively speaking, P is true and P is not true and P is indescribable. Thus, seemingly contradictory statements can be held to be true. A Jaina would say that the statements "Socrates is wise", and "Socrates is not wise" are both true and both false. But if we express such statements correctly, the seeming contradiction disappears: "From a particular viewpoint Socrates is wise, and from another particular viewpoint Socrates is not wise".

The most puzzling aspect of Buddhist logic may be the *catuṣkoṭi*, the "four logical alternatives", which may be given as:

1. S is P. (Ps)
2. S is not P. (—Ps)
3. S is and is not P. (Ps.—Ps)
4. S neither is nor is not P.—(Ps v—Ps)

The *Nikāyas* seem to regard these as the four mutually exclusive and exhaustive expressions of the relation of a subject and predicate. According to this scheme we ween to have in effect a logical calculus in which the principle of excluded middle does not hold. Explanations of this scheme range from exposes of the simple-mindedness of the early Buddhists who obviously couldnot handle logic and thus should have stuck to the problem of salvation, to awe-struck proclamations of the Buddhists' grasp of the essentially self-contradictory nature of reality. Jayatilleke, however, the foremost authority on the subject, insists that even though alternatives three and four above look like contradictories, consistency was as highly regarded in the *Nikāyas* as in Aristotle, and that in the *Saṁyutta Nikāya* there is almost a formal statement of the principle of noncontradiction.[3] Numbers three and four are rather to be interpreted as we would interpret any proposition of these types if they came up in ordinary conversation. If someone answered "yes and no" to the question, "Is he a good student?", we would not castigate him for speaking nonsense but realize that he simply means, "In some respects he is and in some respects he isn't". Obviously such a scheme is closer to the realities of everyday speech than the Aristotelian which insists that three and four are categorically false. The

Buddhist emphasis on the practical problem of communication rather than on the purely formal aspects of language should, by now, not be surprising.

The Buddhists and Aristotle would agree, however, that only one of the two or four (as the case may be) alternatives can be true in a given situation. The other alternatives would, therefore, be false. In any comparison with the Jainas it should be remembered that the *syādvāda* is not a scheme of strict *alternatives*. The Jainas would insist that all seven propositional forms of the *syādvāda* are true in any situation. However, the Jainas do admit the possibility of falsity. Two contradictory statements made from the *same* standpoint cannot both be true. Even the Jainas would here agree with Aristotle that one is true and the other is false.

According to the Buddhists there is one situation where the four alternatives are neither true nor false. If none of the four alternatives adequately describes a situation, then the question for which they are possible answers is to be rejected as meaningless. The most well-known illustration of a meaningless question for which all four possible answers are rejected (rather than negated) is that of the candle flame. If you snuff out a candle and then ask someone, "In which direction did the flame go, north, south, east, or west?", what is he to say ? None of the possible alternatives suffices. Wrangling over such questions is merely vexatious and not conducive to salvation. Other such questions which the Buddhists do not ask are:

Is the universe eternal ?
Is the universe noneternal ?
Is the universe at one and the same time eternal and noneternal?
Is the universe neither eternal nor noneternal ?
Is the universe infinite ?
Is the universe finite ?
Is the universe at one and the same time infinite and finite ?
Is the universe neither infinite nor finite ?
Are the vital principle (*jīva*) and body identical ?
Are the vital principle and the body nonidentical ?

Does the Tathāgata survive death?
Does the Tathāgata not survive death?
Does the Tathāgata both survive death and not survive death?
Does the Tathāgata neither survive death nor not survive death?[4]

In the *Nikāyas* a statement is also considered meaningless if the speaker cannot attach a verifiable content to each of its terms. A standard example of a statement rendered meaningless by such an inability on the part of the speaker is that of a man who builds a stairway in a public square so that he can reach, so he says, his mansion. But when asked to describe this mansion, he is at a complete loss.

It should be remembered that the Buddhists recognized the validity of a much broader verification principle than Aristotle or the logical positivists of the 20th century. Not only sense experience but extra-sensory experience was recognized as a valid *pramāṇa*. The main target of this definitional thrust was, of course, the metaphysical speculators who insisted on discussing and wrangling about such mysterious entities as souls (or prime matter ?) which one could neither see, hear, taste, touch, nor smell but which were claimed to be somehow or other real.

Concerning more formal aspects of logic, the Pāli *Nikāyas* recognized fallacious reasons as a *nigrahasthānam*, "an occasion for censure" of an opponent during a debate, and seem to have been specifically aware of the fallacy of *petitio principii*. But the early Buddhists certainly did not produce anything approaching Aristotle's catalogue of the fallacies. The Buddhists agreed with Aristotle that the truth or falsity of a theory could not be determined simply by noting the consistency, or lack of it, of its reasoning. Though consistency is one criterion of truth (an inconsistent, self-contradictory statement could never be true), the truth of statements depends ultimately on their correspondence with reality.

In general, it may be said that Aristotle's search for the Single Principle should have led him to the Buddhist conception of the direct investigation of the Awareness whereby these distinctions and wherein the questions arise. Aristotle would not give up, however; he still clung to the *nāmarūpa* level, determined to find answers to the questions and adequate designations for all things and ideas. The Theravāda Buddhist allows these at their own level, but goes beyond them, expanding his consciousness instead of investigating everything it seeks to put into determined, closed relation.

NINE

Ethics

Aristotle, in his *Ethics* especially, as in all things generally, along with the Buddha and Confucius, taught the avoidance of extremes, the Golden Mean. For Aristotle the Golden Mean is more than a simple ethical concept; it becomes the unifying principle for his entire psychology, politics, and ethics.

On the whole, Aristotle's conception of blessedness is not quite that of saintliness but rather of well-being; not that of prophecy, but rather of unhindered investigation towards truth; not that of the ascetic or the mystic, but that of one who considers the ordered life, balanced, sane, and completely free from nonreason as the best.

Aristotle recommends that one's material wants be limited to a minimum so that one may be free for the higher pursuits. By no means does he scorn pleasure, and he readily admits a certain pleasurableness in the pursuit of the good. The concept of sacrifice such as one finds in Mīmāṁsā and in many orthodox Hindu texts, as well as in the Old Testament, is quite foreign to Aristotle. Later, the basic trend in the *Gītā* will be to allegorize sacrificial rituals into the 'sacrifice' of knowledge, i.e., discipline of the mind; indeed, anything that will lead to selflessness becomes worthy to be rated as sacrifice. Aristotle simply discards sacrificial ritual altogether.

To Aristotle, happiness (*eudaimonia*) in this world remains the highest good rather than 'salvation' from the world. Even his ethical approach to the nature of God is conditioned by this. For Aristotle the highest good seems to be a matter of quantity more than quality, in contrast to the sharp distinction made in most Sanskrit texts between ordinary happiness (*sukha-duḥkha* : pleasure and pain which alternate) and the divine *ānanda* (bliss) that is eternal and detached from every worldly notion involved in desire.

Quite contrary to the sudden enlightenment expected of "the Orient" by those attracted to Americanized Rinzai Zen, Vaiśeṣika would agree with Aristotle that it is a gradual, accumulative matter. In fact, it is a matter of *enlightenment*, not of *salvation*, the latter being a distinctly Hebraic-Christian-Islamic concept. Also, an intelligent and humane gradualism that does not expect miracles but methodically provides a way of constant improvement of both individual and society is found in the Buddhist *Vinaya-Piṭaka*. It should be noted that the seemingly innumerable details and rules concerning expiation are based on the observation that there are virtually no acts for which one may not find a way of rectification. Violence in punishment is avoided and rehabilitation of a positive nature is always left open. That is the Buddhist spirit.

In all, it is not the good of the whole of humanity (and that strangely, for otherwise his perspectives are so universal) but the well-being of the individual in the *polis* that concerns Aristotle primarily. Thus his long discoursing on friendship (paralleled in Confucius) seems to be focused on the development of excellence in the individual. Aristotle's ethics may show a deficiency in this regard by comparison with the Confucian ethics which focused on the well-being of the entire Chinese empire, i.e., the then known civilized world. An extreme of social emphasis is found in Han Fei Tzu who would have us neglect the rights of the individual almost entirely in order to have law and order in a virtually totalitarian regime such as Wang Mang tried to bring about. As for early Hinduism, the Brahmanical systems are really highly individualistic (if not radically so); there is very little in the Hindu *Śāstras* about salvation of a whole city-state or an empire. It is surely not enough to expect that a merely personal, individual ethics without regard to the society in which one lives is ever going to be adequate. Some sort of balance and harmony must be maintained between the individual and societal groups and ultimately between the individual and the whole world, including, according to the Buddhist ethics, *all* living beings and not only human beings.

Manu has long since become so indigenously traditional that it is virtually impossible to separate his name from orthodox Hindu tradition as such. There is very little discrepancy between the traditions of Manu and Kauṭilya, the latter being only a working out of the theory of Manu in great practical detail. It would seem strange to the Confucianists that there should ever be any discrepancy between the ethics of various groups in society; but in the four Hindu *āśramas* a person's ethics depends on his age and status, and in the caste system the ethical code one follows depends on one's birth. It is better for one to have no *dharma* at all than to attempt to follow the *dharma* of another, i.e., in another caste or trade. The priestly *Brahmin* should not act like a *Kṣatriya*, waging war and engaging in Machiavellian trickery in order to outwit the enemies of his city-state—for India too had her city-states. In turn, for a *Kṣatriya* to conduct his life like *Śūdra*, tilling the soil and doing janitorial labor, was wrong because it infringed on the duties of those whose caste prescribed these functions as the focus for their pride in achievement. One may wonder, if the trade unions became closed shops and if, by a natural association over several centuries, each became pretty much hereditary and developed a carefully guarded pride in its particular craft, would the modern world not also develop all over again what Manu and Kauṭilya were simply recognizing and sanctioning as a realistic sociology ?

By contrast, the Protestant bourgeois ethic, largely inherited from Kant and Rousseau, has too many blind spots. You just cannot demand the same behavior from a Buddhist monk or a Hindu yogi as you can from a New York stockbroker or a denizen of the Pentagon. Thus the question of defending the caste system against the charge of being anti-democratic turns out to defeat itself. Democracy must have room for plurality also. Here Manu and Kauṭilya were perhaps more realistic and 'scientific' than many who through the centuries have followed them.

Essentially the same criticism might be levelled against Aristotle. Does he have a *dharma* for all classes and castes in his society or is he only prescribing (almost without prescribing—a marvellous achievement ?) principles that can perforce apply only to the aristocracy ? If this be true, not only the Marxists but also the orthodox Hindus will complain, for class consciousness is already assumed by Manu as a normal thing, howbeit without a sense of conflict. Aristotle seems blithely unaware of these things, or else he is, almost as much as his master Plato, subconsciously contemptuous of the *hoi poloi*, who cannot be expected to be governed by reason but are, says he, by nature born to be slaves.

In the Jaina and the Buddhist *saṅghas*, the monks, followed a different and much more rigorous code than the laymen followed, a code fitting to their function rather than morally superior. The same is still true in many Catholic and Orthodox countries today where the monastic traditions are respected by the laity. The monk who thinks himself superior to the layman instead of merely having a different vocation is living in mortal sin, the worst of them, pride. The Buddha criticised the caste system and that is possibly one reason why Buddhism did not survive in India, whereas in Ceylon, Burma, and Thailand under the influence of the Buddhist *dhamma* and *saṅgha* no rigorous caste system was allowed to develop. Even today Buddhist and Hindu scholars argue at each other about such matters.

Both Aristotle and the basic Confucian tradition, especially as manifested in Confucius himself and in Mencius, affirmed a humanist Middle Way, an avoidance of extremes, hoping for reform instead of revolution or apathy and basing their opinions on thorough study of their predecessors. They did not give way either to the sentimentalism of universal altruism or to self-satisfaction without regard to social obligations. The Confucianists probably had a greater regard than Aristotle for etiquette and ceremonial observances in a formal, traditional manner, putting aside questions about their literal meanings or their precise historical origins: but, on the other hand, they also had a concern for the whole empire, which was for them the whole civilized world, rather than merely the city-state, and in a definite sense therefore had less of a gap between their ethics of gradualism between individual, primary group, local community, and the total community of mankind than Aristotle who seems to put political science on its own feet virtually independent of ethics as such.

Aristotle probably would not have approved of Mo Tzu and his disciples both because of their pacifism and because of their puritanism. Aristotle, like the Confucianists, thought that man—at least the cultural aristocracy—should live well, avoiding both undue ostentation and rigorous abstenance from the good things of life. Like Confucius, he valued the aesthetic realm, especially music and literature, whereas the puritanical Mohists, very logical in other matters and even experts at mathematics and dialectics, disapproved of music and preferred, like some of their more austere Indian contemporaries, a much more Spartan life of strict discipline in Community. Aristotle also would not have liked their teachings that all people should be treated equally regardless of merit, for Aristotle's ethics is an ethics of merit, not of equality, as was also the case with the orthodox Confucianists.

As for the anarchistic ethics of the Taoists, needless to say Aristotle would definitely disapprove, agreeing with the Confucianists that it was not in accordance with human dignity to live that way. Man is not just a creature of nature but a *rational* animal, and therefore human beings, instead of cultivating a romantic "harmony with nature" and a Rousseauian "naturalness", should conduct themselves with design and a good modicum of regulation because it is simply not reasonable, not truly civilized, to do otherwise. After all, are not the barbarians "close to nature" ? To be truly Greek, as to be truly Confucian Chinese, was to cultivate *excellence* rather than naturalness—excellence in everything from daily speech to scientific *investigation* of nature, rather than *reversion* to the nature out of which civilized man had emerged only after aeons of struggle.

On the other hand, concerning the Legalists Aristotle would have registered disapproval for the opposite reason. Tyranny, government by rigorous laws enforced with merciless strictness, is not conducive to philosophy or science. Knowing fully well that one extreme would breed its opposite, Aristotle might even have predicted the failure of Wang

Mang to effect a successful reform based on legalist principles. The governed as well as the governors must have a claim to justice and, according to Aristotle, without freedom there is no justice. And as for the Legalists' censorship and burning of books, true enough the old stuff did have a lot of useless superstition in it, but the superstition was in the minds of the people, not in the books themselves which are the very embodiment of civilization.

Aristotle is not too clear in the end about the One God in relation to his ethical system. He still speaks freely of the gods and puts his confidence in human participation in the Divine Mind (*nous*). However, we must not be misled by this use of the word "divine" since it is really used in a non-technical way. The Greek philosophers—almost all of them, along with the poets and dramatists—considered anything that was rational as partaking of the highest attainable level of excellence. Excellence itself, being something to marvel at, was something 'divine' in the sense that, inspiring wonder, worship, admiration, and emulation, it is equal to a god or perhaps a quality of God as such; and perforce, the philosopher who is the most rational is most like a god.

It remained for the Jewish (especially Maimonides), Moslem (especially Averroes), and Christian (especially Aquinas) Scholastics to make the technical equation of the Higher Intellect (*nous*) with Aristotle's occasional use of the word God or god, and then equate that with the God of the Old Testament or Semitic tradition in general. But Aristotle himself did not make such an equation. He was not an Israelite or a prophet but an enlightened Greek humanist to whom theological speculations were completely peripheral to the problems of human existence and well-being. It remains for us to adjust Aristotle's humanism to the still wider perspective, integrating the larger Chinese humanism and the Buddhist *Dharma* into the final goal of peace. Dianoetic excellence is not enough in itself, although without it humanity will degenerate into sentimental nonsense. It can be reasonably argued that the entelechy of human destiny lies far beyond dianoetic excellence, in the values of the 'other' world as well as this; nevertheless, the true Aristotelian will not be content with this because the heart too easily gets deluded. He will insist on rational ordering of all things right up to the highest that the 'divine' mind can reach, and will not compromise with the basic faith that it can reach all things that can possibly be known, whether simple percepts and concepts or the Platonic Ideas in the eternal Mind of God.

TEN

Politics

Perhaps the most significant feature in Aristotle's *Politics* is that, instead of writing a 'Utopia' like Plato's *Republic*, or making detailed suggestions for actual administration like Plato's *Laws*, or laying down rules of conduct for the rectification of an empire as with Han Fei Tzu, or providing a system of strategy for success in an almost Machiavellian spirit as with Kauṭilya, Aristotle made a comparative study of virtually all the constitutions of the Greek states that had come before the Athens of his own time and thereby may well be termed the world's first political scientist.

This achievement of Greek rationality is undeniably unique. The other traditions depended on the virtue of the ruler and his counsellors; in both India and China the sage-king is more important than the system he or his subjects set up. Of course it may be objected that a constitution is easy enough for a city-state whereas for a large nation it is not so easy, and the city-states of Greece never did quite achieve a successful confederation even for the sake of defence. Nevertheless, a constitution does represent the entrance of an order of intelligence into the management of human affairs—the triumph of rationality over impulse, the triumph of systematic construction based on deliberate investigation of differing systems over caprice—which was not so clearly accomplished by Aristotle's contemporaries and which still remains a challenge to all.

Aristotle deals with the same problems that concern modern social scientists. In his discussion of the six functions of the state we see what is typical of Aristotle all the way through : he does not propose any sensational revolution nor yet allow any reactionary extreme; rather, balance and harmony, completeness in a rational order and, therefore, simplicity—such is his way, the way of definition based on empirical study.

> First, there must be food; secondly, arts, for life requires many instruments; thirdly, there must be arms, for the

> members of a community have need of them, and in their own hands, too, in order to maintain authority both against disobedient subjects and against external assailants; fourthly, there must be a certain amount of revenue, both for internal needs, and for the purposes of war; fifthly, or rather first, there must be a care of religion, which is commonly called worship; sixthly, and most necessary of all, there must be a power of deciding what is for the public interest, and what is just in men's dealings with one another.[5]

Here again Aristotle is looking for the middle ground. The state should not be reduced to a merely military function as in fascism, nor to an economic function as in communism, nor to a theocracy as in some forms of Islam (it did not work in Pakistan, for example). The last, the judicial function, is most precious to Anglo-Saxon tradition; but without the other functions the state may be reduced to an incohesive nonsociety with nothing organically holding or binding members together in a 'common task'. What's the use, for example, of having courts if there is no way to enforce the decisions of the courts? What's the use of having arbitration in disputes about justice when the people concerned are mere brutes, uncivilized, possessing neither arts nor education? Indeed, what's the use of discoursing in any context about justice when people are starving to death because the state, directly or indirectly, has not been able to provide food, clothing, and shelter? In short, a state must have all six functions in order to attain perfection. In Aristotle's irreducible, even if unelaborated, formula is a key for any who wants to find a viable commune on the one hand or frame a charter for a United Nations on the other.

During the medieval period in every civilization, the canon having been fixed and closed, law, like the Scriptures (Confucian Classics and the Vedas as well as the Bible and Qur'an), was regarded as sacred, whether "revealed" or not. But is law merely a matter of convenience, a social contract which may be broken at any time, if the parties concerned can agree it is no longer binding? Or is it an expression of biological or psycho-physical instincts and drives, man being a social animal, a *zoon politikon* as Aristotle put it? We must leave open for debate the question of whether Aristotle regarded Solon, for example, with the same reverence that the Maccabees had for Moses, or Mencius had for the Sage-Kings Yao and Sun, or Kauṭilya had for the four Vedas. Enough to note that although there was a trend toward law-as-sacrosanct during this period, it was not so strong as to prohibit *rational* new formulations in each case, notably in the case of Aristotle.

> We may cite the Legalist Han Fei Tzu who argues that . . . The sage does not heed injunctions either to change or not to change; he merely rectifies the government [i.e., rationally, by design]. Whether or not ancient tradition should be changed, whether or not existing institutions should be altered, all depends upon whether or not they are suitable . . .[6]

Again, we find Han Fei Tzu proscribing as follows : "Therefore in the state of the enlightened ruler, there is no literature of books and records but the laws serve as the teachings".[7] However, such things can be overdone as indeed they were in China. It was the Legalists, disciples of Han Fei Tzu, who were responsible for the Burning of the Books in 213 B. C. The emperor destroyed all books which he did not want his subjects to read, which included nearly everything except technical manuals and, of course, the laws.

In Kauṭilya we find that reason has become necessary in order to come to an adequate theory over against all the previous authorities who did not agree with each other. His *Arthaśāstra* is scientifically, rationally arranged to cover in minute detail almost every topic that any government will have to deal with sooner or later. The Hindu version of the philosopher-king and Chinese sage-king is recorded by Kauṭilya :

> . . . [He must] acquire wisdom by keeping company with the aged ; . . . keep up his personal discipline by receiving lessons in the sciences; and endear himself to the people by bringing them in contact with wealth and doing good to them.
>
> Thus with his organs of sense under control, he shall keep away from hurting the woman and property of others ; avoid not only lustfulness, even in dream, but also false-

> hood, haughtiness, and evil proclivities ; and keep away from unrighteous and uneconomical transactions.
>
> . . .
>
> Kauṭilya holds that wealth, and wealth alone, is important, inasmuch as charity and desire depend upon wealth for their realization.
>
> . . .
>
> Sovereignty (rājatva) is possible only with assistance. A single wheel can never move. Hence he shall employ ministers and hear their opinion.[8]
>
> . . .

After this follow chapters treating in detail the selection and duties of ministers, the selection and duties of spies ("intelligence service") for which Kauṭilya is as famous as Machiavelli, the business of council meetings, the duties of envoys or ambassadors, and so on until no relevant topic is left untouched.

These discussions were evidently founded on actual experience rather than speculation and thus show anything but the stereotype of that "other-worldiness" with which Albert Schweitzer characterized all Hindu tradition. In Chapter XIX on the "Duties of a King" we are not dealing with obscurities of mystical enlightenment but with hard realities of daily routine which, unless planned carefully, will become hectic beyond control with the result that the whole government will reflect the chaos in the governor's mind. In all systems of government the basic issue is not just the system *per se* but the problem of getting virtuous or charismatic persons to run it. Kauṭilya prescribes a pattern of life such that virtuousness will be necessary, not just laudable:

> At the close of the day, he shall observe the evening prayer (sandhyā).
>
> During the first one-eighth part of the night, he shall receive secret emissaries; during the second, he shall attend to bathing and supper and study; during the third he shall enter the bedchamber amid the sound of trumpets and enjoy sleep during the fourth and fifth parts; having been awakened by the sound of trumpets

> during the sixth part, he shall recall to his mind the injunction of sciences as well as the day's duties; during the seventh, he shall sit considering administrative measures and send out spies; and during the eighth division of the night he shall receive benedictions from sacrificial priests, teachers and the high priest, and having seen his physician, chief cook and astrologer, and having saluted both a cow and its calf and a bull by circumambulating round them he shall get into his court.[9]

The day is also divided into eight parts of which only one part (one and one half hours) is "free time"! Virtually all of Aristotle's six functions of the state are included under Kauṭilya's duties of the king.

The ruler, says Kauṭilya, must have such complete identification with his subjects that

> In the happiness of his subjects lies his happiness; in their welfare his welfare; whatever pleases himself he shall not consider as good, but whatever pleases his subjects he shall consider as good.[10]

Still, Kauṭilya's ideal is more that of the enlightened despot than the Aristotelian Oligarchic-Democratic constitutional polity.

Concerning the caste system Kauṭilya was only codifying to the best of his ability what had been unrecorded tradition for perhaps as long as 4,000 years. It was not a Utopian blueprint, moreover, but a setting forth of some sociological realities which are normal and natural, provided they are not abused. In India the Jainas and the Buddhists offered no specifically political philosophy. Even today the legal codes, the constitutions indeed, of Burma, Thailand, and Ceylon are really derived from Manu and Kauṭilya, who are sufficiently similar that it would be artificial to attempt a separate exposition.

In China as in India and Greece there was a great variety of social and political theories. For example, in some respects we might best compare Aristotle's views to those of Mencius (the Golden Mean, confidence in the goodness of human nature, government by reason rather than by force), but in other respects with Han Fei Tzu (government according to

Hindu Scheme of Life

1	2	3	4	5	6
VARṆA Social Order (caste system or division of labor)	ĀŚRAMAS Stages of Life	PURUṢĀRTHAS Ends to be Pursued	LEVELS OF KNOWLEDGE	PRAMĀṆAS Means of Knowledge	YOGA CAKRAS Psycho-physical Centers
Brahmin philosopher-priest	*Sannyāsa* renunciation	*Mokṣa* emancipation	*Pāramārthika* transcendent	Intuition	Cerebral (pituitary
Kṣatriya warrior-ruler	*Vānaprastha* retirement, social service	*Dharma* virtue, law, order	*Vyāvahārika* theoretical	Reason/Will	Throat (thyroid)
Vaiśya merchant	*Gṛhastha* married householder	*Artha* wealth	*Prātibhāsika* practical	Inference/Analogy	Heart
Śūdra farmer, laborer	*Brahmacarya* celibate student	*Kāma* pleasure	*Mithyā* illusory	Sense Perception	Navel

law, not just adjudication of private cases; an objective code, a constitution as it were; and a strong military organization), or with Mo Tzu (practicality in good balance with theory, not confusing the one for the other but acknowledging that they must go together), or with the Taoists (too much government is really worse than no government). As for Hsün Tzu, all that he offers is simply an explication of the basic Confucian axiom that good government is really a matter of virtue (*li*)—we might say integrity—rather than a matter of political systems.

As with Aristotle and Kautilya, the *Kuan Tzu*—a group of essays probably of the 3rd century B.C. but traditionally attributed to Kuan Chung (d. cir. 645 B.C.)—recognizes that all the functions of the state are necessary in due proportion, and that if the balance between them is upset, there will be trouble, for it is a sort of organic homeostasis that is involved and not just a repairable mechanism. The *Kuan Tzu* bases its polity of long-sustained stability and right motivation on the right relation with nature, harmonizing rather than seeking conquest or transcendence, blending the cyclic alternations of *yin* and *yang* rather than setting them up as struggling antinomies. With characteristic wit that is the necessary counterpart to wisdom (a wit that is healthier than the satire of Aristophanes), it says that the wise ruler is like a bird who sits on her eggs and hatches them without movement or noise.

The three primary concepts in considering Chinese political theory in general are: (1) the Mandate of Heaven, (2) the virtue of the emperor, and (3) the will of the people. Most of the ancient Chinese thinkers, Mo Tzu and Lao Tzu as well as the Confucianists, considered the ruler to be subject to a law higher than human law, whether that law be called the Tao or the Way of Heaven. Also, good government was thought to depend on the virtue of the ruler rather than on any political system as such. But if the emperor should lose his virtue, then he shall also have lost his authority, the Mandate will have been abused, and the people will then have the right, not to say the duty, to overthrow him. In theory, government is for the people and the emperor is subject both to the Will of Heaven above and to the will of the people below.

The greatest contrast in ancient Chinese political theories is between the Confucianists and the Legalists.

> The Confucian Hsün Tzu (fl.298-238 B.C.) goes to the extent of saying that only the right men, not the right laws, can produce and maintain a good government. Mencius is more moderate . . . it takes both the right kind of men and the right kind of laws to produce the right kind of government.[11]

Instead of government through virtue, the Legalists Shang Yang (d. 338 B.C.) and Han Fei Tzu advocated well-defined laws with strict penalties. If the laws are complete, the emperor need not be especially virtuous since the processes of legal rewards and punishments will operate automatically. The basic attitude of the Legalists is that man is naturally selfish and that fear of the law, interpreted to the latter, is the best way to maintain order. Filial piety, moral instructions, and appeal to the past are all of secondary importance to the Legalists.

The classical Chinese philosophy of history began to take shape with Ssu-ma Chien (c. 100 B.C.) who might be referred to as the Thucydides of Classical China. This theory is, in brief, that natural kingship begins the cycle when the charismatic individual comes into power, But if, in the course of time, instead of ruling by virtue and good example, he (or his dynastic successors) begins to rule by force, then he becomes alienated from his people. Thus insulated from the suffering masses, he indulges in sensual pleasures to excess and allows corruption in the court so that he does not get good counsellors. Degeneracy and decline continue and things go to rack and ruin until another charismatic leader, usually emerging from the masses, comes to the rescue and restores *li* and *yi* (righteousness)—somewhat like Chairman Mao now, although it is questioned by many whether the present scene is of this same pattern or is something radically new in Chinese history.

Perhaps the most essential thing about political philosophy is the projection of an ideal to strive for, given the realities from which we must and will, if we are truly human, struggle to gain freedom. We may not accept Aristotle or anyone else of this period as an authority for the 20th century, but the important thing is to examine their methods of rational inquiry and dialectical cross-examination whereby one may no longer be content with naive slogans or folksy sayings as a guide to life, nor with quoting 'scripture' to justify one's own dogmatic position. Although there are aspects of antiquity that are obsolete, a re-examination of the world history of ideas reveals problems that are perpetual and universal.

ELEVEN

Psychology

The *De Anima* became a favorite text during the medieval period among Islamic, Jewish, and Christian commentators, not the least among them Saint Thomas Aquinas. After examining in considerable detail the theories of those who preceded him, Aristotle defines the soul (psyche) as the life principle: the primary difference between organic and inorganic things is the appearance of soul. In the Hindu and Jaina systems the term *jīva* often simply means that which is alive, *ajīva* being that which has no life and is *jaḍa*, dead matter, just brute "stuff" and no more.

Aristotle defines the soul in relation to the body; even though it is dependent on the body, it is neither equatable with the body nor yet (with qualifications) separable from the body. As sight is to the physical eye, so soul is to the physical body. In Aristotle's terms, the soul is the form, entelechy, actuality, final cause (end), formal cause (substance), and efficient cause of living bodies. Aristotle distinguishes three kinds of souls, the higher including the lower but not vice versa: vegetative (plants: reproduction, growth), sensitive (animals: locomotion, sensation), and rational (man: thought). The three *guṇas* of Sāṃkhya—*tamas*, *rajas*, *sattva*—are remarkably parallel to these divisions.

Next in the *De Anima* Aristotle states his general theory of the senses, including the possibility of a sixth sense which he calls the *sensus communis*, the integrating faculty which is the clearing house for the others. Basically his treatment is very much like that in Sāṃkhya although there not only the external senses but the internal senses also are discussed. His *sensus communis* is paralleled in Sāṃkhya and in almost all Indian systems by the *antaḥkaraṇa*, the faculty which unifies the different sense impressions into a concept. From here Aristotle proceeds to an analysis of the intellect and the imagination.

Then we come to Aristotle's discussion of the agent intellect. The rational soul is subdivided into the potential or passive intellect, i.e., capable of being acted upon or of receiving action, and the active or agent intellect, which is not so much "active" as that which *actually is* rather than that which *potentially could be*. His discussion of this agent intellect has vexed all commentators.

In most of the Indian schools the soul (*jīva*) was considered to be of the nature of knowledge(*jñāna*), self-luminous, and separable from the body. However, it was a matter of considerable controversy in what manner this was so and how, being of the nature of knowledge, it could know this. In considering *jīva*, Sāṁkhya emphasizes *jñāna* while Vaiśeṣika emphasizes vital function, and for Cārvāka *jīva* is equivalent to vital function. *Jīva* probably was not used in original Sāṁkhya but was introduced later by way of others' refutations. Whenever and however it appears, *jīva* is distinct from *puruṣa* which is the transcendental self or soul while *jīva* is the phenomenal self subject to the three *guṇas*.

Among Chinese philosophers, Hsün Tzu is usually considered to be most like Aristotle. In metaphysics he was a realist. In ethics he was neither a Taoist recluse nor a rigorist like Han Fei Tzu and the other Legalists but, even more than the 'idealist' Mencius, a rationalist. The extent to which Hsün Tzu's psychology parallels that of Aristotle is not easy to judge since it is difficult to find in any classical Chinese system the equivalents of Aristotle's vegetative, animal, and rational souls. Nevertheless, we do find a text in which Hsün Tzu comes close:

> Water and fire have subtle spirits (*chhi*. . .) but not life (*seng*). Plants and trees have life (*seng*) but not perception (*chih*); birds and animals have perception (*chih*), but not a sense of justice (*i*). Man has spirits, life, and perception, and in addition the sense of justice; therefore he is the noblest of earthly beings. . .[12]

Here there is, as in Aristotle, a consideration of the soul as the vital function plus knowledge and rationally ethical behavior (a sense of justice). Aristotle also acknowledges that other beings share the lesser qualities with man and emphasizes that man alone has those higher qualities of reason and justice. For both Aristotle and Hsün Tzu, man might even be called the all-inclusive animal—a notion that was neglected perhaps too much in the West after Descartes.

Aristotle considers at some length the relation of the emotions to the soul. The norm, the Middle Way again, is in neither fighting nor indulging the emotions but in gaining control of them so that they do not interfere with the functions of the mind but even complement such functions. For Hsün Tzu, "The necessary beginning of knowledge is to consider that desires are permissible and so to guide (but not wholly repress) them. . . .[13] This is in contrast to the extremist Mo Tzu who considered that desires, being useless, should be repressed. Hsün Tzu explains how *li* (propriety) originated as a means to moderate desires:

> . . . man at birth has desires. When these desires are not satisfied, he cannot remain without seeking their satisfaction. When this seeking for satisfaction is without measure or limit, there can only be contention. When there is contention there will be disorder; when there is disorder, everything will be destroyed. The early kings hated this disorder, and so they established the rules of proper conduct (*li*) and standards of justice (*i*) so as to set limits to this confusion, to satisfy men's desires, and give opportunity for this satisfaction, in order that desires should not be stretched to the breaking point by things, nor things be used up by desires.[14]

There is a major point of difference between Aristotle and Hsün Tzu which should not be overlooked, a point wherein Mencius is closer to Aristotle than Hsün Tzu, and that is the question of whether human nature is basically evil or good. One just cannot imagine Aristotle thinking of man as evil by nature, but Hsün Tzu did. His debate with Mencius became the paradigm for all expressions of this controversy throughout the rest of Chinese cultural history and might well become so for the world history of philosophy. But what should be emphasized is that education is a basic necessity with Aristotle, Mencius, and Hsun Tzu, for if the higher faculties are not developed they simply remain potential. The uneducated individual fails to live well and sinks into mere biological subhuman subsistence instead of rising to full humanity. Parenthetically, for both the Greeks and the Chinese generally, music was a basic component of education and not a mere "extra-curricular activity", for music immediately and effectively harmonizes the soul whether man is good by nature or tends inherently toward evil.

There seems to be a strain of quietism in Hsün Tzu suggestive of the Taoists which, if there, would tend to put him at the other end of the spectrum from Aristotle. Some sort of 'quiescence' will be found sooner or later in almost every Chinese philosopher from here on. For Hsün Tzu the quieting of the mind (a sort of "centering down", to use the Quaker expression) is not an end in itself as with the Taoists (and with the much later Ch'an Buddhists) but merely, as with Aristotle, a means to achieving the maximum of rationality.

The atheistic and strongly materialistic emphasis of the Jainas compels them to be all the more rigorous in their ascetic discipline—wherein there is a sharp contrast with Aristotle's Middle Way—in order to purge out grossness. One point which bears some resemblance rather than contrast with Aristotle's psychology is that for the Jainas the soul and knowledge are so intimately related that it is often difficult to distinguish them. The soul is already omniscient though 'covered over' with karma-matter; it is for this reason that purgation of all the hindrances to knowledge takes such a prominent place in Jaina discipline.

The relation of soul to body is worked out with much more subtlety by the Jainas since they distinguish five kinds of bodies whereas Aristotle takes it for granted that there is only one :

> The karmic body (*kārmaṇa śarīra*) is composed of infra-atomic karma-particles. This is the innermost body. It has no bodily functions. The soul transmigrates with the help of this karmic body. All embodied souls have the igneous body (*taijasa śarīra*) which in common persons causes assimilation of food, and in meritorious persons gives effect to their benedictions and curses. Then some saints have the translocation body (*āhāraka śarīra*) which causes their transportation to a Tīrthaṅkara at a distance to consult him and remove their doubts. Gods and denizens of hell have the transmutation body (*vaikri-*

> *yika śarīra*) which they can change at will. All men and animals have the gross physical body (*audārika śarīra*).[15]

Even though Plato did accept transmigration, Aristotle is relatively silent, perhaps taking a sort of noncommittal, agnostic position. We might suggest in passing that there is some resemblance between the *kārmaṇa śarīra* and Aristotle's agent intellect.

For the Jainas the difference between being alive and being self-luminous is a difference of degree but not of kind; hylozoism is taken for granted. All creatures capable of growth, even crystals and invisible creatures in the air, have souls. The Jainas conceived of the souls of sentient beings to be adjustable to the bodies they inhabit, while the other Indian Schools considered the soul as being partless and sizeless. The other differences of the Jaina view cannot detain us for that would involve too much detail, and the Jainas have a mania for detail.

In a much stricter sense than with the Buddhists, for the Cārvākas there is no soul at all but only modifications of bodily atoms. This view is based largely upon the fact that we never actually find consciousness except as functioning in a body, i.e., there is an invariable relation between them such that the body itself must be taken as the cause of consciousness. There was, however, a distinction between the gross Cārvākas, or the *dhūrtta* division, and the cultured (*suśikṣita*) Cārvākas, the former being mechanists and the latter being more like dialectical materialists of the Marxian variety. The distinction is almost as sharp as the between, say, Democritus and Empedocles. Aristotle's refutation of the strict Greek materialists such as Democritus and Leukippus in regard to the nature of the soul is also applicable to the Cārvākas.

It is from the Buddhists and their doctrine of *anātman* (*anatta*) that the greatest challenge to Aristotle comes. There is no such thing as "soul" to the Buddhists. There are only nodes of endless causation, but this causation can be broken through by adequate contemplation, meditation, and observance of rules. Aristotle does not seem to think that this realm of causation, much less its counterpart in the realm of psychology, can be transcended.

Aristotle seems to regard the soul and its faculties as permanent and unchangeable, and at least the agent intellect as unalterable. But the Buddhist regards all faculties as alterable and sets about to make the most of this alterability for the good. When in everyday parlance we say, "You can't change human nature", we are not only differing extremely from the New Testament, which insists on conversion and transformation and the life of the *kainon ktisma,* the new creature, and from the Buddhists, but we are bound by the Greek doctrine of necessity, *ananke,* which even Aristotle did not quite transcend, probably because he never found a way of modulation between the actual and the potential.

For the Buddhists all experience can be treated, not strictly as illusory, but as *only experience* and therefore not of much value, for the important factor is the observing consciousness, which is infinite and capable of observing the infinite. Observing-the-observer allows a perspective from which all things may be balanced out in a complete detachment which brings the realization that all "things" are only processes and not Aristotelian substances. From the Aristotelian point of view, however, as from the Vedāntic point of view, the question may constantly be put back to the Buddhists, "But what is this observer consciousness? Is it not substantial also, or do you admit an infinite regress (observing the observer which observes the observer which observes that obesrver etc., *ad infinitum*)?" This is also the Jaina criticism of the Buddhists, for the Jainas simply admit the relativity of both the infinite regress and these substantial views and assert that in the attainment of the omniscience which is available only in complete 'isolation' (*kaivalya*) all possible views are included. The question continues, "Or does not your view simply cancel out all possible speculations, leaving us in complete nihilism?" The Buddhist will answer "yes" as far as metaphysical speculation is concerned, arguing only for the moral way of going ahead with relief of suffering.

It is difficult to determine which has the better and more ultimate foundation. To a great extent Aristotle's refutation of the Buddhists may already be found in his refutation of Heraclitus; but there are some sharp differences between the Buddhist *kṣaṇavāda* and the Heraclitian flux, at least for the

Theravāda Schools. The flux is completely nonsubstantial whereas the momentary accretions, the occasions (almost in the Whiteheadian sense), on whatever scale, whether infinitesimal or the whole of the cosmological—which is included within the psychological for the Buddhist and not the other way around as the Aristotelian holds—are, *qua* experience, *actual* but *completely transitory*. This is all that we can know, and the question of the metaphysical ultimate beyond this transitoriness should therefore not arise. The best that we can do is to cultivate awareness without any preconceived commitments.

Thus the dialectic goes on. There may not be any way of reconciling these two views. It may be that one simply has to choose. But then even this predilection for choice is observable. One day there is this choice, another day that choice. What chooses? The Buddhist would say that this is also only a coming together of aggregates of psychological influences, of passing "moments" in the totality of the world of cause and effect. And, says the Buddhist, it is rather by emptying than by further multiplication of postulations that this totality can be seen as such. Still, Aristotle's systematic inclusiveness does give us a possible integration of the relativistic and the absolutistic, the process and the substantial views. All possible views must be ordered and given their proper place, and to do this it is necessary to *think*.

TWELVE

Cosmology

A. Nature

For Aristotle, nature (*physis*) is the basic given. His problem is not that of distinguishing nature from anything else, but the problem of the One and the many within nature. To establish his own position here he must refute all the Pre-Socratics from Democritus to Parmenides. Can he also refute Sāṃkhya and Vaiśeṣika, the Theravāda Buddhists, Chuang Tzu and Hsūn Tzu, and the others we have encountered ?

It will be remembered that Aristotle in the *Physics* goes through a rather thorough examination of all the views that had preceded his work, including those that claim a Single Principle for everything, those that claim that the phenomenon of polarization is the key to everything, and those indeed who tend to triadize, hoping thereby to achieve greater harmony, and finds them all unsatisfactory in themselves. What then is left but some sort of synthesis of them all ? But what sort of synthesis ? What is involved here, of course, is the age old controversy between monism, dualism, and pluralism. These are matters in which empirical observations do not help much since no matter what observations one makes about any aspect of natural phenomena, these observations are meaningless unless one has some conceptual framework into which to fit them. Among conceptual frameworks the numerical ones are the most obvious and therefore probably the most fundamental; and since they cannot be proved or disproved from empirical observations alone, Aristotle has to use other methods. His conclusion concerning the Single Principle is that even if there be such it must be basically three-fold :

> To suppose then that the elements are three in number would seem, from these and similar considerations, a plausible view, as I said before. On the other hand, the view that they are more than three in number would seem to be untenable.[16]

It is difficult to discern the exact number for the simple but profound reason that unicity denies change, but change implies something that changes. At the maximum there is a triad constituted of change, permanency, and their relation.

This triad reminds us of Sāṃkhya's division of *prakṛti* into the three *guṇas*, while his emphasis on the polarization between mind (*nous*) and nature reminds us of the basic antithesis of *puruṣa* and *prakṛti*. The primary difference here between Sāṃkhya and Aristotle seems to be that it is *prakṛti* in a state of disturbance that moves whereas for Aristotle the Prime Mover (*puruṣa*) as the "attracter" is the cause of motion *ab extra*. *Prakṛti* is supposedly not moved by *puruṣa* even though in the classical metaphor *prakṛti* "dances" for *puruṣa* until the balance is restored.

In a definite sense *prakṛti* in Sāṃkhya is the Single Principle as far as nature is concerned, *puruṣa* being in a purely nondynamic hyperstatic situation, not influencing the operations of nature at all. So here Aristotle is searching for a Single *natural* rather than supernatural or metacosmic Principle, at least in this particular work. The Single (natural) Principle moves, changes, takes on dyadic or polarized or even pluralistic forms. In either system the problem is not solved since if one says that 'mind' (*puruṣa*) itself is the Single Principle, how can we account for the existence and multiple operations of matter (*prakṛti*) ? But if we affirm matter alone, then how can we have a basis of intelligibility since matter of itself must necessarily be (and Aristotle and Sāṃkhya alike say "necessarily" as an unavoidable presupposition) unintelligible ?

Sāṃkhya simply admits that *prakṛti* moves and *puruṣa* does not, leaving the dualism there as such. But Aristotle seems to be always trying to find a unity between them, linking the moving and the nonmoving, the ideal and the actual, Being and Becoming, coming-to-be (*genesis*) and passing-away (*phthora*), hoping that that would be the dynamic Single Principle; but he does not find it. And of course the reason he does not find it is that he is confronted with a dilemma : if anything moves, it must move either from itself toward another or else move internally in a sort of self-othering or be moved from the outside by some other. So motion implies, necessarily, not a Single Principle but at least some 'othering' principle. Moreover, any duality presupposes a *hypokeimenon*, a primordial unity out of which or into which or within which the polarization occurs or operates. Hence, perhaps—and who knows ?—even Aristotle's 'Matter' also "dances" in order to be or to become intelligible. But intelligibility itself cannot exist in isolation out of relation with the intelligibles.

Another factor common to both Sāṃkhya and Aristotle is the consideration of nature from within nature. But Sāṃkhya also has the perspective of seeing the whole of nature as undergoing a process of evolution and involution until the final *pralaya* is reached and all is in equilibrium again. Then the tension between *prakṛti* and *puruṣa* is resolved and there is the possibility of liberation for the soul. One may find evolution in Aristotle but certainly not involution.

Chuang Tzu seems to have developed a rather sophisticated doctrine of emergent evolution, indeed, with an expertise that may slightly exceed Aristotle's in this particular aspect of his total system. Hsün Tzu, however, rejects this. In fact, in almost everything that Chuang Tzu, was and said and did, Hsün Tzu appears as his polar opposite. If Chuang Tzu put all his hopes on the Infinite or on Emptiness, Hsun Tzu—who ought to be rather popular with North Americans for that very reason—would simply respond with a "where does it get you anyway ?"

Perhaps the more natural comparison would be to link Plato with Sāṃkhya and Aristotle with Vaiseṣika wherein the pluralistic trends within the greater unity, the emphasis on individuation, and the demand for precision prevail. Even though it did not have an all-embracing concept of nature, Vaiśeṣika is very 'naturalistic' in its handling of the *pramāṇas*, in the delineation and use of categories, and in its general interest in natural phenomena. Indeed, by interpolation, we may speculate whether this was the philosophy which gave encouragement to the scientific achievements in India during this period. Thus, as far as the concept of nature as such is concerned, it may be conceded that whereas in Sāmkhya nature is sharply, even dualistically, contrasted with spirit, in

Vaiśeṣika nature is, as it were, taken for granted as all-inclusive. Everything is more or less natural to Vaiśeṣika as it is to Aristotle. Although neither materialists nor mystics, they are both realists with heavy pluralistic emphases in many areas.

From a first reading, however, one may wonder whether the Vaiśeṣikas had not, unlike Aristotle, given up the search for the Single Principle and become frank and overt pluralists. Contrary to the stereotype concerning Indian philosophy as idealistic, monistic, and mystical, to say the least there is no overt mysticism in classical Vaiśeṣika at all. Of course it must round out its system with an ethics and a philosophy of religion in order to attain perfection but the emphasis seems to be not there as, however, it is in some other Indian systems.

All "things" are real for Aristotle and Vaiśeṣika in virtually the same sense, in contrast to Plato's dualistic idealism. But this contrast between Plato and Aristotle, as for that matter between Sāṃkhya and Vaiśeṣika, can be overexaggerated. In the broader scope, we may be reminded that although Vaiśeṣika shares with Aristotle the greater proclivity towards precision, Sāṃkhya seems to come closer to Aristotle's organicism of nature in which or by virtue of which both have serious doubts about atoms and, instead, want a more uniform Principle, whether it can be found or not. Vaiśeṣika does not have a general concept of *prakṛti* in the same sense that Aristotle and Sāṃkhya have; and although there is a sort of hierarchical ascent by abstraction from sense perception to the higher levels of intellection in both Aristotle and Vaiśeṣika, to the latter the plurality of souls is absolute whereas, if one takes the Averroist interpretation of Aristotle's Higher Intellect (and it is as reliable as any available thus far), there seems to be a sense in which Aristotle is to some extent, like Sāṃkhya, a panpsychist as Vaiśeṣika is definitely not. There is definitely no Unmoved Mover in Vaiśeṣika. Also, all knowledge is objective, whereas in Sāṃkhya and Aristotle reflexivity of self-knowledge does have a place and an important place at that.

To Sāṃkhya-Yoga the antithesis between *prakṛti* and *puruṣa*, the changing and the unchanging, is real but it can be transcended by adequate *ascesis* (spiritual discipline). But for the Buddhist the antithesis does not really arise. The whole of nature as only "name and form" (though there was disagreement as to the relative reality of this) was considered a field of constant change in a more radical sense than Aristotle considered it. For the Buddhist there is no Aristotelian substance behind the change; nothing is permanent. Since the Theravāda view is that there is no (permanent) soul and *everything* changes, there was controversy as to whether even the achievement of that spiritual state whereby this is realized is also changeable, i.e., can one lapse back into ignorance? The later Buddhist (Mahāyāna) interpretations, however, definitely have a "once saved always saved" doctrine and almost posit something like a permanent soul or identity of person which substantially transmigrates.

Aristotle was only observing the change and its characteristics, but the Buddhist was not content to observe and philosophize about it; through his psychic power generated in meditation he sought to spiritualize it, transform it, and bring at least all sentient creatures to deliverance from it. Not observation only, but complete detachment and salvation are the Buddhist's aims. Clinging to life is equally for the Buddhist as for the New Testament Christian a basic, if not the basic, source of evil. The chief thing to note, perhaps, is that whereas Aristotle makes propositions about the components of nature, the Buddhist seeks deliverance from them by transcending them—but a transcendence, we should add, not like that of a Kierkegaard or a Nietzsche where transcendence means *triumph* as over an enemy, but by a profound dissolution of the bondage that holds the contemplator.

It should be mentioned that the Hindu, Jaina, and Buddhist traditions, in contrast to the Greeks and the pre-Buddhistic Chinese, had the concept of a vast number of worlds, past, present, and future—a view which Aristotle explicitly rejects. These multitudes of worlds and all that they contain are really *kṣaṇas*, events, unsubstantial moments according to the Theravāda Buddhists. Since they are observable, at least by the imagination, they are not eternal, for eternal things could not be observed by finite observers such as we are.

The Chinese concept of nature has been well explicated by Needham. The following is a rather over-generalized statement although in regard to the emphasis on harmony it remains valid :

> We are thus in presence of a thorough parallelism at the three levels of cosmos, human society and individual body. But it seems that the Western conception was deeply different from the Chinese. The former saw justice and law at all levels, closely associated with personalized beings, enacting laws or administering them. The latter saw only that righteousness embodied in good custom represented the harmony necessary for the existence and function of the social organism. It recognised also a harmony in the function of the heavens, and, if pressed, would have admitted one of the functions of the individual body also, but these harmonies were spontaneous, not decreed. . . in China, the phenomenalist conviction of cosmic-ethical unity gave no stimulation whatever to the idea of laws of Nature.[17]

In Chinese tradition it was assumed that there is a universal nature of all things to which they conformed according to principles of harmony and separation from that harmony. The sense of wholeness seems to have predominated over the contrast between Being and element. There was not so much the abstraction towards universals as the other way around : each integer in nature (*hsing*) took its place in the Great Oneness and the problem was to keep it thus rightly related rather than to separate it out in order to distinguish it from its fellow components. Nevertheless, it can readily be seen that the results are almost the same in both cases; the individual component must be distinguished regardless of the basic motivation. In both cases, combination and distinction were not neglected.

The Chinese sages were not so prone to separate physics, psychology, logic, ethics, and metaphysics into distinct fields but usually sought out general principles that would govern them all. Of course in the Legalists and the Dialecticians we have sharper distinctions and a rather sophisticated attempt at formal arrangement of principles. In the Yin-Yang/Five

Agents School as represented by Tsou Yen (305-240 B.C.) there is a heavy emphasis on a 'naturalistic' attitude towards things and an early attempt at a foundation for scientific endeavor. In this School we find the most developed cosmology of elements and principles in a sense comparable to that of Aristotle. Still, Needham makes the claim that the Mohists had anticipated Newton's first Law of Motion which had received little explicit formulation in the Latin West until the time of Galileo due to the authority of Aristotle.

Detailed cosmological theories in China are not readily available until the Han period; however, we may mention the Taoists. The ultimate principle for Lao Tzu is, of course, the Tao. But the process of evolution also involves Being (*yu*), non—Being (*wu*), and the Great Ultimate (*T'ai Chi*). Out of nonBeing comes Being (Heaven and Earth) through the force of the Tao. This opposition of Being and non-Being is paralleled by the evolutes, i.e., nothing is produced which does not have its opposite : light—dark, good—evil, short—long. Part of Verse 42 of the Lao Tzu says:

> Tao produced the One.
> The One produced the two.
> The two produced the three.
> And the three produced the ten thousand things.[18]

Concerning this verse, Chan remarks:

> It is often understood that the One is the original material force or the Great Ultimate, the two are *yin* and *yang*, the three are their blending with the original material force, and the ten thousand things are things carrying *yin* and embracing *yang*. . . .[19]

Although both Lao Tzu and Chuang Tzu made references to a "Lord" or "Creator", it is generally held that the Tao alone is responsible for the universe (or one might better say that the universe is responsible for itself).

It may well be that many of the Chinese views need more sharpening of distinctions, but then perhaps Aristotle needs more rounding off at the edges. The Single Principle which he seeks but never quite finds and therefore only postulates as necessary—is it not the Tao ? The Indian Schools, on the other hand, do not need any more rigor of distinction-making. They have, for one thing, a more exacting language than even Greek in which to express themselves, wherein a single word can have both comprehensiveness and precision such that it would take a thousand years to explicate. But at that level they might learn from Aristotle a little more of the importance of mathematics as a basis of philosophizing and allow a little more room for the investigation of nature and for the scientific classification of phenomena therein.

B. Actuality and Illusion

It is by the ordering of concepts that Aristotle avoids the problem of illusion. He believes that by refining distinctions all error can be eliminated, but this refining of distinctions does not provide an ultimate foundation for his concepts. Even after all the means of knowledge (*pramāṇas*) are brought into play, there is no absolute guarantee that real, indisputably valid knowledge, good for all time and all places without qualification, has been made available or has been arrived at. In the face of this, Plato in the earlier dialogues had often ended in *aporia*, open-ended Socratic 'ignorance', without any conclusion; only in the later dialogues did he propose *orthe doxa*, right opinion, as the best we could do even though we should still strive for more. Aristotle hopes for something more than this *orthe doxa* by exercising scientific precision and refinement of distinctions between genera and species and by right classification or, if we may interpolate the Chinese phrase, Rectification of Names. But this is also subject to the same dialectical critique as any other *pramāṇa*; for dialectic, far from giving us positively any validity of concepts, only eliminates the false ones negatively.

It is just this lack of any ultimately valid means of getting a guarantee of absolute certainty that we call *māyā*. The word "illusion" which is commonly used for translating it, therefore, is often misleading or woefully inadequate since in English it carries the connotation of illusory sense perception at best or affirmation of a false dream as though it were real.

Thus Aristotle has no absolute guarantee, at least in the cosmological field, that his concepts can be validated by observation and abstraction or by dialectic and practical application. Such validating is rather radically challenged by the Mīmāṁsakas who, in opposition to Nyāya, argue that the knowledge of the whole of the realm of nature may come under the same difficulty that one may have in distinguishing between a rope and a snake in the twilight. Unless the concept of "snake" were already in the background, the appearance of the rope would not be able to evoke it. Thus, dialectically, the appearance at once conceals the reality and reveals it. *Māyā*, in other words, has a positive function, as it were, and not a mere negative one after all, for although it is not really real in itself, it has the capacity to provoke almost a negation of negation whereby, coming to the realization of the falsity of our affirmations, we seek for the real thing even though we may never find it.

Moreover, this is not a merely epistemological matter, for the whole range of the phenomenal world is subsumed under the ambivalence of*āvaraṇa* and *vikṣepa*, concealing and revealing the One Reality that is Brahman, and may be seen as such only by ascetic discipline which, at the time of liberation or attainment of *mokṣa*, is supposed to end in the dawn of the final *jñāna*. That is to say, since the normal means of knowledge never give any reason for their own validity, nor does even the mind afford us any more than an infinite regress of observing the observer, we either have to give up the search for a locus of ultimate validation or else find some means of attaining certainty in meditation and ritualistic worship, or else admit that at some link in the chain of perception and conception knowledge is selfvalid or selfilluminating, i.e., it is simply recognized as "already there", as it were, and we are fooled all the time not only by false perception (or inadequate perception, rather) but by trying to find an ultimate validity which is already afforded in the intrinsic nature of every object itself. This "being fooled", that most frequent of human experiences in everything that we do, is what is meant by *māyā*, illusion.

Thus there remains a certain radical ambivalence to all

knowledge situations : we never attain to absolute certainty by normal means at least, and yet it is only by dialectical examination of these inadequacies of the means of knowledge that we know that they are adequate. Every knowledge situation both reveals and conceals (*āvaraṇa* and *vikṣepa*) knowledge at the same time. The ambivalence remains a difficulty that an Aristotelian will object to even though he may be unable to produce any better alternative. It is an ambivalence and not an antinomy, and it remains almost unresolvable because the observer is bound up within it as well as the observed—a perspective which Aristotle with astounding naivete disregards. It is a very unAristotelian question to ask about "illusion" except in the very elementary psychological sense of being fooled by our senses once in a while. True, Aristotle speaks and thinks in terms of actuality; but the opposite of this is not illusion but potentiality. Aristotle simply assumes that he really is observing a real nature and really making postulates about *it*, the order of whose workings he discovers and codifies, without inquiring adequately into the question of who or what part of the Cosmic All it is that treats it as such. Has he already committed *hybris*, even against the Socratic humility ?

Ultimately, are there any 'answers' to Aristotle's inquiries, or is there only a constant opening of a wider question ? In the Hindu schools, and later in the Mahāyāna (but not the Hīnayāna which preferred to be concerned almost exclusively with moral disciplines and practical contemplations until *nirvāṇa* is reached), this opening of the wider question is what is really meant by *māyā*, and not "illusion" in the lesser sense of a merely pessimistic attitude towards a world that others cherish as lovely and enjoyable. For behind the doctrine of *māyā* is the radical Search for the Single Principle against which all else is falsely seen as separated. The opening of the wider question is almost synonymous with the concept of *māyā* itself. Those who never search for reality are never bothered by the unreality of their lives. The wider question is the devastatingly simple one, "What is really real ?", and it is only after this question is asked that māyā becomes, inevitably, a problem—a problem which Aristotle evidently did not quite realize, at least not as much as most of the Hindu Schools.

Aristotle is very keen at codifying the fallacies of logic, but there is some question whether he has quite the equivalent of the dispute we find in the Indian Schools over the theories of illusion where the problem is the allocation of the source of illusion and the possibility that it can be operative at all if Brahman is perfect. This problem of perfection is clearly seen in almost all the Indian Schools : in order that there be any valid reality at all, there must be a Reality that is unquestionable, unatlerable, partless, etc. We see that everything within experience is subject to the opposites of these; therefore, it must be beyond our usual experience. But by virtue of what do we know this or have the ability and the courage to assert that it must be ?

It is certainly true that in general this problem of appearance and reality concerns much more than language since it parallels the problem of the relation of conflict and harmony and is part of the great phenomenon of polarization which permeates and governs all activity. Still the problem does include language and some of the Dialecticians and Neo-Mohists in China, along with the extremists among the Naiyāyikas in India and some Sophists in Greece, came to the conclusion that by cleaning up the language one has rendered the ultimate service to philosophy and civilization.

The Later Mohists further refined the concept of *ho* (harmony) by equating it rather closely with correspondence, e.g., the right designation of things by the correlative right name (Rectification of Names). These Mohists dealt with the broader cosmological problem of the actuality of the things designated by the names and the rather odd phenomenon that there can be correspondence between the thing known and the knowledge which embraces both knower and known, for such is the function of the 'name' (or harmony). In other words, they seem to share with Aristotle a contentment with the proximately known even though this is the realm of *māyā* from which no technique as such will deliver us completely; but also, unlike Aristotle, they still affirm the openness to enquiry beyond that because of a belief that there is an *a priori* harmony or correspondence between the realm of the proximate and the realm of the ultimate.

It might be argued that the Taoists in their monastic retreats were even more keenly aware of the problem than Aristotle or the Neo Mohists. One may well take the approach : "If it's all illusion, why not enjoy it ?", as indeed the later Han Neo Taoists did; or more profoundly, one must cultivate the Tao by contemplation and emptying the mind instead of cramming it full of definitions and arguments, and then maybe the veil will become transparent, the clouds will part, and you can see forever.

Aristotle is looking for the Single Principle, the object of the Upaniṣadic search is the Single Identity behind or beyond *māyā*, while the Taoists emphasize the fundamental Harmony behind individual phenomena but which permeates the phenomena in such a way that no (sophisticated) theory of illusion is really needed. How these views can be synthesized remains for the student to think about; or perhaps he would rather resort to the Buddhist method of contemplation and see Aristotle's postulates from the perspective of 'no-difference'.

C. *Time*

In the controversy between Sāṃkhya and Nyāya-Vaiśeṣika over the nature of time we find that both reject Aristotle' view of time as measure. To Sāṃkhya time (*kāla*) is a creation of the intellect (*buddhi-nirmāṇa*) as a representative or communicative device. It has no real existence of its own but is simply a modification of ether (*ākāśa*). Time is all pervading and thus does not cause bondage since even liberated souls are 'in time'. Vaiśeṣika, on the other hand, considers time to be a real *dravya*, a substantial level in the hierarchy of Being, followed by space (*dik*), *ahaṁkāra*, and *ātman*-Brahman. Time is objective and not merely a subjective form of perception. It is the substance which causes the intuition of its own attributes. For Vaiśeṣika, time and space are not essentially different from ether. Both Sāṃkhya and Vaiśeṣika are concerned with both the least possible unit of atomic time and with the grand stretches of cosmic time in evolution and involution.

Vaiśeṣika denies the basic Buddhist view that time cannot be disassociated from actions (rather than from motion as such, as is the case with Aristotle). According to Vaiśeṣika, time and space are 'efficient' causes of all effects—a fascinating view since they might even make a fifth and sixth cause in Aristotle's scheme. The idea of efficient cause is used here in a loose, nontechnical sense still; that time should be a cause is not necessarily any less acceptable an idea than that "form" should be a cause.

Plato has difficulty with the problem of eternity versus time. The realm of the Ideas, like the realm of the *puruṣa* in Sāṃkhya, is eternal in the sense of being beyond time. The Ideas are "brought into time", so to speak, along with all the rest of the world, only in their material manifestations. This is like Sāṃkhya's association of time with *prakṛti*. Both Plato and Sāṃkhya remain rather dualistic in basic orientation.

By contrast, Aristotle, like Vaiśeṣika, tends to keep his focus on the worldly operations, on details and precision rather than on broad metaphysical speculations (though certainly not lacking in these either). As Solmsen says :

> As he eliminates Plato's metaphysical point of view—the opposition between time and eternity—from his own account of time, so he at least limits the cosmological motif to a minimum significance.[20]

Even the sense in which he uses the term "infinite" seems to take on a different color; for him it means the ultimate limit of measurability rather than the undifferentiated primordial "Ground" of reality beyond all appearance.

Aristotle does not discuss the idea of cyclic time in spite of saying that the cyclic motion is the most perfect. Time is serial, and beginning, now, and end follow in regular sequence. But from our comparative-comprehensive perspective the most important thesis Aristotle develops in regard to time is that of the relation of time to consciousness.

> And if nothing can count except consciousness, and consciousness only as intellect (not as sensation merely), it

> is impossible that time should exist if consciousness did not; unless as the 'objective thing' which is subjectively time to us, if we may suppose that movement could thus objectively exist without there being any consciousness [psyche]. For 'before' and 'after' are objectively involved in motion, and these, *qua* capable of numeration constitute time.[21]

In his association of time with soul (*psyche*), Aristotle's treatment is rather more similar to Sāṃkhya than Vaiśeṣika. Since it takes time to measure (observe) time, there must be a timeless observer (*sākṣi*) which, for Aristotle, is the soul.

The Sāṃkhya and Vaiśesika systems which we have been comparing with Aristotle are the systems as fully developed and without internal inconsistencies. It might well be that if these systems were reduced back to their first formulations of Kapila and Kaṇāda—a reduction which has not been accomplished because, in part, of the lack of precise Indian chronology—then these systems would show discrepancies similar to those found in Aristotle.

For the Jainas, space, matter, and time are inseparable. They alter the usual terminology somewhat, using for "space" the word *ākāśa*, which the others, including Aristotle, interpret as "ether" or, by definition, the most refined etherial element of the material order. The Jainas seem to treat space (*dik*) as virtually identical with *ākāśa* as a sort of punctuation of their atheism and materialistic tendencies.

According to the Jaina view, time is a substance—a substance moreover, which is the auxillary cause of all change.

> Time is the real substance that assists the continuity of substances through their successive modifications and insures orderliness of evolution . . . Time causes evolution and dissolution. Creative evolution of the world is aided by *utsarpiṇī kāla* [evolutionary time]. Dissolution of it is aided by *avasarpiṇī kāla* [involutionary time].[22]

Time is divided into two basic types : absolute time and relative time. The temptation here is to assert that the Jainas have come across the same problem that Aristotle did vis-a-vis

Plato; but the emphasis seems to be, even more than with Aristotle, on relative time. A time distinction evidently unique to Jaina conceptions is that between real time and empirical time. Sinha explicates :

> Real time (*kāla*) is one, eternal, formless, without beginning or end, and devoid of varieties. Empirical time (*samaya*) has a beginning and an end, and consists of varieties, seconds, minutes, hours, and the like. Moments are momentary, but hours, days, weeks, and the like have long duration. Real time (*niscayakāla*) is an eternal substance. Empirical time (*vyavahārakāla*) is momentary or temporary because it is a modification (*paryaya*) of real time. It is the material cause (*upādānakāraṇa*) of empirical time. One time (*kāla*) is modified into infinite moments (*samaya*).[23]

We may risk the opinion, subject to much more detailed research, that Aristotle is aware of this distinction between real time and empirical time but sees no real problem there, whereas for the Jainas it seems to be very important. It is enough to point out that the basic Jaina concepts of time are definitely un-Aristotelian and sufficiently distinct to compel us to reexamine our presuppositions which, after all, may be considerably more naive than those of this and other early Indian systems.

For the Buddhists time is circular, without beginning or end. This is difficult indeed to reconcile with an Aristotelian system where almost everything, if not everything, is caused in a one-to-one sequential pattern. Aristotle has a theory of the eternity of time, but for him it is a sort of nexus at best or an endless straight line.

There is hardly any controversy in the whole of the history of the world's philosophies greater than that within the various Schools of Buddhism over the definition of the *kṣana*, the moment, and its corollaries as to the relative reality of the existence of the past and the future. The Theravāda School regarded the past and the future as having at least derivative existence since they are dependent on the present. However, this "present" is almost undefinable, for it may be only the most infinitesimal moment of an eternity or it may be the whole of phenomenal existence.

According to the Theravāda Buddhists, meditation on time brings one gradually out of bondage to time. Such meditation led the Buddhists to a high degree of expertise in the discernment of time psychologically considered. The age-old problem-paradox that it takes time to think about time—much less to measure it in the external universe—may be an inherent impasse to be surmounted or a barrier to be penetrated before any valid, unquestionable observation about objective time can be made. For time is subject to no particular sense like sound, light, and smell. Some psychologists even in the modern world have posited a separate time-sense as a part of the human psyche, and certainly the phenomenon of biological "time clocks" in the unconscious workings of many living creatures has been definitely proven. There are other arguments to the effect that, assuming it is the same time that is observed "out there" and "in here", the introspective method is a better and more definitely empirical approach to the problem than the so-called objective methods.

What results these Theravāda monks obtained in meditation is probably more difficult to understand now in a modern, secular university environment. Their attainments were the result of a very specialized environment especially provided for the purpose—the Buddhist *saṅgha*.

> Now it is clear from the *Kathāvatthu* that, for Buddhism, time-distinctions have no objective existence of their own, and that reality is confined to the present. The past reality has perished; the future reality is not yet become. And when Buddhist doctrine says that reality is present, both these terms refer to one and the same thing *per se*. When this gives up its reality, it gives up its presence; when it gives up being present, it ceases to be real.
>
> Now what time is to life, space is to matter. Space, like time, is a permanent concept or mental construction, which constitutes a sufficing condition for the movement of bodies. It is void, unperceivable, without objective reality.[24]

In their efforts to penetrate the barrier of time itself, they were affirming a quest for timelessness rather than for eternity, in contrast to their contemporaries in Eurasia during this period. Also, they were making very minute and precise observations about the reality of (psychological) time itself. Indeed, it was not long before the Buddha's injunctions against bothering about 'metaphysics' themselves began to be a theme for metaphysical speculations. Observation was not enough. They needed a theory to make their experience intelligible. And, of course, there was anything but unanimity of opinion about the theory.

Through all of the controversies and differences, the doctrine of momentariness remained central. Over against the Brahmanical assertion of permanence, perduration of unchanging time, eternity, or transcendence of time, these Buddhists asserted momentariness, timelessness, and the power to observe time as constant change of all things, including the observer of the changing process. The momentariness doctrine is inherently tied up with the *anatta* or *anātman* (no-soul) doctrine. If everything else is subject to time, change, momentariness, how can we expect the soul, the self, or any psychological entity or function to be exempt from this change? This presents a very serious challenge for Aristotle as for the Brahmanical systems. In his famous treatise of *genesis* and *phthora* Aristotle consistently insists that there must be "something there" that undergoes this process of change. But the Theravāda Buddhists, or at least most of them, insisted that there is no substance which undergoes the change but the process of change itself is primary.

It seems that the Chinese did not develop such a sophisticated notion of space or of time as did their Indian counterparts, while those in turn, with all their fascination about time and causation, did not develop such a sense of history as did the Chinese. Although the consideration of time as a metaphysical category or as a matter of scientific speculation, such as we find in Aristotle, Vaiśeṣika, the Jainas, and even in Sāṃkhya to a great extent, is very difficult to find in their Chinese contemporaries, and although it may be true that the pre-Han Chinese philosophers did not consider time and space as cosmological problems *per sc*, still one suspects that the definitive study of ancient Chinese philosophy has not been written yet and that later one may be better able to discern implicit theories of time and space in such philosophers as Chuang Tzu and some Mohist philosophers. For now, given the scarcity of specific sources, we must necessarily generalize.

To most of the ancient Chinese philosophers, time equals change, not a measure of change. There is no concept of time as a substance as in some of the classical Hindu Schools. Concerning the Chinese concepts of time, Needham says :

> For the ancient Chinese, time was not an abstract parameter, a succession of homogenous moments, but was divided into concrete separate seasons and their subdivisions. Space was not abstractly uniform and extended in all directions, but was divided into the regions, south, north, east, west and center.[25]

Again, Needham's book *Time and Eastern Man*, as summarized by Chan, maintains that

> . . . to the Chinese time is a continuum and not atomistic, that the Chinese have treated history not as compartments but as a continuity, that their cyclical concept of time is minor and largely Taoistic, that Chinese historians have worked out a coherent "single track" theory of dynastic legitimacy, that they have regarded time as going upward, but that the element of compartmentalized time, which has not been entirely absent, has worked against the development of natural science.[26]

Perhaps the most dominant view was that time is simply understood in relation to events. For the Confucianists we would expect time to mean historical time. There must be rectification of virtue on the part of the emperor and rectification of names in the administration of the empire so that the people may have knowledge of history and of the proper ceremonials according to the time of the year ; thus the Blessing of Heaven may not fail. Still, there were other views. In contrast to Confucius, Chuang Tzu considered time to be not only endless but beginningless. Cultivation of the Tao must have led the Taoists to detachment and to freedom from anxiety about time. Nature as a whole being essentially timeless, one should cultivate such timelessness and not become aroused by temporal crises which will, no doubt, turn out to be not so cosmically significant after all. Even more suggestive of a metaphysical view of time is that of Hui Shih who, like Zeno the Eleatic, had considered the paradox of the flight of an arrow through discrete units to time and space. Some of Hui Shih's paradoxes have been interpreted as advocating the unreality of time.

D. Causation

The scheme for which Aristotle is most famous is that of the four causes material, efficient, formal, and final. The theory of the four causes is a synthesis: Aristotle gathered together the works of his predecessors and put them into a comprehensive framework which has been a field of orientation from which scientists and philosophers have been working ever since. Virtually everything Aristotle discusses under the title of causation can be found in Indian and/or Chinese thought but in scattered references. Schematically pulling them all together was a stroke of original genius which stands out in world history as prominently as it does in the history of Western civilization, just as, for example, in the field of logic his square of opposition stands out.

Although it is not easy to find the exact parallel to these four causes in our other Schools, it must not be thought that the Chinese and Indian Schools did not philosophize about causation. The most basic teachings of the Buddha is that through adequate contemplation one may and must get beyond the endless chain of causation (*pratītyasamutpāda*). Especially between Sāṃkhya and Nyāya there is endless argumentation over theories of causation, the leading question being whether the cause is inherent in the effect, changes into its effect, or whether the effect is inherent in the cause, or whether in some sense causation is an illusory superimposition on the basic Ground of Reality. Aristotle is on similar ground when he raises the question as to whether a particular cause is invariably bound to a particular effect, or whether several causes may produce the same effect, or whether one cause may have several effects, or whether the cause exists before it produces its effect. These questions suggest a comparison between Aristotle's discussion of the relation of actuality and potentiality and the Indian *satkāryavāda-asatkāryavāda* controversy. When Aristotle speaks of all change being the actualization of that which *is*, potentially, is he espousing a form of *satkāryavāda* ?

The Buddhist tendency is to consider causation to be operative primarily in the psychological realm, whereas the Hindu Schools and Aristotle alike considered the soul and the mind to be above, and not affected by, nature even while observing all natural processes and making hypotheses about the laws, causal and otherwise, that govern them. But the Buddhists—anticipating the development of scientific psychology in the West by almost 1500 years—considered the mind to be subject to definite patterns of causal operation.

The Neo-Mohists, who were within a century after Aristotle, had this view of how to explain causation:

> . . .To use 'statements to set forth causes' means not only to set forth the material causes of things, but also the causes (i.e., the steps of reasoning), by which we arrive at a certain statement.[27]

In other words, if the causal relationship obtains in the things operating according to the causal pattern, it almost necessarily follows that there must be the same causal pattern governing the ordering of the ideas that bring the understanding of these events.

The Neo-Mohists conceived of an organic harmonious nexus in which there was a natural concomitance of *thought about causation* and *causation of thought.* All human thought is a part of nature, and nature is basically harmonious, therefore how could there be anything but harmonious relations between thoughts about (nature and therefore about) causation and the actual causation in nature? There could be only one set of laws operating in both nature and mind. This really makes more sense than the assumption in Western cultural heritage that nature and the mind are at odds with each other and operate with two different sets of laws. In the long run, Aristotle is reduced back to the Neo-Mohists; he must necessarily assume, as an axiom, that there is some, if not a high, concurrence between these two sets of laws since any attempt to prove or disprove the concurrence requires using the laws of thought, which leads to a circular argument. Thus, in a way that the Aristotelians did not, the Neo-Mohists conceived the nexus of causation to be inclusive in such a way that is complete in itself; thus explaining how the mind acts causally on things as well as understands things causally. Whether the Neo-Mohist view involves us in a parallelism or a conceptualist-realist controversy as it did in the European medieval period and in China in the same period is difficult to determine.

The whole conception in the Neo-Mohist School, then, is perhaps more Platonic, or even exemplarist in a way that does not come into European tradition until Saint Augustine at least, than Aristotelian. This, however, involves another term, *fa*.

> The *fa*, in other words, is the common model which may be applied to any particular things falling in its class. In the class of squares, for example, there are such differences as that some are made of wood, others of stone, etc., but this does not prevent them from all being squares. Extending this principle, the model through the imitation of which things become like this model, is a *fa*, and the things that are modelled upon this *fa* are imitators or *hsiao*. The *fa* for making a circle, for example, may either be the concept of the ideal circle, or it may be the compasses used for making circles, or it may be another circle which has already been completed. Once this *fa* has been fixed, all the things which imitate it become circular in form.[28]

Fa has been associated with Platonic "Form" and compared with Aristotle's final, efficient, and formal causes; in short, it is too broadly defined for us to be sure how Aristotelian or Platonic an interpretation the Neo-Mohists may have intended it to have.

It is fairly clear that the Israelites did not develop, in the strict sense, a philosophy of causation at all. God is the cause of everything—except a few things where, inconsistently,

Satan does or is allowed to do something quite outside the ordinary sequence of the Lord's being the cause of everything. This seems strange and is as yet to be explained, for in other cultures where the poetic genius was developed to such a degree as we find in *Isaiah* and the *Song of Songs* and some of the Psalms we usually find an equally high degree of philosophical development.

THIRTEEN

Metaphysics

A. Being/non Being

There is much overlapping between the Physics and the *Metaphysics*; Aristotle probably never intended that they should be constituted as separate fields or disciplines. He begins the *Metaphysics* by saying that all men by nature desire knowledge. By means of the senses they seek to know, not in terms of the One or of God, but in terms of causes (*aitiai*) and principles (*archai*), the knowledge (*episteme*) of which will give, or rather is, wisdom (*sophia*).

Aristotle's determined intention is to come to a single focus such as the Buddhists achieved. In his search for the Single Principle he employs the technique of classification by genera and species. But invariably as soon as he begins to analyze he multiplies distinctions; and though finding plurality in every possible definition, he still refuses to abandon definition. It might well be said that if he did achieve his single focus, it was in the science of definition as such (*horismos*), not in the principles thus defined.

Can we really make definitions ? Aristotle cogently argues that we can because we must. Reason (*nous*) is the divine faculty within us that we cannot avoid following. To try to refute philosophy is only further to philosophize, 'surrender' to any higher authority is impossible, and abdication to anything lower—skepticism or return to the merely sensate life—is beneath our human dignity.

With some crypto-Buddhist Hindu idealists who come later (Gauḍapāda, for example) the inference is drawn that since "the son of a barren woman" is a meaningless 'definition', how do we know that any of the other definitions which we make are any more valid than this extreme test case ? And if our knowledge by definition falls down, is there any other way by which we can validate our knowledge of things ? If we cannot validate our knowledge, then we must conclude that all our knowledge is *māyā*, except, perhaps, that by which we know this. Whether personal or impersonal, or whether some neutral category including this dichotomy, the "that by which" is somehow both Knowledge and Being. There may be a slight advantage here over Aristotle for he never seems quite to make the final reduction of the knower-known identity back into itself, i.e., the "reduction to identity" of soul to self, self to ultimate reality, and in parallel sequence the reduction of the known to the knower and this in turn to ultimate reality likewise, in such a way that all that is not so reducible is to be considered as *māyā*. In fact, he never quite discovers the method of *re*duction, which is the sublating synthesis inclusive of the methods of *in*duction and *de*duction. In insisting on definition by distinction he is only further separating the ontologically inseparable within which we must function, or rather, which we are. This is the extreme, of course, and was scarcely proposed before Aristotle. However, the basic components of the argument had been around since early Upaniṣadic days if not since the era of the Ṛg Veda.

In Aristotle's method of classification and definition, similitudes and differentia naturally group into genera and species in an hierarchical order giving us a sort of ladder of the sciences themselves, the higher being inclusive of the lower and necessarily more abstract. At the top of the ladder is Being which, as the most general possible prerequisite of the existence of anything, is also, unfortunately, the most abstract. Being is the abstraction of the highest possible order of the one and only common characteristic that pertains to all possible entities.

In Aristotle's procedure the particular sciences are not unified so much as properly placed or assigned—almost in the sense of Hsün Tzu's Rectification of Names. In Hsün Tzu's treatment of the Rectification of Names we ultimately get something very closely resembling the famous "tree of Porphyry". Hsün Tzu says :

> We press on and generalize; we generalize and generalize still more, until there is nothing more general. Then only we stop. . . . We press on and classify. We classify and classify still more, until there is no more classification to be made, and then we stop.[29]

The "tree of Porphyry" is also virtually laid out in Aristotle's *Metaphysics*.[30]

The essential point is that without the science of predication there can be no physics or metaphysics no, matter how loudly one shouts the magic words "Being", "Idea", "Tao", or "Brahman". Even these terms are not exempt from the basic rule—which turns out to be not merely a technique for classification but a metaphysical principle of dialectic—of constantly balancing off likeness and difference against each other. This seems equally realized by both Aristotle and Hsün Tzu.

Thus Aristotle comes in Book IV to a consideration of Being *qua* Being and the properties inherent in it by virtue of its own nature. He cannot separate Being *qua* Being from its properties nor allow any manner of consideration wherein the properties are transcended or in any way left behind. He leaves the "ladder" there ready for the descent in case it be necessary instead of being content, once the "point" or "field" of Being is purely conceived in itself, to remain there. In other words, he considers the *pravṛtti* and the *nivṛtti mārgas* to be of equal value, and he will not allow the transition from *saguṇa* Brahman to *nirguṇa* Brahman, from the *tao* of earth to the Tao of Heaven. This is not necessarily an adverse criticism, however, for he is by no means alone here. Hsün Tzu as against the strict Taoists, and Vaiśeṣika as against the Mīmāmsā, will continue to support him.

What then is Being *qua* Being ? Aristotle says that in a sense a definition of Being is not only impossible but unnecessary for the simple reason that it is by Being that other things, substances (*ousiai*) in particular, are defined. Being does not 'be' in its own right but only has existence insofar as it is dialectically related to actual existents, things that do 'be'. But although things 'have' existence as their most necessary description or the most essential prerequisite before they can be described, since a nonexistent thing cannot be described, Being does not in the same sense 'have existence'. It is not a "thing" but a logical operation, a class of all classes which, if it truly exists at all, exists in an entirely different mode. According to this realist metaphysics, things exist (have existential import) whereas abstract classes do not 'exist' but are only a mental tool for calculation concerning the things that are members of the classes concerned.

This may be compared with Ingalls' discussion of Nyāya :

> 'Sattā' means existence or reality. It is traditionally defined as a generic character, the broadest of all such characters . . . Broad as it is, however, there are many things one can talk about that do not 'exist' or are not 'real' in this terminology. Among them are the generic characters themselves . . .[31]

But even more pertinent is the controversy between Nyāya and Mīmāṁsā on the nature of *sat* (Being). Whether we can arrive at the correct designation of *sat*-in-itself remains as problematical as it does in Aristotle.

Still the question remains whether the search for a Single Principle is itself only the assertion of a presupposition. As soon as we seek to reduce statements to their presuppositions we end either in redundancy or in a vacuum of naivete. Without logic we cannot even prove or demonstrate or clarify any existence at all, but with logic we can only fabricate demonstrations about what we must presuppose without really grasping the presuppositions. Shall we admit that the Jainas were more nearly right than Aristotle—presupposition only leads back to presupposition *ad infinitum*? We are inherently trapped in relativity, and until by some yogic or other discipline we come to omniscience, the best we can do is to admit relativity.

Then, too, having arrived at the concept of Being *qua* Being the basic question inevitably arises: what is the relation of Being to beings? How can such a concept be considered without a certain extrapolation away from "things", a certain abstraction that exceeds universalization? Likewise, if we begin with Being *qua* Being, how can we bring it down, as it were, to its proper function of imparting existence to things without compromising its essential quality of exaltedness as the one Universal of universals upon which we can depend as the final end of our Search for the Single Principle? Even if we say that Being *is* the One, our proposition does not necessarily exclude the possibility of its being other things also, or of other things being, in spite of their inherent plurality or severality, included in the One making it rather the All than the One in pristine purity.

Aristotle insists that Being is faced with the necessity of being *something* or not 'being' at all. The counter-argument to this, nevertheless, is that things really do not exist except as *māyā* since they are finite, limited, evanescent, and unstable, and by definition existence entails much more than constant change and unreliability; therefore, only Being as a Pure and Eternal Idea truly exists. Things only reflect or obscurely participate in Being like moonlight shadows in relation to the sun, or else the being of things is only a sort of imitation plastic copy of the original ivory carving, as it were. It is against such a view that Aristotle is arguing, and if he does not swing to the complete other extreme, denying Being altogether or anything abstract as divorced from reality in an extreme naive empiricism, it is all to his credit. He is seeking for a valid middle position, a rational positive synthesis, not merely a catalytic analysis of others' views.

Modern Indian realists and materialists tend to put quite a different interpretation on Sāṃkhya than has been done traditionally by the Advaitins, who tend not only to adopt Sāṃkhya but to adapt it to their ends, so much so indeed, that one must be cautious in trying to get to the original pre-Vedāntic formulation by stripping off the Advaitic overlay. Sinha is recommended since he is less prone to follow this Advaitic overlay than most contemporary interpreters, Sharma and Das Gupta for example. *Puruṣa* usually takes the primary attention of Advaitic interpreters almost to the exclusion of *prakṛti* which, in their view, is only *māyā*.

If we equate *prakṛti* with Aristotle's nature, we are left with precious little to deal with in Sāṃkhya that we can call metaphysics. If *prakṛti* enfolds almost all, if not all, that we can know by experience and is inclusive of all the categories and the levels of psycho-physical functions corresponding to Aristotle's vegetative, animal, and rational souls, what then is *puruṣa*? Is it the same or almost the same as the Single Principle for which Aristotle constantly seeks? In a sense it seems to be except that, like Plato's system, it is too much apart from nature (*prakṛti*) to be an absolute Unifier. It is not a *single* principle, therefore, but only one of two principles. That Sāṃkhya is more radically dualistic than Descartes, not to mention Plato, should not be denied by any stretch of interpretation.

If *puruṣa* is almost or even entirely removed from the realm of experienceable nature, then how do we know it exists? What are its characteristics? What function does it have? What are its duration and location in time and space or in some dimension other than the spatio-temporal dimension of *prakṛti*? The answers to these questions, not being self-evident or derivable directly from the *Sūtras* themselves, have been favorite themes in Indian Philosophy ever since the first formulations of the system in oral tradition.

As distinct from the monism of later Vedānta—and we must reiterate that monist trend does not explicitly emerge in Indian thought until later even though it may be extracted out of some Upaniṣads—and as distinct from the pluralism of Vaiśeṣika, Jainism, and Mīmāṁsā, Sāmkhya is neither monistic nor pluralistic but dualistic. Perhaps it is a "middle way" after all? Still Aristotle would not have approved of it because to him the Middle Way was rather a qualified monism, which he could never formulate completely even though he was as equally dissatisfied with the Pre-Socratic materialists—pluralists and monists as with Plato himself.

As to the specific problem of Being/non/Being, it is difficult to find this in Sāmkhya without spueezing pretty hard or reading into it what is not explicitly there. Is *puruṣa* to be equated with Being? There is no evidence that Sāṃkhya makes any such claim. Then with *prakṛti*? Perhaps in a realistic sense, since all that is or functions in the realm of the known or knowable is taken as real without questions about non-Being even in the sense of *abhāva* (absence) not to mention *māyā* which, please note, does not figure at all in the original *Sāṃkhya*. Essentially the same thing can and must be said about original Vaiśeṣika. The question does not arise concerning non-Being, just as there is no doctrine of *māyā* in either system in their early formulations.

For Nyāya, "non-Being" (*abhāva*, absence) is merely a logical function as a variety of negation. There are four varieties of *abhāva* : prior nonexistence, posterior nonexistence, mutual nonexistence, and absolute negation. *Abhāva* refers to particular entities and not to Being since such a denial would be an absolute impossibility for the Nyāya-Vaiśeṣika realistic metaphysics. *Abhāva* is only theoretical or logical denial; moreover, it is the denial of the existence (not the "being", whatever that might be) of some particular impossibility, such as a square circle.

It might be argued that *bhāva* and *abhāva* are not the key terms, but rather *sattā* and *asat*—a distinction which is not easy to make in the English language, although it roughly parallels the distinction nowadays being emphasized by the phenomenologists between Being (*sattā*) and existence (*bhāva*). But in the early Nyāya-Vaiśesika virtually all of these distinctions, even that between *bhāva* and *sattā*, are primarily, if not completely, logical rather than ontological. It was the later Navya-Nyāya that enlarged and developed the concept of *abhāva* and ascribed reality to it.

As in the other sections, when it comes to Mīmāmsā we are in difficulty chronologically since almost all traditional treatments go into great detail over the controversial differences between Kumārila and Prabhākara who live in an entirely different world than our present period. Specifically Jaimini, or even Śabara Mīmāṁsā, is very difficult to extricate from all the overlay. First, we are again confronted by a radical realism and, according to many interpretations, even a radical pluralism, and from such a system it is difficult to derive anything resembling a Platonic ontology or even a moderately qualified one like Aristotle's. The temptation is very strong, even more so than in the case of Sāṃkhya, to read back from Advaita into the Mīmāṁsā something of *māyāvāda* and therefore a doctrine of non-Being. But right at the outset we are reminded in the Jaimini *Sūtras* themselves that even the early Mīmāṁsā regarded *abhāva* as primarily if not exclusively involved in epistemology rather than ontology as such.

Abhāva in Mīmāṁsā has a nuance of connotation that is

quite different from its use in Vaiśeṣika. It is not a pramāṇa in Mīmāṁsā, and because of this status it has an at least quasi-causal power insofar as it can cause knowledge about what is "not there". From these admissions it might even be argued that Mīmāṁsā attributes reality to non-Being. But that would be going far too far since it would contradict other aspects of the system in addition to forgetting that *abhāva* is only a logical function, no more. Even the concept of *pralaya*, which is about as close to non-Being as a realist might ask to go, is rejected by Mīmāṁsā.

Some mention is certainly available of the *sat-cit-ānanda* definition of Brahman in early as well as late Mīmāṁsā, but there seems to be nothing like the full development of ontology in the strict sense or of *māyā* in the full technical sense of non-Being until the time of Gauḍapāda and Śaṅkara. In other words, as far as we can find, virtually all schools of Indian philosophy contemporary with Aristotle would be in agreement with him that Being must be the being of something, as we have explained above.

It is virtually impossible to find anything in Hsün Tzu's views which would indicate any treatment of the problem of Being/non-Being in the Aristotelian sense. In fact, his realism went much further than Aristotle's; and although in most cases he is very close to Aristotle, in matters of metaphysics he is sufficiently positivistic or pragmatically humanist that he either deliberately neglects or consciously rejects anything that does not bear practical consequences for explicitly human affairs.

Although in some respects Hsün Tzu is supposed to have been influenced almost as much by Lao Tzu as by Confucius, he reads out of the Tao any possible mystical interpretation and says in effect that what is referred to is really simply the way (*tao*) that human beings think and act, and that is all. Likewise, in his interpretation of *T'ien* (Heaven) he is anti-theological, anti-ontological; or rather it may better be said that such questions simply do not arise. About the closest he comes to metaphysical speculation is in his interpretation of *ming* (fate), yet even here he discards every intimation of any transcendental factor.

Hsün Tzu does have a method of abstraction for the purpose of practical classification of things in his Rectification of Names discipline. But this stops when it comes to matters of nonexistence or non-Being. It would appear that insofar as he has a doctrine of negation at all, it is strictly for the purposes of lexical definition and logical operations. The notion of nothingness as such, or the idea of the conflict between phenomena and noumena which seems to underlie Parmenides (and later Advaita Vedānta), just never could bother him. He is a realist out-and-out and would probably have asked Aristotle why he was clinging to so much of Plato and Parmenides in these matters anyway.

Being for the Taoists remains as the Tao, the Great Mystery (*Hsüan*), and definition is denied as a method whereby knowledge of the Tao is to be attained. We shall mention those aspects of Chuang Tzu's "Way" which most disagree with Aristotle's "Thought" in order to suggest a means beyond the strictly rational techniques of induction, deduction, and dialectic whereby one may better complete his search for the Single Principle. We shall consider, not Chuang Tzu's Tao or *teh*, but his *hsü*, *ling*, and *ming*.

> "Hsü" means to be vacuous and receptive . . . Chuang Tzu, followed by Hsün Tzu and the Neo-Confucianists, takes *hsü* as one fundamental nature of the mind and connects it with the word *ling* which means knowing freely, spontaneously, and without attachment.
>
> . . .
>
> . . . Chuang Tzu uses the idea of *ming*, which means the lasting actual state of the mind when his nature, as purely vacuous and receptive, is fully realized in its knowing. Literally, *ming* means "light". As a state of mind, it is enlightenment of mind.
>
> . . . according to this type of thinking, there is neither world nor individual. The state of mind of this type of thinking is thus neither subjective nor objective. Instead, it resides in the center of subject and object, and, hanging *in vacuo*, escapes from the duality of these two.[32]

Obviously, this is not in Aristotle. According to the metaphysics of *yin* and *yang*, Aristotle is a *yang* philosopher, as is

Hsün Tzu to a very great extent, while Chuang Tzu is a *yin* philosopher.

Chuang Tzu's story of the frog in his well-defined universe is a good illustration of the meaning, existentially, of *māyā* in a moderate interpretation. Aristotle might simply classify these concepts as metaphors instead of definitions, however, leaving us, dialectically, with a problem which has a history almost coterminous with civilization itself thus far. For we may insist that metaphors open up new meaningfulness where definitions confine us and tie us down eventually to dogmas. Chuang Tzu might say in response to Aristotle's systematic rigor : "Poor Aristotle ! He wanted to stop the top and then wondered why it kept flopping over refusing to be defined."

In the Parmenidean and Platonic traditions, as well as in the Taoist and Upaniṣadic traditions, there is a wondrous infatuation with the mystery of non-Being. But for Aristotle non-Being is no more a mystery than Being since as soon as one affirms the actual or potential existence of anything one has introduced negation into his *thinking*; but non-Being does not exist in nature, nor could it. Hence, in order to understand or posit or recognize such a concept as that of Being, Aristotle is fully aware that it is necessary to admit the dialectically opposite of Being, namely non-Being, not as something that 'exists' but as the logical or dialectical opposite without which Being could not be thought.

Perhaps the basic difference is that the Taoist or the Platonist attempts to become his own 'other' and to reascend from the differentiation to the undifferentiated Ground, whereas the Hsün Tzu-Aristotelian type is quite content to let the 'other' remain in its proper place without trying to be or become that also, having confidence in the natural and logical order of things, each with both its selfhood and otherness, its being and, in proper proportion, its non-being—non-being in the sense of limitations rationally considered, not some phantom of itself that "non-be's" in some other non-world.

In refuting Parmenides' and in criticizing Plato's views on non-Being, Aristotle distinguishes three senses of non-Being. Prime Matter is non-Being in the sense that potentiality is non-Being. Form is non-Being in the sense that the oak which the acorn will become does not 'exist'. Privation is non-Being in the sense that absence (*abhāva*) is non-Being.

But none of these three designations seems to cover quite the sense of non-Being found in the Taoists or the Buddhists. In the former the term is *wu*, which is only the counterpart of Being (*yu*), the antinomy being resolved in the concept of the Great Oneness (*t'ai i*). In the latter the antinomy is resolved in the concept of the *śūnya*, 'emptiness'. The Taoists also had this *śūnya* to a very profound degree and termed it *hsü*. The connotations of *śūnya* are more moral than ontological for both.

The Buddhist concept of *śūnya* is more highly developed in the Mahāyāna than in the Hīnayāna which is closer both chronologically and ideologically to Aristotle; but even the *Majjhima Nikāya* a Hīnayāna text, devotes two major sections to it. The question of non-Being in the sense of *abhāva* which troubled the Naiyāyikas does not trouble the Buddhists so much, largely because they are not so much interested in ontology as in psychology and ethics (*dhamma*). *Śūnya* is thus not so much non-Being as an emptying out of the mind of all conceptual thinking—even the concept of emptiness. This is commended as the only way to avoid the multiplication of distinctions which plagues any Aristotelianism in spite of what Maritain says about *distinguer pour unir*.

This implicitly raises the question of the relation of mental states to the actual world. Certainly the senses and the ego do blind us, keeping us from right perception and from impartial judgments; Aristotle would have no quarrel with that. But he might question whether it is honest simply to meditate on the 'emptiness of things', for this involves ontology and not just epistemology.

The point is that the Buddhists of Aristotle's time did believe in the impermanence of things, as we have previously noted in many contexts. And impermanence meant absence (*abhāva*) of anything to cling to. Just as 'no soul' is pivotal in their psychology, so 'no being' is pivotal in their ontology. In fact they insist that *śūnya* is absence rather than logical impossibility (e.g., son of a barren woman), or mere denial, or some mysterious something or other out there which somehow must exist even though it is all too like nothing or non-Being since it cannot be described. In other words, Theravāda does not hold to Being or to non-Being. *Śūnya* is, for want of a better word, sheer neutrality untrammelled by any dualistic conception or affirmation or negation.

Whether Aristotle's *theoria*, the *noesis noeseos*, includes the complete imperturbability of the *śūnya* is for the student to determine by whatever method is needed. Probably Aristotle would have considered even this imperturbability as subject to critical investigation, but then the Buddhist would claim such investigation to be at a lower level. It may be that the two ways are not reconcilable and one must choose between them as simply different types. And yet this certainly compromises both Aristotle's and the Buddhist's intention of arriving at a single perspective that will include all choices and varieties and differences.

B. Being/Becoming

Change is perhaps *the* major problem for metaphysics and for all the rest of philosophy; and the problem of motion seems to attract Aristotle's attention almost more than the problems of Being and the nature of God. Aristotle asserts that there are some things that are not subject to process, to beginning and ending, and it seems that behind this statement is a marked preference for permanence against Heraclitus's preference for change. Though he prefers permanence, he does admit, unlike Parmenides, that change is real. The here-and-now is certainly not permanent, but the universal is. Geometrical figures as pure forms remain permanent even though we may erase exemplifications of them and draw them anew. Here Aristotle is dangerously close to Plato's Ideas which he has so painstakingly avoided and even attempted to refute at great length. Aristotle thinks that it is the attributes (termed "accidents" in Scholastic language) that change while the substances, the substrates of the attributes, do not change. Change is not chaotic but orderly in a sort of semi-permanent or at least stable way.

Becoming is the realm of the transition from the potential, the unknown, into the realm of the actual, the known, the definable. Thus, insofar as becoming comes within our grasp or can be brought under our dianoetic faculties, it simply becomes another variety of Being.

Aristotle discusses change in relation to everything except us, the observers. But if we are just as changeable, both in the sense of being subjected to changes from without and also changing ourselves and other things from within, or indirectly by changing our environment so that the externals will not change ourselves so much—if we are no more reliably unchanging, in some sense 'absolute', then how are we capable of making judgments about all the rest of the phantasmagoria? Some, like Averroes, have interpreted the agent intellect as the unchanging judger which satisfies this need.

For Aristotle, mystical apprehension is neither necessary nor convenient for knowledge of that which does not change, for the only necessity is our dianoetic postulations derived equally from experience and from dialectical crosschecking of possible theories, i.e., we 'logically' derive Being *qua* Being Prime Matter, and substance. We, therefore, have no reason for despair, for this dianoetic faculty joins mind with reality, regardless of the form whereby we may deal with it. But the antinomy between the permanent and the changing, as two of these forms, remains. The best that we can do is to hope for an adequate mathematics, a calculus, which Aristotle almost comes to formulate at the end of the *De Generatione* when he deals with the cyclic (usually mistranslated as the circular) motion which will mediate these two basic categories; but we can never expect to prove that one is more ultimate than the other.

In discussing the substratum of change, that which lies under all things (*to hypokeimenon*)—and it is strange that this term, which he takes from Plato almost without variation in meaning, should be chosen rather than a term indicating a total dependence as seems the case with the Mīmāṃsakas—Aristotle himself was not completely satisfied with his own attempts at solving the difficulty about the relation of the substratum (Prime Matter) to unqualified, undifferentiated Being (Being *qua* Being). Are they identical or at opposite ends of the hierarchy? If Randall in stressing the dynamic side of

Aristotle's philosophy[33], is more faithful to the original Aristotle than, say, the interpretations we have inherited either from the Thomistic tradition or from the German idealists, then he, the 'real' Aristotle, is closer to Mīmāmsā.

The popular notion of Brahman in Indian philosophy is something all-too-Platonic, all-too-mystical, all-too-spiritual. We should remember that during this Axial Age the realist rather than the idealist trend was predominant, the latter not becoming dominant until the late Han-Hellenistic-Bactrian Period with the emergence and flowering of the Mahāyāna. With the Mīmāṃsā and other realist schools the term "Brahman" is really almost synonymous with our word "Reality" with a capital "R", with Reality *as such.* That Reality-as-such, whatever its nature, must underlie or undergird, or permeate and/or transcend, or lie in some hierarchical relation to, all its many material or worldly manifestations, itself remaining One or retaining Unicity of a comprehensive sort that embraces all the manifold or finite realities as we know them. Now according to Mīmāṃsā, such a Reality could not be merely ideal, even though it is by ideas (in our *heads*) as instruments that we come to knowledge about that Reality-as-such or anything else that might be real as included in It.

Likewise, if all that we know as real is moving and changing all the time, then how could one say that that Reality-as-such is not also changing somehow and to some extent since the changes are also really real and not outside Reality-as-such (Brahman)? Therefore, Brahman is also dynamic, not static, in a way that Randall so cogently argued that Aristotle's Being is not static but dynamic. Instead of the *to hypokeimenon* being, as it were, "down there" at the bottom of the hierarchy of being (s), it should be taken as really identical with Being, which therefore is not merely Ideal but actually existing, the "real stuff", whatever it may be, out of which the world is made.

Thus, according to Randall and Sinha respectively, Aristotle and Mīmāṃsā have a realistic metaphysics in common. They both allow for the phenomenon of Change or Becoming as almost primary, but not quite. They insist that it is real change, not just the appearance of change; and yet they both insist that there is an unchanging permanence of some sort or other which is also real and which undergirds all that does change. Aristotle and Mīmāṃsā may differ in many other details, but their remarkable similarity in at least these basics should not be overlooked.

In the light of the Vaiśeṣika system, as well as the Jaina and Sāṃkhya systems and most of the general trends in Indic civilization, Aristotle's *genesis* and *phthora* take on a fresh significance, insofar as, instead of the particularities which fascinate Aristotle, there is in the background of these systems an emphasis on the vast cycles of time between *pralayas*. Equal importance is placed on evolution and involution. The Greek view does not include speculations about such grand cosmic cycles even though it presupposes the eternity of the world. Aristotle does seem to incline toward a qualified cyclic theory of time but he does not seem to see this as having the same great significance for his philosophy of Becoming that Vaiśeṣika does.

The purpose of Becoming in Vaiśeṣika according to Basu is to explain, account for, make possible and help the evolution of the souls under the influence of *Adṛṣṭa* and according to the law of *karma*. The system of the universe has no internal purpose of its own and the evolution of the world is not an end in itself: it exists for the sake of the souls. Basu defines *adṛṣṭa* as an unseen principle capable of initiating changes. It consists of *dharma*, merit and demerit, and is intended to denote the potential after-effects of volitional acts from previous births. *Adṛṣṭa* inheres in the Soul.[34] Is *Adṛṣṭa* comparable to the Chinese concepts of *li* or even *teh*? Or is it the Single Principle which Aristotle did not find because he insisted on reducing it to something that would be less than what he was looking for? *Adṛṣṭa* is like and yet unlike Aristotle's Unmoved Mover, which seems to have nothing to do with the souls. Would the Latin Scholastics have found in *Adṛṣṭa* a middle ground between Aristotle and the Biblical views? Whether there is any factor in Aristotle's system comparable to the Vaiśeṣika *Adrsṭa* is debatable; still, this is only a typical point where comparative methods cross-culturally might be a more fruitful way of viewing and explicating Aristotle historically than the present trend of critical examination of the text in the light of later developments only in the Latin West.

In contrast to Plato and Sāṁkhya (all in the realm of *prakṛti* is changing but *puruṣa* is unchanging), in the Vaiśeṣika and the Aristotelian systems the spiritual (*jīva* and *psyche*) realms are also subject to change and operate within the realm of Becoming, although release (*mokṣa*) is supposed to be the deliverance from Becoming and the entrance into Being, as it were.

It is difficult to compare Aristotle and the Buddhists, for although the Theravāda schools in particular depend largely on the *kṣaṇa* doctrine of momentariness, this is not strictly a doctrine of Becoming. Rather, the emphasis should be placed on the *pratītyasamutpāda*, the wheel of endless causation, and the regularity of change which it stresses.

Bhāva is used in quite a different sense in Buddhist circles than in most Hindu contexts. Its simplest meaning is "presence" as opposed to "absence". In connection with the *pratītyasamutpāda*, it is the tendency to remain within the wheel of *saṃsāra*, within the endless round of causation, and thus within the realm of Becoming rather than in transcendence or deliverance from it by the Noble Eight-Fold Path. Just as in psychoanalysis when one traces tendencies back to their origin one is released from them by bringing them into consciousness and then into conscious control—a reversal of the natural process, a sort of un-becoming or de-becoming so, if one puts a sort of Whiteheadian interpretation on these things, one might even come to an explanation of how it is claimed that not only chains of causation in one's own psyche can be cut or stopped by this reversing process, but chains of causation in the outside world also (if there is really any difference) so that the universe won't 'remember' them any more. (Whitehead speaks of the "memory" of the universe; too bad he never had the opportunity to become more overtly a Buddhist.)

As for the matter of Becoming, both Aristotle and (according to Sinha) the Sarvāstivādins believed that change is real and that there is really something 'there' that changes, illusion being ruled out and replaced at best by mistaken identity.

In both, although only latently, one moreover finds a tendency towards a theory of cosmic homeostasis as the possible basic pattern of the universe, such that there could never be a total coming-to-be or passing-away but rather a dynamic balance between these two extremes. However, according to Das Gupta and others, no Buddhist school ever admitted permanency, and the traditional view is to see Aristotle as thinking of permanency as primary. Thus, depending on the interpretation, Sarvāstivāda may be seen as a contrast with Aristotle rather than a comparison. Certainly earlier Buddhist tradition was reluctant to admit much more than the basic insight that since *everything* changes, one of the causes of suffering is clinging to things, even to metaphysical notions of "substance", "essence", and all the rest of the indefinables. So perhaps the final question in this context from the Buddhist point of view is: Was Aristotle only clinging to a (false) notion of permanence, and should not he have 'let go' so that the truth—if truth there be—could continue to flow ?

As with Theravāda Buddhism, the emphasis in the early Jaina *Sūtras* is so almost completely ethical that it is difficult to squeeze any metaphysics out of them. It might seem that since the Jainas put so much emphasis on relativity they would go along with the Buddhists toward emphasis on change over against the typical Hindu views of emphasis on permanence. But such is not the case. For the most part they lean heavily towards permanence rather than change, toward Being—but only in the realistic, pluralistic sense of beings—rather than Becoming, even in the presuppositions of their ethics. As realists, the Jainas are not interested in such ideal abstractions as Being as such, even though they are interested in the problem of permanence and change as related to substances. To the Jainas substances are definitely real in themselves in such a way that they need no ontological underpinning. Insofar as they can be known, substances are permanent. Thus the Jainas criticized the Buddhist doctrine of *kṣaṇavāda* ; and just as the Parmenidians and the Heraclitians in the West are still debating, so in India, Ceylon, Burma, and Thailand the Buddhists and Jainas are still debating this issue which is vitally important for the intelligent development of an organic philosophy of science.

Not only the Taoists but virtually all Chinese sages presuppose that change is primary and that what is permanent, or appears to be permanent, or is relatively permanent, is only the patterns of change. Aristotle does not co⌐cede so much, even though Randall's interpretation does challenge the traditional interpretations on this very point. Hellmut Wilhelm gives the general Chinese view :

> Reflection on the simple fundamental facts of our experience brings immediate recognition of constant change. To the unsophisticated mind, the characteristic thing about phenomena is their dynamism. It is only abstract thinking that takes them out of their dynamic continuity and isolates them as static units.[35]

With Aristotle there can be rest or stop (*stasis*) and this concept no doubt influenced the whole of Western tradition right down to Newton. But for this Chinese view the opposite of change is not rest or *stasis* for this is still an aspect of change. There may be either forward or backward change, but never can we validly assert complete stop even as a possibility. There may be slowing-down or speeding-up in either direction, but never complete cessation.

> The opposite of change in Chinese thought is growth of what ought to decrease, the downfall of what ought to rule. Change, then, is not simply movement as such, for its opposite is also movement. The state of absolute immobility is such an abstraction that the Chinese, or at least the Chinese of the period which produced this book [*I Ching*], could not conceive it. Change is natural movement rather, development that can only reverse itself by going against nature.[36]

This concept of change as natural movement is comparable to Aristotle's concept of entelechy. To Aristotle the principle of entelechy was inherent within the natural order and did not appear from any extra-natural source. Things move toward their natural end, but this 'final cause' has nothing to do with anything supernatural. Purposive behavior of animals is the most evident example of entelechy. An egg becomes a chicken, a child becomes a man, and so on. Somehow the whole balance of nature depends on inter-reciprocal entelechies.

The most likely exception to the general Chinese idea of the primacy of change or Becoming over permanency or Being is Hsün Tzu, although even there the evidence is rather scanty that he opposed it.

From Heraclitus Aristotle no doubt inherited the notion that flux (Becoming, process, change) is associated with *conflict* and not with harmony. With the Taoist tradition, if not with other Chinese traditions as well, that is not the case. The polarization of Tao into *yin* and *yang* is one of complementariness. This contrast between the Heraclitian "war is the father of all things, of men and gods and all that is" vis-*á*-vis the *yin-yang* harmony may partially characterize the history of the two civilizations ever after. Could it be that Aristotle really does not like change because of associating it, at least subconsciously, with disorder, chaos, irrationality, conflict? And why the wish, the will, the preference for permanency? Why not admit with the Theravādins that everything—observed, observer, observation—is impermanent, or admit with the Jainas that all is relative?

FOURTEEN

Theology

In Europe the word "theology" had had a long history before Aristotle. It was an invention of the Greek mind, not of the later Judeo-Christian developments. The Judaic religion never quite developed a scientific or systematic approach to the subject in spite of some rather advanced insights in the specifically religious but not theological field.

According to Jaeger, God became a problem to the Greeks (and has remained so ever since). It might be said that in the Chinese as in the Hebraic tradition, but for entirely different reasons, God never became a problem. In the Hebraic instance, intensity of piety seemed to render systematics unnecessary, whereas with the Chinese, so basically humanist after Confucius, the problem just did not arise because attention was shifted to the social and political reality and other matters specifically human. At least this was so among the Chinese aristocracy, while evidently superstitious and popular religion continued undisturbed at the village level.

However, in the Six Systems of Indian philosophy we do find doubts and disputes and an amazingly wide variety of standardized arguments concerning the existence and nature of God and the gods. In India as well as in Greece philosophy emerged out of a polytheism with the theological aspects of philosophy taking their place along side the other problems of philosophy. Once again, although the trend in the first half of the twentieth century was to emphasize Greece as the cradle of science and India as the cradle of mysticism (and never shall these ever have any common bond—strange notion!), as for doubts and iconoclasms, both India and Greece contain the full range from blind credulity to crass hedonistic cynicism. For India also, God became a major, but not necessarily *the* major, problem.

It is difficult to determine how early the Vaiṣṇava mythology of Kalki, the Avatar to come, or the Mahāyāna Maitreya, the Bodhisattva that is yet to come, began to be current. But of course the prophetic teaching of the Messiah has remained very strong in general world history, and that somewhat strangely considering the total perspective, for the Greeks especially, and the Chinese and the Hindus to a notable extent, looked back to a Golden Age from which mankind had degenerated. Aristotle had no eschatology. He was concerned primarily with his own time in history as he knew it. As for the future, certainly no *parousia*, no coming Messiah or Avatar, no Mahdi or even "withering away of the state" and long awaited Utopia—none of these futuristic foci can be found in his whole system. And to the Greeks generally, the premedieval Hindus, most pre-medieval Buddhists, the Confucianists and the Taoists, such a notion of a coming Savior of the world would have been completely foreign.

Aristotle does not theologize in separation from the rest of his work. Here and there we catch glimpses of his developing opinions, but always in some other than specifically theological contexts. To skim off from other works what are virtually parenthetical remarks and thus attempt to write a theology into Aristotle's system is therefore perhaps a perversion at the outset. Anaxagoras and Anaximines and the others had gone through the crisis of outgrowing their 'fundamentalist' heritage, as had many of their contemporaries in the Axial Period such as the Buddha, Mahāvīra the Jaina Tīrthaṅkara, Confucius, and most of the other Chinese sages. Aristotle in a sense should be considered more neo-orthodox or humanist than either traditionally orthodox or rebellious. Once again, the rational Middle Way prevails : neither atheism nor superstitious uncritical acceptance but intelligent reappraisal of all previous notions, one against the other dialectically, to yield at least suggestions towards system by eliminating contradictory views, thus giving a challenge to exceed what had accumulated in the past instead of discarding it altogether. Net result: Aristotle's theology has very little to do with popular religion or piety; it is a matter of physics and metaphysics almost entirely

Considering his grandiose and detailed structure of proofs, demonstrations definitions and distinctions, it seems strange that Aristotle's conception of God is so relatively unsophisticated. In a sense his conceptions of Being and the One are really more primary than his conception of God, who is merely *a* Being, *somehow* the Prime Mover, *somehow* the ultimate Focus, the unexpressed Entelechy towards which all process tends, whether it ever arrives or not. It is doubtful whether Aristotle ever saw God as the Reconciler of all his antinomies and antitheses.

Working against the background of Greek polytheism in much the same way that the philosophers of India were working against the background of Vedic polytheism, Aristotle is faced with the alternative of either discarding the concept of "God" altogether and finding or constructing a purely pansophical concept of the One Ultimate Principle undergirding all reality, including the gods, or of arriving at a concept of God that would be inclusive of the Principle whereby Being, as inclusive of many "beings", tends to be subject to description. In Being, in other words, is the solution to the problem of the One and the many—or is it necessarily only a quasi-solution as long as there remains any possible equivocation between the Being of God and the Being of the world?

Without the equivalent of the term "Brahman" Aristotle is trying to arrive at a similar concept but refuses to admit that it will not be conformed to his logical formulations. That God should be this concept does not quite occur to him. Aristotle's God, in other words, is too closely linked with his concept of nature and not, as is generally supposed, with the final resolution of the problem of Being.

To Aristotle there is very little identification of God with Being as such, and in a sense, therefore, in a way that perhaps he was not aware of, Being is above Deity in his system (and thus from later perspectives constitutes an inconsistency). As far as theology is concerned, Aristotle puts almost all the stress on God as Prime Mover and as the Supreme Contemplator (*noesis noeseos*) rather than as Being. It might even be argued that for Aristotle there could be no God without the world, whereas for the Hebraic tradition there could be a God without a world and, indeed, He could create as many possible (and perhaps impossible) worlds as He pleased. It might be mentioned that in these matters Aristotle is perhaps nearer to early Hindu than Hebraic theism. However, these things should not be quibbled about overmuch since once again, they were not that important to Aristotle himself. Like the early Buddhists and Confucius, he was primarily a humanist rather than a theologian. There is Being as the category of all categories, scientifically ; and if God does not explain nature to him, scientifically, then he is not interested and would probably consider theological disputes as such a waste of time.

In considering theological matters, Aristotle often resorts to a form of analogy that is strange by comparison with the rest of his considerations : "If, then, the happiness which God always enjoys is as great as that which we enjoy sometimes, it is marvellous ; and if it is greater, this is still more marvellous."[37] God's blessedness may be analogically inferred from the best that we may know even though God may have some attributes of which we can have no notion. Again Aristotle is avoiding the *via negativa* by presupposing that by the science of definition we may proceed with equal ease in the realms of man, nature, and God. He simply assumes the adequacy of human discourse to deal with what will be recognized in Plotinus and what is already pointed to in the Upaniṣads : the ineffability of Deity. Aristotle is trying to derive a doctrine of God from his doctrine of nature (and/or man, for man here is still at least partially bound to necessity without the opening of any 'salvation' but nevertheless given the capacity to *think* about anything in all three levels), rather than beginning with God as self-subsistent, self-luminous, indescribable, and then discerning how nature and man may be accounted for as coming forth from Him.

Aristotle has attempted a non-mythological, non-symbolic, imageless approach to God, and he is the first in Western tradition to attempt this seriously. After the destructive clearing away of the false, inadequate, and limited conceptions of deity of Anaximander and Anaximenes, Aristotle begins a systematic and deliberate reconstruction using a 'scientific' approach to theology. This sort of thing was not to be found in most of the Chinese schools where the primordial Tao is already sensed as subject to neither symbol nor logic, howsoever the Dialecticians may quibble. But Nyāya was as rigorous as Aristotle, and the Patañjali Yoga prescribes definite methods for arriving at this imageless thinking. Above all, the Buddhists clearly mapped out the route to the Greater Awareness that includes all these things in a perspective of complete detachment and liberation from being bound even to discursive thought. *Nirvāṇa* admits of no definition, and from the perspective of *nirvāṇa* every experiencible as well as every definition of experience and non-experience may be treated as *completely optional.*

That both the mind in *nirvāṇa* and Aristotle's Unmoved Mover are in the condition of 'rest' as the antithesis of motion (for all motion suggests imperfection, even for Aristotle) is a remarkable point. However, most of the Buddhists would argue that unmoved and unmoving remains a possibility still higher than unmoved and moving. It is necessary, if we are to be theists, to reconcile the paradox of motion and the nature of God. Otherwise we are left with a bad dualism of God and world. And we must not allow a naīve pantheism to creep in. The problem ensnares us in the nets of *māyā*, and from beyond the play of opposites the solution must come. It is doubtful whether Aristotle came to a satisfactory conclusion, even for himself.

In many contexts one finds references to the arguments for and against the existence of God in the various schools of Indian philosophy. Classical Sāmkhya is no doubt technically atheistic although by no means materialistic. It rather borders on panpsychism in one aspect of its radical dualism, although more recent interpretations have stressed the materialism as far as its extended doctrine of matter (*prakṛti*) is concerned. Patañjali Yoga, on the other hand, is mildly theistic, acknowledging, but not insisting, that meditation on God is helpful in attaining *siddhi* (supernormal powers) and/or reaching the ultimate goal of moksa as release from *karma*; but it offers no proofs or disproofs of a formal or systematic nature for God's existence or nonexistence. Classical Jainism, as we have observed in several contexts, is definitely and even aggressively atheistic, while early Buddhism of all the Theravāda schools is better described as rather agnostic or mildly nontheistic.

In the cases of Nyāya and Vaiśeṣika there are cosmological and moral arguments for the existence of God which become quite sophisticated at a relatively early period, although again we must be cautious since the chronology of their developments from root traditions to definitive systems, influenced by a long series of commentaries, is still very confused. Later researches will probably vindicate the hypothesis that most of the technically theological arguments and counterarguments are largely a development of later periods, especially between about 750 A. D. and 1600 A. D. Nevertheless, as many sources suggest, the germ out of which these argumentations developed was undeniably there by the time of Aristotle. The earlier if not the earliest Vaiśeṣika was atheistic, the theism being added by later philosophers amending the system, somewhat as was the case of Sāṃkhya.

Perhaps some distinctions are in order, for the Sanskrit language is very rich with words that can be translated as "god", "God", "the gods", etc. *Deva* usually refers to any deity, such as any member of the Hindu pantheon. *Īśvara* is the more usual word indicative of God as the Supreme (individualized) Being, whether or not identified with *saguṇa* Brahman or with Viṣṇu and Śiva as henotheism emerges out of the polytheism that seems perpetually endemic to popular religion even today in India. *Bhagavān* is the word usually used in reference to God as a personal being to whom one is familiarly devoted. *Hari* is a term popularly used in the Bhakti traditions as still more intimately personal than *Bhagavān*. *Antaryāmi*, in close association with *antaḥkaraṇa* in some but not all later systems, is the Inner Controller or something closely resembling the Holy Spirit idea. Sometimes God is associated with the terms *adṛṣṭa* and *avyakta*, the Unmanifest, the Hidden Principle, the Unspeakable. In the Vaiṣṇava tradition, but only remotely in the Śaiva systems, *Avatāra* refers to the incarnate forms of Deity and *Vyūha* to the angelic or ultra-symbolic forms of Deity. There are still other terms which are used but it must by now be clear that all in all, instead of a dark dichotomy between theism and atheism, or between God and satan in a radical dualism as inherited from the Zoroastrian influence in the Judeo-Christian heritages, there is a very elastic continuum between the extremely abstract and philosophical concepts through the technically theological concepts to the intimate personal-relation concepts of God. There is scarcely the sense of continuum in Greece or China to parallel these Indian heritages. The words go very far back in history, although again it is not until the medieval developments that they become specifically distinct and take on technical meanings.

There is no exact word in classical Chinese to correspond very closely to the word *theos* in Greek as it came to be used to translate Hebrew and Aramaic conceptions of Yahwe, much less words to correspond to all the fine distinctions available in Sanskrit. Insofar as there were attempts at formulating theological concepts as in Europe and India, they are not so prominent in the classical Chinese era as in medieval times, e.g., 12th-17th centuries. Hence, when the Jesuits first tried in the 16th century to translate the Bible into Chinese, they ran into trouble since they used the ideogram for *T'ien*, more usually translated as "Heaven". The Dominicans, however, ruled this out and coined a different word for the purpose. This led to a hot and bitter controversy in the Vatican itself which occasionally still echoes down to the present day.

In the Confucian tradition, on the part of both Protestants and Catholics as well as modern Chinese apologists, literature about the various shades of meaning of *T'ien* is certainly plentiful enough, but there has been little intensive study of similar concepts in the other schools. It should be mentioned that one should not confuse the word usually translated as "spirits" (*shen*) with a polytheistic listing of gods although there are remote similarities. These are more on the order of a high animism than a polytheism.

The relation between Tao and *T'ien* is not always explicit; in fact, it seems more often to remain deliberately ambiguous, both of them being at best indefinables and therefore not really reducible to an Aristotelian system. Correspondingly, the intimate relations between *T'ien* and *ming* (destiny/fate) and *hsing* (human nature) are difficult to separate out into distinct Aristotelian definitions. *T'ien* and *ming*, as far as man is concerned, are so all-pervasive that they are only a sort of numinous milieu within which human affairs are conducted. Likewise, the manner in which *T'ien* and *Ti*, Heaven and Earth, are so frequently paired together is scarcely to be found in Aristotle or any Greek thinker.

The "Will of Heaven" is absolutely essential in running the empire since if the emperor merits it all will be well, but if not, then revolution! Evidently that's what happened to Chiang Kai-shek? Heaven blesses only those who have a vital and even sacrificial concern for the masses; thus if Chairman Mao is an atheist communist, that does not matter. We shall see whether Heaven has, dialectically or not, blessed the latest cycle in Chinese civilization—even without being invoked!

It is certain that *T'ien* is not the Unmoved Mover of Aristotle or the "self-thinking Thought" or even the abstract locus of any reductive logical process connected with infinite chains of causation, as with the Hindu concepts (and with Aristotle somewhat). Although not so personal a Deity as Yahwe of the Old Testament, *T'ien* does seem to have a numinous quality which neither the Greek nor the Hindu concepts have.

FIFTEEN

Conclusion

It is strange that traditional histories of philosophy seem to ignore almost completely the field of aesthetics even though the most elementary introductory textbooks on philosophy at least acknowledge that aesthetics is as much a part of philosophy as is epistemology or ethics. And in the case of Aristotle this is doubly odd. Scarcely anyone who makes even the most superficial acquaintance with Plato can deny or ignore the aesthetic component in his contributions to the history of wisdom, whereas with Aristotle, if the aesthetic field is included at all, it is as though it were not a serious matter for him. But nothing could be further from the truth. Not only is there the *Poetics* and the *Rhetoric*, but one finds references to beauty and art, and the problems involved in consideration of them, in the *Metaphysics*, the *Nicomachean Ethics*, the *Parts of Animals*, the *Physics*, and even in the *Politics*. If one remembers that one of the basic dicta of Aristotle is that philosophy begins with *wonder*, that for him contemplation is more important than the practical arts, that for Aristotle (as for virtually all Greek thinkers of the classical period) art is connected with *techne* and/or *poiesis* as that which distinguishes man from the beasts, then one cannot consider aesthetics as an afterthought in Aristotle's philosophy.

What, then, about Aristotle's contemporaries in India and China? Again, we find neglect. The aesthetic field philosophically considered has been largely unexplored, no doubt in part due to stereotypes as to what one should search for. Almost *a priori* one looks in courses on Indian philosophy for metaphysics and epistemology alone, in spite of the fact that courses in the history of art as such take Indian art very seriously and tend to present the whole of Indian civilization from its aesthetic aspect. In the Upaniṣads, not to mention the *Mahābhārata* and *Rāmāyaṇa*, one reads that Brahman is equally *sat*, *cit*, and *ānanda* (Being, Consciousness, and Bliss), which so closely parallel the Platonic triad of Beauty, Goodness, and Truth (which Aristotle most likely simply took for granted as common ground of operation) that it is strange that the parallel is not taken more seriously.

Our records of systematic aesthetics as a distinct discipline not necessarily tied in with the rest of the inquiry into Brahman do not antidate the Tamil Saṅgham (cir. 100 A. D.), and one has to wait until almost the 9th century A. D. before Bāṇa and the other Kashmiri aestheticians set forth their sophisticated canons for poetry and drama. Nevertheless, even if it should prove true that archeology does not uncover evidences of much earlier explicit formulations (which seems unlikely), the implicit information is plentiful enough. For example, there is *kāma* in the exposition of the *puruṣārthas*, the ends of life; and *kāma* is aesthetic pleasure, including everything from *ars amoris* to the fruits of ascetic discipline preparatory to making an image which will become an incarnation of some deity or other.

Unfortunately the works which have been done on aesthetics, even comparative aesthetics, usually neglect historical perspectives, lumping so much together that it would be like trying to draw some conclusions about "European" aesthetics from Plato Saint Bonaventura, Fenelon, Kant, and John Dewey without any reference to periodization. The subject is often treated as though there were no differences between the art (not to mention the canons) of India, China, Japan, and Iran—as though Europe were unique and all the rest of the world just somehow happened as an afterthought or almost as an embarrassing mistake in the Demiurge's play with forms.

On Chinese aesthetics not much has been reported before Ku K'ai-chih (344-406 A.D.), which for our purposes is not much help. But does this mean that there was nothing that could be called aesthetics before that date? We are not in a position to do the necessary spadework research since this involves specializations beyond our scope of operation. But at a minimum we may be reminded of the aestheticism—usually designated as "hedonism"—even in the *Lieh Tzu*; of Confucius' fondness for music and poetry as a necessity for the cultivation of one's true humanity ; of Mo Tuz's puritanism in the matter (a controversy which engendered still more as it must have issued out of a high degree of sophistication); of the marvellous ***objects d'art*** recently excavated, which surely could not have been brought forth without some canons of excellence deeply rooted even in pre-Confucian tradition; and, not least of all, we may be reminded of the researches into the mathematics and physics of sound in general and of music in particular in ancient China, thus questioning the Pythagoreans' uniqueness in this regard. We might also note that Confucius' major work was editing the pre-Confucian (literary) Classics, and that in doing so he was attentive both to historical accuracy and aesthetic excellence.

In all three civilizations the variety of types and styles of poetry and other literature had developed to a very high degree of sophistication, and we might well expect that canons of excellence must have likewise developed in all three areas with equal expertise. These things deserve much more attention than we can give them until the researchers and builders come—bridge builders especially, across these cultural isolations that still plague mankind, because while so much money is exchanged, so few ideas ever cross the oceans.

* * *

One's judgment of Aristotle in his position in the history of Western philosophy alone, as well as one's preference for either Plato or Aristotle, often seems to depend not just on one's training and heritage but also on one's temperament. Very few have succeeded in reconciling Plato and Aristotle although, as we shall see later, many made valiant attempts at doing this, especially in Byzantium. But when we see essentially the same sort of difference prevailing in this Axial Age in India between Sāṃkhya-Yoga and Nyāya-Vaiśeṣika, and in China between the Confucianists and the Taoists (with a few exceptions on the periphery in all three cases admittedly, but that need not bother us in the broader perspective), we must infer that there is something rather radical about this pattern of polarization of types of philosophies. In later periods of world history we shall repeatedly see that this polarization seems still to prevail: philosophies historically occur in pairs

For this reason it may be argued that it is not *just* a matter of temperament whereby one arrives at his own preference but rather that this matter of temperament itself is an exemplification of a metaphysical principle, that of *yin* and *yang*, which seems to be a much better way of designating what is afoot than the traditional dichotomizing of subjective and objective upon which has been strangely built the myth of the mystical 'Orient' and the corresponding myth of the materialist 'West', neither of which has any historical validity in the period we have covered nor in the periods yet to be surveyed.

From this it should follow that our overall judgment of Aristotle in the ecumenical perspective should be based primarily on the degree to which he surmounted this polarization or was aware of it sufficiently to account for it. But here he may fall short of the Taoists. On other scores what judgments may likewise be made, since obviously judgment on one count only should not be adequate for any thinker so comprehensive and/or versatile as Aristotle ? That's it: *comprehensiveness*; and here he does rate very high indeed, perhaps higher than anyone within his period in world history.

And yet, is comprehensiveness enough? For one could be comprehensive and yet be lacking in precision. But that is the remarkable thing; Aristotle also has precision. Of course it can and should be claimed that Nyāya-Vaiśeṣika also has precision and therefore we must avoid prejudice in the face of empirical facts. Still, even with this qualification, although Aristotle may not be exceptionally outstanding, he does not lag behind but holds his own very well in all fields.

Are these criteria yet enough ? Not necessarily. There are qualities like resiliency, freedom from (the risk of) dogmatism, aesthetic appeal, ease of comprehension and simplicity on the one hand and profundity on the other. And there are many others possible, one's list itself being a manifestation of what one's own philosophy is or is becoming. Whatever the criteria, Jaspers, for example, must be satisfied as well as those in the so-called analytic school currently popular in the English-speaking world, and the Marxists of the many varieties that have emerged within the last century, not to mention all the others in the rest of the world. Thus, the very criteria of judgment as to what philosophy consists of, much less the criteria of judgments as to its excellence, constitutes one of the most difficult of all philosophical problems. With Aristotle we have begun to wrestle with it in earnest, and we shall continue to do so for many centuries ahead.

What emerges in turn from these considerations? Perhaps *historical perspective* has at least this advantage, that it enables us to make judgments in terms of a multiplicity of criteria. But there again Aristotle should have taught us something of this, as in the case of his constant empirical historical reviews of his predecessors in Greek civilization and his comparative study of constitutions in the political sphere. We may well continue to take Aristotle, not necessarily as the 'greatest' of his period, but as perhaps the most adequate rallying point for a synthesis of all the rest.

Before Aristotle, man became aware of almost all of the basic problems of his existence: man has a destiny, the full meaning of which he only dimly surmises; man must make laws; man must investigate nature; and man must excel above all else in self-knowledge and in self-conquest; he must rise out of his naive subjectivity to the rules that govern the operation of truth; he must learn to think both imaginatively and logically. But in so doing he is still limited in spite of his will towards non-limitation which is the Divine within him. And his efforts towards that non-limitation shall be unceasing, perhaps even if he comes to know it all, until the whole of creation is again brought into the Greater Cycle of the Grand Return, the Final Withdrawal back to its partless uncaused Cause.

Thus, having discarded the local gods, he must, after expanding his own psychic aptitudes to include the whole range of the knowable and suffering world, still acknowledge a Deity which is higher and more noble than his own conceptions. This Deity must be One, Being, Absolute, sublime, perfect, eternal, and above all the alterability of nature and man's own nature. This Deity must also be the Source of the Moral Law and the Giver of Salvation, or at least the Restorer of the good in man, if not in nature also. Although man thinks in terms of enemies and battles, this Deity operates from above the region of conflict and the dualities, and eternally wills the predominance of the greater Good that is not subject to comparison.

All differentiation, all process, all motion, all imperfection moves towards this God-beyond-all difference; while at the same time, all that *appears* to be imperfect and illusory, all time and space and material, all embodied existence, reveals His unmanifest Being. It is by knowledge as well as obedience that He and all things and all things in relation to Him must be known, for He has made man primarily a knower wherein man excels the beasts and the birds. For other beings are in a sense more blessed, happier than man and more beautiful; but man, as capable of both tragedy and harmony, is destined by knowledge to become most divine, most like the Deity which or whom he worships.

APPENDIX

MO TZU

(c. 470—c. 391 B.C.)

> Love only exists when it has reached everybody; love has disappeared the moment it fails to include all; when love is not pervasive, it cannot be called love.—*Mo Tzu.*

Mo Tzu (also called Mo Ti, Motse, Motze, and Micius) founded the classical Chinese School of Mohism. Although Mohism has been overshadowed by Confucianism and Taoism, from the 5th century B.C. to the beginning of the Han Dynasty it presented the greatest challenge to Confucianism. Mencius, in his defense of Confucianism, picked out Mohism as its greatest enemy. The two Schools may represent class conflicts in that Mo Tzu was apparently from the lower class (though well-educated in the Classics) and attacked the Confucianists as "aristocrats."

Mo Tzu may be seen as a combination of Robin Hood, Gandhi, and Thomas Hobbes : he was against war yet came to the defense of the attacked; he observed ascetic discipline and devoted his life to social change; he taught that the state of nature was "nasty, brutish, and short" and that thus the state must have "authority equal to God's". All about he saw people being wasteful because certain things were supposedly right in themselves (the Confucianists with their elaborate and costly rituals) and others being wasteful because of emotions and lack of order in the country (the war lords fighting for supremacy). In response to this, Mo Tzu taught the principle of utilitarianism : only that which is profitable is good.

Mo Tzu's philosophy (and his life) was an attempt to bring order out of chaos. Mo Tzu taught that if all people would love one another without distinction (universal love) there would be harmony; but the Confucianists were teaching love with distinction, viz, first love the family and then others to a lesser degree. Universal love would be profitable both to those who love and those who are loved; but since people are blind to these benefits, and since human nature is neither naturally good nor evil but tractable, certain sanctions should be employed to induce men to love one another. First, there should be a central authority (the Son of Heaven) with whom all must remain in absolute agreement. Secondly, men must be taught that Heaven and spirits reward and punish men according to their conduct. Also, frugality is a necessary measure for increasing the population and allowing everyone enough food, clothing, and shelter. Music, war, emotions, and elaborate rituals are all wasteful, do not help the state, and should be eliminated—in other words, these are not conducive to the greatest happiness of the greatest number. Clearly, Mo Tzu meant universal love in a strongly social sense.

There were no Mohist philosophers after the 3rd century B.C. A recent revival of Mohist thought is due to his utilitarianism and the supposed resemblance of his "Heaven" to the Christian God. Although Mo Tzu's philosophy has been criticized as shallow, barren, and impracticable, Mo Tzu the man is usually praised (even Mencius acknowledged his altruism), the highest laudation coming from Liang Ch'i-ch'ao : "For depth of sympathy, for vigor of altruism, and for richness of the spirit of self-sacrifice, there is none like him, save Christ, in the whole world".

HSUN TZU

(c. 320—c. 238 B.C.)

> People desire and hate the same things. Their desires are many, but things are few. Since they are few, there will inevitably be strife.—*Hsün Tzu.*

During the Warring States Period (403-221 B.C.) Chinese feudalism continued its decline with ever increasing violence until China was finally unified for the first time in its history by Ch'in Shih-huang in 221 B.C. Hsün Tzu, the most eminent scholar of his time, was concerned with good government and even served as a magistrate; but effectively serving in an office was a precarious affair and he was either dismissed or gave up his post. Hsün Tzu's sober, realistic attitude was no doubt in part a result of his awareness of the conditions of his day even as his philosophy is a reflection of those conditions.

Confucius, Mencius, and Hsün Tzu form the magnificent Confucian triumvirate which is often compared with Socrates, Plato, and Aristotle. Mencius is the idealist, Hsün Tzu the hardheaded realist. The extensiveness of his thought and his matter of fact manner make Hsün Tzu an obvious comparison with Aristotle.

Some of Hsün Tzu's basic views were : (1) human nature is evil in that natural desires lead to conflict and anything which leads to conflict (which is evil) is itself evil; (2) it is by education that man becomes good, and any man can become a sage through hard work; (3) man's natural desires, the source of evil, must not be entirely suppressed but regulated, especially through music and ritual; (4) nature should be mastered rather than (as well as) meditated on; (5) a teacher is one of a man's greatest treasures; (6) authority (the Classics), law, and discipline are essential for social order and individual advancement. Hsün Tzu was one of the few early Chinese philosophers to discuss language theory, and he was a most astute critic of other philosophers. His philosophy is not especially speculative, and his Tao lacks the sublimity of the Taoist concept. To this tough-minded naturalist, nature is almost mechanistic, ethical laws are man-made, and religious rituals are largely practical and aesthetic affairs.

Hsün Tzu is a mean between the Legalists (law) and the Confucianists (rites). His most famous student, Han Fei Tzu, became the leading Legalist and another student, Li Ssu, became the Prime Minister of the emperor of the Ch'in Dynasty and helped to put Legalist concepts into practice. It is with Hsün Tzu that the longstanding Confucian authoritarianism really begins. Though an unorthodox Confucianist himself, he has been called "the moulder of ancient Confucianism", yet compared with Mencius, he has been mostly unknown outside of China. His influence was great in the Han Period (206 B.C..220 A.D.) but almost disappeared in the 9th century with the rise of Neo-Confucianism. Because of his strong emphasis on law, rationality, hard work, practicality, naturalism, and authority, some modern day Chinese might find an especially enticing authority in Hsün Tzu.

His teachings are found in a book of thirty-two essays bearing his name, the *Hsün Tzu.*

MENCIUS

(c. 371-289 B. C.)

> If there is a desire that the world should enjoy tranquillity and good order, who is there today, besides myself, to bring it about?—*Mencius*

Like Plato, Mencius elaborated the thought of a great teacher—Confucius. Excepting Confucius, Mencius is the greatest teacher in the Confucian tradition. Until the 20th century, the *Mencius*, the book containing his thought, was memorized by every young student in China ; thus, the extent of his influence is obvious.

Mencius' explicit intent was to become another Confucius. Like Confucius he was a man with a mission in a troubled world, but more so than Confucius, he had to compete with other schools. In the 4th century B. C. in China there were so many different philosophical schools that the *Chuang Tzu* refers to them as "the hundred schools". Mencius attacked primarily the views of Mo Tzu and Yang Chu (a precursor of Taoism who taught a kind of Epicureanism).

The careers of Mencius and Confucius were very similar. Mencius spent much of his time travelling from state to state looking for a prince who would give up aggressiveness and power-seeking and attempt instead to create good government for the people. Like Confucius, he did not find one. This was during the Warring States Period, thus he met with a few sympathetic listeners when he spoke of benevolence and righteousness. His lack of success could more likely be attributed to boldness than diffidence ; he could call an emperor a scoundrel to his face and he once refused to be summoned to court because he believed that scholars are superior to aristocrats. Like Confucius, he eventually gave up his active quest for reform.

Mencius is best known for his doctrine of the goodness of human nature. It is man's mind (or heart, the same word is used for both) which distinguishes him from the beasts. All men are born with four seminal virtues : wisdom, propriety, righteousness, benevolence. But these virtues must be cultivated or there will cease to be any distinction between man and beast. Man is basically a moral being and the 'thinking heart' must be developed by moral thinking and action. Mencius said : "The end of learning is nothing but the search for the lost heart."

According to Mencius, all men are equal and all are capable of becoming sages. Government should be for the people and the people should be the judge of government. When a government does not help the people, they have the right of revolution. In asserting the right of revolution, Mencius broke from tradition and established himself as an authority for all subsequent revolutionaries. In his tremendous social concern, Mencius demonstrated that he recognized the close relationship which exists between the moral and the external economic conditions of a state.

To what extent Mencius was a mystic has been debated throughout Chinese history. Mencius said : "All things are complete within us." The elements of mysticism in his teachings have strongly influenced the views of some later Confucianists.

By his elaborations of the *Analects*, Mencius insured the success of Confucius' teachings ; but later Confucianism is really as much Mencius as Confucius. The idea that human nature is good is still the dominant view in China.

CHUANG TZU

(c. 369—c. 286 B. C.)

> Let us forget the distinctions of 'right' and 'wrong'. Let us find enjoyment in the realm of the infinite and remain there. —*Chuang Tzu*

As Plato was to Socrates, so Chuang Tzu was more than a mere interpreter of Lao Tzu. He was a mystic, a romantic, and one of the first of the great Chinese thinkers to express a deep love for and to advocate absorption in Nature. And yet he followed reason and did not teach a denial of the world; rather, one should expand his world to include the universe. Very little is known about Chuang Tzu's life. He and Mencius were contemporaries but did not know each other. Many legends grew up about him, even that he performed miracles. As with some other Chinese philosophers, he probably would be better known except from confucius' overshadowing position.

Chuang Tzu's basic doctrines are naturalness and spontaneity. He said: "Cherish that which is within you, and shut off that which is without; for much knowledge is a curse." Intuition is the key to harmony. Everything has its own particular nature and happiness comes when each thing follows its own nature. The original state of nature was one of Unadorned Simplicity. With government came artificiality. Government attempts to force people to follow the same patterns and standards. Thus, the best government is no government. Chuang Tzu said: "Everything in the world longs for peace. Why should there be some who address themselves laboriously to govern the empire?" Each person should have complete freedom to do things in his own way. The Confucianists wanted to educate man; Chuang Tzu wanted men to follow the way of Nature rather than the way of man.

The way of Nature is one of constant flux, constant self-transformation from the simple to the complex and back to the simple again. Through identification ('pure experience'), one avoids making distinctions. Between life and death there is no distinction, says Chuang Tzu, and yet fear of death is one of the major causes of man's unhappiness. All is Tao. If a man identifies with Tao, then he shall discard beginnings and endings, subject and object, reality and unreality. Chuang Tzu said: "Heaven and Earth came into being with me together, and with me all things are one."

One of Chuang Tzu's central doctrines is the equality of all things. All the world is a play of opposites, but the opposites through a dialectic not unlike Hegel's, cause each other and are ultimately resolvable in the Tao. All values are relative and all viewpoints may be equally right, thus arguments can solve nothing. There is unity in diversity and one should hold all positions equally and cultivate 'emptiness'.

Chuang Tzu's concepts of Tao and *teh* (Tao as manifest) are not greatly different from those of Lao Tzu, the traditional founder of Taoism. His stress on individual nature and spontaneity greatly influenced Neo-Taoism. He also exerted great influence on Zen Buddhism and Chinese art. Since about the 5th century A.D. he has not been explicitly adopted by any major Chinese philosopher. The Confucianist Hsun Tzu criticized Chuang Tzu by saying that he is "prejudiced in favor of Nature and does not know man."

HAN FEI TZU

(C.280-233 B.C.)

> The sage, in governing a state, does not trust men to do good of themselves; he makes it impossible for them to do wrong.—*Han Fei Tzu*

Kuan Chung (d.645 B.C.) was probably the first major Legalist. The *Kuan Tzu*, a book containing Legalist ideas, was attributed to him but was actually written much later. Though there were many who adhered to a "Legalist" philosophy, there was no Legalist school until Han Fei Tzu, who not only synthesized the doctrines of the previous Legalists but who was also influenced by Confucianism (he was a student of Hsün Tzu), Mohism, and Taoism. Legalism as taught by Han Fei Tzu and practised by Li Ssu (a schoolmate of Han Fei's and the chief minister of the first emperor of Ch'in) was responsible for the unification of China through the establishment of the totalitarianism of the Ch'in Dynasty. This dictatorship lasted only until 206 B.C. and with its overthrow went Legalism—there have been no Legalist schools since.

Like Mo Tzu, Mencius, and Hsün Tzu, Han Fei Tzu wanted to see order and social welfare established through governmental reform. He was born an aristocrat in the state of Han and experienced the period of that state's greatest destruction. The ruler of Han refused his services and Han Fei refused to serve any other state; thus, he remained a theoretician primarily. Through the machinations of his rival Li Ssu he was put into prison and induced to commit suicide by poisoning.

Han Fei Tzu's answer to the chaos of the Warring States Period was the most extreme of all; rather than re-establishment of virtue or the ideal of universal love, he proposed the setting up of a monarch who would exercise absolute power through strict and comprehensive laws. There are three essential Legalist principles, all of which can be found before the time of Han Fei Tzu: law (*fa*), power and position (*shih*), method and art of governing (*shu*). Han Fei's treatment of these plus his other views results in his Legalism.

According to Han Fei Tzu, human nature is selfish and naturally leads to violence. The only way to make men act in a way beneficial to the whole (i.e., the state) is to make it very unpleasant for them to act otherwise; thus, there should be a corpus of well-defined laws with correspondingly severe punishments for law-breakers and generous rewards for those who obey. Motives are irrelevant in 'legal' justice; external actions must conform to the law regardless. To secure and maintain an all-powerful state, Machiavellian methods are quite acceptable. Rites should be discarded. The farmer-warrior class should be elevated over the official-scholar class. Scholars are useless parasites. The Legalist concept of a good state is one wherein material needs are met and the populace are capable of securing the state in time of war. Han Fei Tzu makes little appeal to virtue or religion. In sharp contrast to the Confucianists, the Legalists saw progress in history and considered any appeal to antiquity for solutions to modern problems to be futile.

During the Warring States Period the feudal system was giving way to central authority, and in some ways Han Fei Tzu and the Legalists were only giving a foundation to what was happening.

JAINISM

Because of their similarity in some respects and because of the initial scarcity of available materials, some scholars at first thought that Jainism was merely a branch of Buddhism. But it was soon confirmed that Jainism is probably even older than Buddhism. Jainism comes fom "Jina", "one who conquers" all obstacles and becomes emancipated. The Jainas believe in twenty-four Tīrthaṅkaras or 'prophets' of which Mahāvīra ("The great hero"), a contemporary of Buddha, was the last. He did not found Jainism but shaped it into its present form.

The first systematic exposition of Jaina doctrines, Umāsvāti's *Tattvārtha-adhigamasūtra*, is not found until c. 300 A.D. Like the Buddhists and the Cārvākas, the Jainas are *nāstikas*, i.e., do not believe in the authority of the Vedas. Today there are about two million Jainas. Jainism is found only in India.

Jainism is atheistic, pluralistic, and realistic. It might be argued that the Jainas are really materialists, i.e., that the soul is only very subtle matter, but almost all interpretations find a dualism of spirit (*jīva*) and non-spirit (*ajīva*) which are separate and independent. Their realistic metaphysics is called *anekāntavāda*, "manyness of reality". There are innumerable atoms and souls (*jīvas*, which are simply embodied *ātmans*). *Ajīva* includes matter (*pudgala*), motion (*dharma*), rest (*adharma*) space (*ākāśa*), and time (*kāla*). The world and the souls are eternal and uncreated. The Tīrthaṅkaras have been deified, but any liberated soul would be equally divine.

According to their *karma*, souls become embodied in virtually all material forms: earth, fire, water, air, plants, animals. The universe is full of life. As light fills an entire room, so the soul fills the entire body it happens to be occupying, whether that of an ant or an elephant. Life, consciousness, and knowledge are the essences of the soul. As with the material atoms, each soul is qualitatively the same and different only quantitatively. The liberated soul has omniscience (*kevalajñāna* and pervades the universe.

The Jainas think of *karma* as subtle matter which defiles the otherwise perfect soul. The object of Jaina teachings is to recover the purity of the soul by practising the Three Jewels (*triratna*) of faith (*darśana*), knowledge (*jñāna*), and conduct (*cāritra*). They emphasize asceticism perhaps more than any other school. The central virtue is *ahiṃsā* (non-injury in all possible meanings). Jainism is a philosophy of self-help. Without external aid one must, through ascetic penances (*tapas*) and meditation (*dhyāna*), stop the beginningless influx of karma-matter (*āśrava*) and burn away the karma-matter sticking to the soul. Devotion gains good *karma* and heaven, but the goal is liberation through destruction of good and bad *karma*.

Each atom and each soul possesses innumerable qualities;

to know all of them requires omniscience. Thus the Jaina theory of the relativity of all knowledge (*syādvāda*) exemplified in the story of the three blind men each of whom thought to describe an elephant by examining only part of it. The Jainas believe that most disputes arise when men confuse a partial truth for the absolute truth.

CĀRVĀKA

Cārvāka is the oldest of the classical Indian schools. It was probably formulated between the 8th and 6th centuries B C. There were materialist views before this school, but there does not appear to have been a materialist School as such. There is no extant literature of the Cārvāka school; all that we know about it comes from others' attempted refutations. Thus Cārvāka is always presented as rather crude and unsophisticated. Cārvāka is possibly derived from "cāruvāk" (a man of beautiful word or sweet tongue) from "vac" (to speak). They are also known as Lokāyatas, which means "that which is found among people in general". Lokāyata is also taken as a general term for materialism. The name Cārvāka possibly was given to the Lokāyatas by their adversaries as a depreciating designation, or possibly Cārvāka was the disciple of Bṛhaspati, the traditional founder of the School, or possibly Cārvāka himself was the founder of the School. The two Schools of Cārvāka are the Dhūrtta and the Suśikṣita. The extreme and unorthodox views of Cārvāka probably stimulated, through reactions, the development of the other Schools. At one time Cārvāka School was probably very influential; it was refuted by all the other Schools. There is evidence that it was still a force in the 4th century B.C.

Cārvāka was a reaction against the domination of *Brahmin* priests and Vedic rituals. The Cārvākas strongly attacked the authority of the Vedas and pointed out their contradictions while the Mīmāṁsakas were trying to establish the authority and reconcile contradictions. The Cārvākas were atheists, materialists, naturalists, positivists, and naive realists. There is no soul surviving the body and consciousness is only an epiphenomenon of the body. Only matter is real; life is due to a special configuration of matter. Everything is a result of the combination of four elements: earth, air, fire, water. These are eternal and uncreated. There is no God, no heaven, no hell, no law of *karma*, no rebirth after death, no power (*apūrva*) in sacrifices. Religion is a fabrication of the priests who cannot make a living honestly. If sacrificed animals go to heaven as the priests say, then why not sacrifice your father?

The only valid *pramāṇa* is sense perception (*pratyakṣa*). All things which are real are perceptible; thus the smallest particle of matter is perceptible and *ākāśa* (ether) is unreal since it is not perceptible. Inference can only give us probability but not certainty since all possible cases, past, present, and future, cannot possibly be observed. Also, there are no universal causal laws or laws of nature. There is no necessary connection between a sequence of events; we cannot examine all such sequences and prove an inevitable causal law.

Cārvāka is the only hedonistic Indian school. The highest good and the end of life is to enjoy as much sensual pleasure as possible and to avoid as much pain as possible. There are no objective ethical laws; any means is justified to gain pleasure. In short, the view is "eat, drink, and be merry," for when we die there is neither reward nor punishment but simply an end to it all.

SĀMKHYA

Kapila, the traditional founder of Sāṃkhya, supposedly lived before the Buddha. The oldest extant literature of the School, however, is the *Sāṃkhya kārikā* of Īśvarakṛṣṇa (c.200. A.D.). Thus very little is definitely known about its origins. One meaning of the word "sāṃkhya" is "right knowledge"; Sāṃkhya was one of the earliest attempts to answer metaphysical questions by reason alone. Sāṃkhya is primarily theoretical; it is the theory behind the practices of the Yoga School. Though Sāṃkhya is no longer very influential, historically only Vedānta has been more influential than Sāṃkhya-Yoga.

Sāṃkhya is dualistic and atheistic (though originally it may have been theistic and monistic). The two parts of the

Sāṃkhyan dualism are *prakṛti* and *puruṣa*. *Prakṛti* is the material cause of all physical and psychical manifestation. All evolutes, including thoughts, emotions, and bodies, are modifications of it. *Prakṛti* itself is nothing but three *guṇas*: *sattva*, *rajas*, *tamas*. *Sattva* is the principle of pleasure, lightness, love. *Rajas* is the principle of motion, pain, restlessness. *Tamas* is the principle of darkness, resistance, heaviness. The three *guṇas* are the substantial constituents of *prakṛti*. They are infinite in number, eternal, ever-changing, and always found together. All things (except the *Puruṣas*) are made up of the *guṇas*.

The *puruṣas* are individual souls or selves. *Puruṣa* is pure consciousness. All things except pure consciousness are transformations of *prakṛti*. *Puruṣa* is uncaused, co-eternal with *prakṛti*, and nothing but the infinite number of individual *puruṣas*. *Puruṣa* is always the subject of knowledge, never the object; always the observer, never the observed; not a cause or an effect; inactive; beyond time and space; free from pleasure and pain. *Puruṣa* is supremely the spectator. As there is no God, *puruṣa* and *prakṛti* were not created.

The world is the result of the periodic evolution of *prakṛti*. *Prakṛti* evolves to serve *puruṣa*. Evolution is teleological; it is for the purpose of offering the *puruṣas* experience in the world (*bhoga*). Though the *guṇas* are ever active, they periodically attain a state of equilibrium (*pralaya*). Evolution begins anew when this equilibrium is disturbed. Sāṃkhya's most difficult problem is accounting for the disturbance of this equilibrium since *puruṣa* and *prakṛti* are not causally related. In one way or another, the disturbance is attributed to *puruṣa*.

Because *buddhi* ('intellect'), the first evolute of *prakṛti*, has a predominance of *sattva*, it can and does 'reflect' the consciousness of *puruṣa*. Thus all thoughts, emotions, and volitions are falsely attributed to *puruṣa*. But it is really the *jīva* (the 'reflected self' or modified *buddhi*) which experiences the pleasures and pains of the world. This ignorance of the distinction between the *jīva* and *puruṣa* is the cause of bondage. Liberation is the attainment of discrimination (*viveka*) between *puruṣa* and all modifications of *prakṛti*. *Puruṣa* is never really bound by *prakṛti* but only 'reflected' in it. In a sense, one is always free; cessation of bondage is simply the attainment of the knowledge of one's true identity.

YOGA

Sāṃkhya-Yoga may have originally been one school which later divided. The dates of Patañjali, the traditional founder of the Yoga school, are uncertain—probably between the 4th and 5th centuries B.C. He was certainly not the first yogin but rather a systematizer who grafted the yogic principles onto the Sāṃkhya metaphysics. The word "yoga" means "union". For Patañjali, yoga is a method, and in the *Bhagavadgītā* it is also the name for the highest attainable spiritual state.

Yoga accepts the metaphysics and epistemology of Sāṃkhya with only slight modification. Yoga differs from Sāṃkhya primarily in that it insists on the use of the yogic method and posits a God. Yoga is theistic (*seśvara*) and is called "theistic Sāṃkhya" while Sāṃkhya is atheistic (*nirīśvara*). For Yoga, God (*iśvara*) did not create *prakṛti* but out of compassion He moves it as efficient cause for the benefit of the *puruṣas*. *Īśvara* did not create the *puruṣas* but indeed is one of them, although He is omniscient and omnipotent and has never been subject to *karma*. *Prakṛti* and *puruṣa* are co-eternal with God. The *puruṣas* can attain liberation without the help of God; but if a *puruṣa* is devoted to God then He will remove hindrances to liberation. In Sāṃkhya there is unconscious teleology, but in Yoga there is conscious teleology, i.e., God directs *prakṛti* for the *puruṣas*' ends. The yogic method is more important than devotion or metaphysical speculations. Sāṃkhya is theoretical, but Yoga is supremely practical.

The objective of yoga is not union with God but *kaivalya* (liberation, 'isolation'). Sāṃkhya-Yoga, like the Buddhists, thinks that life in this realm is suffering. The purpose of philosophy (in the broadest sense) is to dispel *avidyā* (ignorance), the cause of bondage. Here *avidyā* is the illusory identification of *puruṣa* with *citta* ('mind' in the most general sense, *buddhi*). Sāṃkhya considers *avidyā* to be the result of non-discrimination or a lack of complete knowledge; but Yoga regards it as misapprehension or false knowledge, thus liberation is not the result ofgaining correct knowledge so much as dispelling false knowledge.

The yogic practices are designed to gradually control the incessant modifications of *citta.* All knowing (except that final 'knowing' of enlightenment) is the result of the transformations of *citta*; and since *citta* is an evolute of *prakṛti*, these transformations must result in false knowledge. The yogic method consists of the Eightfold Path of Perfection : (1) ***yama*** : abstention from injury by thought, word, or deed; (2) ***niyama*** : self-development by austerities, study, and devotion; (3) ***āsɪna*** : the discipline of physical postures; (4) ***prāṇāyāma*** : breath control; (5) ***pratyāhāra*** : control of the senses; (6) ***dhāraṇā*** : focusing and steadying the mind; (7) *dhyāna* : meditation; (8) *samādhi* : concentration, the identification of subject and object in meditation. In the last state all modifications of *citta* have ceased and the *puruṣa* realizes itself to be, and to have always been, independent of *prakrti*.

Yogic methods (without the Sāmkhyan metaphysics) have been employed by all Indian schools except Cārvāka.

VAIŚESIKA

Just as Sāṃkhya and Yoga may be seen as one School, so Vaiśeṣika and Nyāya together form one school. Vaiśeṣika is concerned primarily with philosophy of nature while Nyāya is concerned with epistemology. The *Vaiśeṣika sūtras* of Kaṇāda, the founder of Vaiśeṣika, are probably pre-Buddhistic in origin. The name of this School is derived from the term "viśesa" which means particularity. Vaiśeṣika is atomistic, realistic, and pluralistic. Complex existents are reducible to atoms, all existents are ontologically independent of the mind, and reality consists of several simple substances which are irreducible and have ontological 'particularity'. Unlike the idealistic monisms which followed Vaiśesika historically, and unlike the Sāmkhyan dualism, Vaiśesika emphasized a plurality of particularities and differences as the essence of the universe. In its realism, Vaiśesika holds the common sense view of reality, i.e., things exist independently of perception.

Vaiśeṣika is generally considered not to be materialistic since it admits spiritual substance.

In its analysis of nature, Vaiśesika discerns six categories which allow the metaphysical classification of all things. Each category (*padārtha*) is distinct from the others and they are not to be seen as manifestations or modifications of some single category. The original six categories of Kaṇāda are : substance (*dravya*), quality (*guṇa*), action (*karma*), generality (*sāmānya*), particularity (*viśeṣa*), inherence (*samavāya*). A seventh category, non-being (*abhāva*) was added later. Substance is the primary category and all others depend on it. Compound substances are transient, but simple, substances are indestructible and permanent : earth (*pṛthivī*), water (*ap*), fire (*tejas*), air (*vāyu*), ether (*ākāśa*), time (*kāla*), space (*dik*), spirit (*ātman*), mind (*manas*). Generality is that the possession of which allows individuals to belong to the same class, e.g., "manness"; and this "manness" is an objective reality. Both individuals and universals are separately and equally real. Each simple substance, e.g., each atom and each *ātman*, though alike in other ways, has a unique particularity (*viśeṣa*)- which makes it absolutely irreducible and eternally distinguishable. To mention one other of the categories, inherence is "inseparable relationship" such as the relation of part and whole or quality and substance.

Concerning *ātman* (spirit, soul, self), these are innumerable, independant, individual, eternal, and all-pervading. Consciousness and other qualities are adventitious attributes of *ātman* and are due to its embodiment. Bondage is due to ignorance of the true nature of *ātman*. Liberation appears to be a rather neutral state—no feeling, no actions, no bliss, no thought, no consciousness.

Kaṇāda himself does not speak of God, thus he may well have been an atheist although his later followers were theists. The material cause of the universe are the atoms of earth, air water, and fire. The atoms are naturally motionless; motion is supplied by the Unseen Power (*adṛṣṭa*) which is, potential energy, inherent in karmic merits and demerits. God, using *adṛṣṭa*, is the efficient cause of creation. Atoms and souls are uncreated and co-eternal with God. God is only the Supreme Ātman (*paramātman*).

NYĀYA

The word "nyāya" means "argumentation". Nyāya was the first school of logic in India, and Gautama (c. 400 B.C.), the traditional founder of the school, can be considered the first systematizer of logical principles, although no doubt the rudiments of logic had developed before his time. Believing that knowledge of reality was essential for enlightenment, Nyāya considered it important that we investigate the means of gaining valid knowledge (*pramāṇas*) and learn to distinguish fallacies. Thus Nyāya is primarily concerned with epistemology and right argumentation. Nyāya accepts the authority of the Vedas, and it is probable that one reason for the development of logic by the Naiyāyikas was in order for them to refute the Buddhists and Jainas who were presenting arguments against Vedic authority. Indian logic developed in the context of dialectical confrontation and the need to insure as nearly as possible that truth rather than cleverness would determine the victor of a debate. Nyāya shows an outstanding faith in the ability of reason and analysis to discern truth. Later Indian logic is called Navya-Nyāya and developed from Nyāya logic. Nyāya has had a beneficial influence on all of the Indian schools.

Vaiśeṣika is metaphysical while Nyāya is primarily epistemological. Nyāya accepts the Vaiśeṣika metaphysics except for two major differences : (1) Vaiśeṣika accepts only perception and inference as *pramāṇas* whereas Nyāya accepts perception, inference, comparison, and verbal testimony; (2) Nyāya includes all seven of the Vaiśeṣika categories in a single category called "object of knowledge" (*prameya*) and then adds fifteen other categories. The names of these categories clearly indicate Nyāya's concern for right reasoning rather than ontology : *pramāṇas*, doubt, purpose, example, established tenet, members of syllogism, confutation, ascertainment, discussion, cavil, wrangling, fallacy, quibble, futility, occasion for rebuke. Gautama held the theory of correspondences :

valid knowledge must correspond to reality. The test of knowledge is pragmatic : valid knowledge leads to successful activity. One of the outstanding achievements of Nyāya was the formulation of the classical syllogism with five instead of three propositions and using both induction and deduction in the same syllogism.

Like Vaiśeṣika, Nyāya views the innumerable souls as substances which have consciousness, cognitions, and feelings as accidental rather than as essential attributes. Bondage is due to our ignorance regarding the natural, pure condition of the soul. We attempt to increase the accidental attributes thinking that they are essential attributes. Originally Nyāya was probably atheistic, but the later Naiyāyikas developed a theory of grace, arguments for God's existence, and introduced the devotional element. Still, knowledge of God and union with God were not the objectives, but rather knowledge of nature and of the soul (*ātman*). Nyāya also believed in teleological creation, the purpose of this world is to allow souls the opportunity to attain liberation. The Nyāya-Vaiśeṣika doctrines of atomism, pluralism, and their concept of *ātman* were severely attacked by the later Vedāntins.

MĪMĀṀSĀ-VEDĀNTA

As with Sāmkhya-Yoga and Nyāya-Vaiśeṣika, so Mīmāṁsā and Vedānta are closely associated. Both place much emphasis on the authority of the Vedas. Mīmāṁsā is primarily concerned with the first part of the Vedas (the Brāhmaṇas) and is thus called Pūrva-Mīmāṁsā or Prior Mīmāṁsā, while Vedānta is primarily concerned with the last part of the Vedas (the Upaniṣads) and is thus called Uttara-Mīmāṁsā or Posterior Mīmāṁsā. Also, Mīmāṁsā emphasizes action (*karma*) while Vedānta emphasizes knowledge (*jñāna*). Vedānta is idealistic and monistic. The only reality is *ātman*-Brahman, all else is *māyā* (illusion). Vedānta officially begins with the *Brahmasūtras* of Bādarāyaṇa whose dates are probably somewhere between 200 B.C. and 100 A.D.; thus, Vedānta develops as a distinct school only after the Axial Age.

Jaimini is the founder of the Mīmāṁsā school. The traditional date given to his *Mīmāṁsā-sūtras* is around 400 B.C. However, a complete development of the Mīmāṁsā theories is not found until the 8th century with establishment of the two major schools of Mīmāṁsā : Kumārila Bhaṭṭa founded the Bhaṭṭa school and Prabhākara Miśra founded the Prabhākara school.

Mīmāmsā literally means "attempts at rational enquiry." Its basic motive was to set forth canons for the correct interpretation and performance of the Vedic rituals and sacrifices. It endeavors to explain the apparent contradictions in the Vedas, establish on rational grounds the authority of the Vedas, and present philosophical justification for the various aspects of Vedic ritualism.

Mīmāṁsā is a philosophy of *dharma* (duty) and *karma* (action). Original Mīmāṁsā was not so much interested in speculation and transcendental knowledge as in the proper performance of ethical actions as prescribed by the Vedas. Thus Mīmāṁsā is supremely a philosophy of action. The Mīmāṁsakas held that the Vedas were uncreated and eternal. They did not have an author, either human or divine. To justify this view they held that words and their meanings are eternal. Language is a natural phenomenon; it was not created. Just as the world was not created. Specific sounds and symbols are manifestations of the eternal letters and words. The particular arrangement of words in the Vedas is self-determined; no author arranged them. The Vedas are self-revealed and of absolute authority. Thus total obedience to Vedic injunctions was required by the Mīmāṁsakas.

Mīmāṁsā is both realistic and pluralistic. Its categories are about the same as those of Nyāya-Vaiśeṣika. The world is self-existent, not created. There is no God and the 'gods' serve no function except to be the object of sacrifices. In sacrifices a positive potential power (*apūrva*) is generated which results in a positive effect at some future time. Physical causation is subordinate to the law of *karma*, There are a plurality of souls (*ātmans*) which are very similar to those of Vaiśeṣika. Later Mīmāṁsakas became theistic and sought liberation, but originally they considered that to be alive was to be active and to be active was to be involved in *karma*.

Original Mīmāṁsā did not consider liberation, which entailed no consciousness or feeling or knowledge, to be desirable. In short, they did not find the life of the monk to be respectable.

BUDDHISM

About a century after the Buddha's death the Buddhists split into two major schools, the Sthaviravādins (sometimes called Theravādins) and the Mahāsāṅghikas (ca. 343/383 B.C.). We can find references to other schools of Buddhism which seem to have flourished during this period, but we know very little about them and they are rarely discussed except in the most meticulous and comprehensive works.

Sthaviravāda, the first prominent school of Buddhism, is usually viewed as the ancestor of Hīnayāna or Southern Buddhism (so called because it continues to flourish in South-east Asia) and Mahāsaṅghika as the ancestor of Mahāyāna or Northern Buddhism (so called because it continues to flourish in Tibet, China, and Japan).

The doctrines of the Sthaviravādins are to be found in the group of works written in Pāli known as the *Tipiṭaka* (Sanskrit-*Tripiṭaka*) or the "Three Baskets", which was probably compiled at the Third Buddhist Council at Pāṭaliputra (ca. 249 B.C.). The first 'basket' or group of writings is called the *Vinaya-Piṭaka*) and deals exhaustively with the rules governing the *Saṅgha* (the Order of Buddhist Monks). The second is the *Sutta-Piṭaka* (Skt. *Sūtra-Piṭaka*) and is a collection of the utterances of the Buddha. The third or *Abhidhamma Piṭaka* (Skt.—*Abhidharma-Piṭaka*) is a collection of (more or less) philosophical works. Other important sources of information about the Sthaviravādins are the *Visuddhimagga* (a compendium of Sthaviravāda Doctrines) of Buddhaghoṣa (ca. 400 A.D.) and his *Atthasālinī*, a commentary on the *Dhamma-saṅgaṇi* (one of the works of the *Sūtra Piṭaka*).

Sthaviravāda is the basic, ethically oriented, anti-metaphysical Buddhism so often referred to in this Volume. The emphasis is on the basic message of the Buddha called the Four Noble Truths (*ārya satya*). The Buddha begins with the insight that existence is a vicious cycle of causation (*pratītya-*

samutpāda) which does not end in death, for death is only the beginning of a new life of suffering (first Noble Truth) But there is hope, for suffering has a cause and that which has a cause can be halted by removing the cause (second and third Noble Truths). The root cause of all suffering is ignorance (*avidyā*) and, therefore, knowledge (*prajñā*) is the sole means of liberation from the endless round of rebirth. Such emancipating knowledge is the fruit of a rigorous course of discipline (best followed in a monastic euvironment (called the Noble Eight-Fold Path i.e., right faith, right resolve, right speech, right action, right living, right effort, right thought, and right concentration. This right knowledge leads to the cessation of all desire or craving and the aspirant becomes an *arhat*, one who has managed to get 'outside' the realm governed by the law of *karma* and whose deeds will bear no fruit. Final extinction of sorrow (Pali-*nibbāna*, Skt.-*nirvāṇa*) then takes place as the natural result of the destruction of desires.

The Sthaviravādins began to decline in importance after the Third Council until they disappeared altogether from India. A branch of the Sthaviravāda—the Theravāda—has, however, continued to thrive in Ceylon, Burma and Thailand for over two thousand years. But as Sthviravāda declined in importance in India, another, more philosophically oriented, school was developing—the Sarvāstivādins.

The relationship between the Sarvāstivādins, Vaibhāṣikas, and Sautrāntikas is particularly unclear. Though Vaibhāṣika and Sautrāntikas are sometimes treated as sub-schools of the Sarvāstivāda school, in this sketch 'Sarvāstivāda' and 'Vaibhāṣika' will be used synonymously and contrasted with Sautrāntika. The differences between Sautrāntika and Vaibhāṣika (Sarvāstivāda) do not seem to be pronounced and their basic affinities as schools of Buddhism out-weigh them.

Sarvāstivāda (Vaibhāṣika) was the major school of Indian Hīnayāna Buddhism after about the second century B.C. The Sarvāstivādins used Sanskrit but only fragments of their works in that language are preserved. However, Sarvāstivāda, as well as the other schools of Indian Buddhism, migrated virtually intact to China and the entire Canon is available in

Chinese translation. The Sanskrit version of the *Tripiṭaka* does not agree entirely in content with the Pāli version and Theravāda seems to have had little or no direct influence on the development of Buddhist schools in India. When the "Abhidharma Philosophy" is referred to, the Sarvāstivāda school is invariably meant.

The most important Sarvāstivāda works are the *Vibhāṣā* and the *Mahāvibhāṣā*, commentaries on the *Jñānaprasthāna Śāstra* (a commentary, in turn, on the works of the *Abhidharma-Piṭaka*) of Kātyāyanīputtra, and it is from the word *vibhāṣā* (exposition) that the Vaibhāṣikas supposedly got their name. The Sautrāntikas, on the other hand, emphasize the works of the *Sūtra-Piṭaka*, the *Sūtrāntas*, and reject the Abhidharma works as unauthentic. An important source of information about both schools is the *Abhidharmakoṣa* of Vasubandhu (who is sometimes said to have originally been a Vaibhāṣika and sometimes a Sāutrantika)

Their respective theories of perception have traditionally received the most attention from non-Buddhist writers as the distinguishing characteristics of Vaibhāṣika and Sautrāntika. The Vaibhāṣikas are characterized as Presentationalists, insisting that 'external' objects are directly known in perception, while the Sautrāntikas are Representationalists, saying that external objects are not directly perceived but only indirectly inferred. We cannot know the thing-in-itself, we can know only ideas which are 'copies' of reality and from these we infer the existence of the 'originals'

Both Vaibhāṣika and Sautrāntika accept the *kṣaṇabhaṅgavāda* or theory of momentariness, but their interpretations of it differ radically. According to this theory matter is an aggregate of indivisible, imperceptible, momentary atoms (*paramāṇu*). These atoms are the minutest form of matter and combine, in turn, to form the four elements (earth, air, fire and water). In each element the atoms with its special characteristic are predominant. The antisubstantial tendencies of early Buddhism are carried out in the psychical as well as in the physical realm. As matter is only an aggregate of momentary atoms, so the person is only an aggregate of momentary *skandhas* (physical and psychical constituents) Look as hard as you will, you will find no substantial soul in the 'heap' of constituents forming a person (doctrine of 'No-Soul').

Both schools are atheistic and accept the *arhat* ideal. Both agree that *nirvāṇa* is the cessation of all misery that follows the extinction of all desires and passions. The Vaibhāsikas, however, say that *nirvāṇa* is a 'something', an eternal *dharma* (ultimate constituent of existence) which causes the particular stream of consciousness which is the *arhat* to remain disassociated from all impure (misery producing) *dharmas*. The Sautrāntikas, on the other hand, argue that *nīrvāṇa* is not some real and distinct entity but the absence of the tendency to act and the liability to be reborn.

The Vaibhāṣikas accept 75 *dharmas* (ultimate constituents of Reality) and the Sautrāntikas accept 53, claiming that the rest are simply mental constructions. But there is a more profound disagreement here than that over numbers. The Vaibhāṣikas say that the *dharmas* themselves are eternal but are cognizable only when they manifest themselves. They manifest themselves for a single instant (and thus *appear* to be instantaneous) and then (appear to) disappear. But their disappearance is not a return to non-existence but a return to an unmanifested state. Thus from the phenomenal point of view *dharmas* are impermanent and momentary, but from the noumenal viewpoint they are eternal. The Sautrāntikas insist that the doctrine of the eternality of the *dharmas* is a heretical perversion of the Buddha's teaching. They oppose it with a more radical application of the theory of *kṣaṇavāda* (*kṣaṇabhaṅgavāda*—momentariness), holding that not only is Reality momentary from the phenomenal viewpoint but from the noumenal as well the *dharmas* are as impermanent as the things composed of them.

The Vaibhāṣikas further argue that the past and future are as truly existent as the present and that the eternal *dharmas* "travel through the three periods of time". The Sautrāntikas object that since dharmas are momentary it makes no sense to distinguish between a *dharma* and its moment of existence. But this unreality of enduring entities has as its corollary the unreality of time. Therefore, neither past, present nor future are truly existent.

The starting points of the Sautrāntika version of the theory *kṣaṇavāda* are an equation of Reality with efficiency and an extremely strict criterion of identity. The permanent, it is argued, as unchanging cannot be efficient, productive of an effect, and is therefore not real. Further, the criterion of identity states that "that cannot be one of which two or more opposed characteristics can be predicated." According to this, even difference in time means a difference of things. The only real things, once you accept the basic tenets, are the momentary, self-identical, unique 'things' (*kṣaṇas*) we imagine to be the more or less permanent empirical things we deal with in our everyday life. If you took the observation that "I'm not the person I used to be" and carried it to its logical conclusion, "I'm never the person I used to be, not even the person I was a second ago," you'd be thinking along similar lines.

One conclusion drawn from the doctrine of *kṣaṇavāda* is that the universal is just a thought construct. Change, therefore, cannot be a change in the attributes of a permanent underlying substance but the replacement of one distinct entity by another. Permanence is an illusion and *satkāyadṛṣṭi*, the inveterate tendency to see as permanent and identical what are really momentary and discrete, is caused by beginningless *avidyā* (ignorance).

The Mahāyāna emerged during the period from 100 B.C. to 100 A.D. Its sources are the *Prajñāpāramitā Sūtras* (Perfection of Wisdom Treatises), anonymous works that are supposedly transcriptions of the words of the Buddha. The most important of the *Prajñāpāramitā Sūtras* is the *Aṣṭasāhasrikā*. The *Astasāhasrikā* is also considered to be one of the "Nine Dharmas", works held to be canonical by all Mahāyāna schools, which also include the *Saddharma Puṇḍarīka* ("Lotus of the wonderful Law") and the *Laṅkāvatāra*. Most of these Mahāyāna *sūtras* were composed during the first three centuries A.D.

The roots of the Mahāyāna are usually traced back further to the Mahāsāṅghika school. However, no original works of this school survive and our only knowledge of them comes from references in the works of other (usually hostile) schools.

Aśvaghośa (*ca*, 80/100 A.D.), who was a learned Brahmin scholar in his early life, is credited with being the first systematic expounder of the Mahāyāna. His most important work is the *Mahāyāna-śraddhotpāda-śāstra* (the original Sanskrit version is lost and it is available only in Chinese). Almost all important doctrines of the various Mahāyāna schools can supposedly be traced to him.

All things, says Aśvaghoṣa, are simply manifestations of the uncreate and eternal *bhūtatathatā* ('thatness'). The *bhūtatathatā* transcends all intellectual categories and at best can simply be 'pointed to' linguistically at 'thatness'. Through a beginningless, instinctive, creative tendency (*smṛti*) the mind superimposes a false duality on the *bhūtatathatā*. Just as when the wind blows, waves appear upon the surface of the water, and when the wind ceases the waves disappear, when the mind is disturbed by the 'wind' of *avidyā* (ignorance) the multiplicity of things is produced, but when the mind is quieted, the multiplicity of things disappears.

But just as *avidyā* 'perfumes' or influences *tathatā* (Reality) and the world-appearances spring forth, *tathatā* also 'perfumes' or influences the product of *avidyā*, the phenomenal world, and the result is the striving for good. Thus there is, in effect, an inherent principle causing human beings to loath the misery of birth and death and seek *nirvāṇa*. We are deluded, but not completely so. The *tathatā* within us causes us to long for the transcendent.

Also found in Aśvaghoṣa is the first flowering of the doctrine of the Bodhisattva, the saint who out of his Infinite Compassion (*mahākaruṇā*), defers his own *nirvāṇa* for countless eons in order to liberate those who are still bound to the wheel of birth and death. Along with this comes an emphasis on the more positive aspects of *nirvāṇa*, the Goal. Emphasis shifts from *nirvāṇa* as extinction (an admittedly drastic way to end suffering) to *nirvāṇa* as bliss (*ānanda*). The paradigm analogy is no longer the snuffing out of a candle flame but the orgasm.

According to Aśvaghoṣa it is his intention to explain the real meaning of the Buddha's teachings, not to introduce innovations. The Buddha was forced, provisionally, to make use of language, but we must always be aware of the limitations of speech and not be too literalistic in our interpretation of scripture. This, coupled with the basic Mahāyāna tenet that the Buddha taught according to the capacity of his Disciples, led to some interesting developments. According to school A, school B was not absolutely wrong, they were just not advanced enough to understand the *true* import of the Buddha's words. The Mahāsāṅghikas had shown this spirit when they insisted that the Sthaviravādins were mere literalists. In Śūnyavāda and Vijñānavāda the tendency is manifested in the rather simple division of scriptures into *nītārtha* (those which give the ultimate teaching) and *neyārtha* (those of secondary import). In Chinese and Japanese Buddhism it led to more and more refined hierarchical arrangements of the scriptures according to subtle differences in the intellectual and spiritual prowess of the reader until it was finally decided that the most profound and obscure of the *sūtras* were meant only for gods and Bodhisattvas.

Śūnyavāda, also called Mādhyamika, is often viewed as the basic school of Mahāyāna Buddhism, but occasionally it is contrasted with Vijñānavāda and the two are viewed as complementary but equally important schools. Nāgārjuna (*ca.* 100/200 A.D.) is considered to be the first systematic expounder of Śūnyavāda. Nāgārjuna's major work, the *Mūla-Mādhyamika-kārikā*, is the basic text of Mādhyamika. Āryadeva (*ca.* 200/300 A.D.), Nāgārjuna's chief disciple and successor, is the author of the *Catuḥśataka*, a work secondary in importance only to the *Mūla-Mādhyamika-kārikā*. Candrakīrti (*ca.* 550/650 A.D.), author of the *prasannapadā*, is the major commentator on the writings of Nāgārjuna and a basic source of information about the Mādhyamika. Shāntideva (*ca.* 600/700 A.D.) is referred to as the last great philosopher of Śūnyavāda, for Śūnyavāda died out as a major force in the Indian philosophical tradition around the eighth century A.D., though it continued to thrive in China as the San-lun or "Three-Treatise' school.

According to Śūnyavāda, Reality is *śūnya*; language cannot express it and the intellect cannot grasp it. Śūnyavāda is, therefore, referred to as espousing *śūnyatā*, "The view of no views". Since reality is beyond language and intellect, *all* philosophical views are equally worthless. Ultimately silence is the highest philosophy.

Speculative metaphysics, the Mādhyamikas claimed, can never give us knowledge, only illusion. This was not simply asserted dogmatically, the Mādhyamikas actually tried to prove the worthlessness of speculative metaphysics. Through dialectic the inner contradictions implicit in any metaphysical system were ruthlessly brought to the surface by the Mādhyamikas. The implications of the view were simply drawn out in extensive and exhaustive *reductio ad absurdum* arguments (*prasaṅga*) until its self-contradictory character became evident. The views with which the Mādhyamikas were particularly concerned were the Sautrāntika, Sāṃkhya, and Vaiśesika metaphysical systems.

A basic tenet of the destructively dialectical process is the Mādhyamikas' distinctively epistemological and linguistic interpretation of the doctrine of *pratītyasamutpāda*, 'Cause' and 'effect', 'substance' and 'attribute', 'whole' and 'part', 'subject' and 'object', etc.—all are mutually dependent and hence relative concepts. Their relativity, their dependence upon one another makes it impossible, in particular, to define one term of the pair without reference to the other. The terms, therefore, lack 'own-being' (*svabhāva*) : i.e., neither term has an essential characteristic by which it can be defined without reference to the other term of the pair. It is this chronic lack of essence which is the basic mark of unreality. 'Cause' and 'effect', therefore, are simply labels and the two different labels can easily be applied to the same thing "depending on how you look at it." It's the "depending on how you look at it" that expresses the basic relativity of the concepts. Therefore, terms like 'cause' and 'effect' do not represent ultimately real and distinct metaphysical entities. Categories like these are just so many conceptual devices (*vikalpa*) by which the discursive intellect (*buddhi*) attempts, unsuccessfully, to grasp the Real.

Since the phenomenal world (*saṃsāra*) is Reality (*nirvāṇa*) looked at 'through' thought forms, *saṃsāra* and *nirvāna* are, from an absolute standpoint, identical. Corresponding to these two aspects of Reality are the two levels of truth. *Saṃvṛti* is the practical makeshift, the necessary compromise required for everyday life. This is truth from the viewpoint of the ordinary man. The authority of the intellect in this sphere is unquestionable. *Paramārtha* is absolute truth, truth from the viewpoint of the Bodhisattva. Intellect is totally worthless in this sphere.

Though Reality transcends thought (discursive intellect), it is 'accessible' in intuition or Pure Knowledge (*Prajñā*). *Prajñā* is most often characterized as knowledge "devoid of distinction". Intellect is to be transformed into Pure Knowledge in the course of progression through the ten stages of Bodhisattvahood. The '*śūnyatā* discipline' (critical philosophy) is necessary for the dawning of *Prajñā* and final release. But it is necessary in a rather negative sense. Only by participating in the dialectic, engaging in philosophy exhaustively—until we have "wrung it dry"—can we finally come to realize that it is a dead end. Only then can we transcend it in Pure Knowledge.

Maitreyanātha (ca. 270/350 A.D.) is generally credited as the founder of the Vijñānavāda (also called Yogācāra) school of absolute idealism, but his disciple Asaṅga (ca. 350/480 A.D.) and Asaṅga's brother Vasubandhu (ca. 280/400 A.D.) are conceded to be the most important philosophers of the school. The most important Yogācāra works are the *Sandhinirmocana* and *Laṅkāvatāra sūtras*, Vasubandhu's *Viṃśatikā* ("Twenty Verses") and *Triṁśikā* ("Thirty Verses"), and Asaṅga's *Mahāyāna-Saṃgraha*. Also important, though variously attributed to Asaṅga and Maitreyanātha are the *Mahāyānasūtrālaṃkāra* and the *Madhyāntavibhāga*. Vijñānavāda, like Śūnyavāda, died out in India around 800 A.D., although it continued to thrive in China as the Wei-shih or "Consciousness Only" school.

The differences between the Yogācāra and Mādhyamika schools are not profound and they are often spoken of as supplementing or complementing one another. Mādhyamika, true to the basically antimetaphysical, antispeculative tendencies of the Buddha, concentrated on showing that Reality is truly beyond the capabilities of language and that speculative metaphysics should be avoided, while Yogācāra, true to the basically psychologistic tendencies of the Buddha, concentrated on explaining the phenomenon of consciousness. The tendencies exemplified by the two schools are paralleled in the twentieth century by the followers of Wittgenstein and Husserl. In both schools the traditional Buddhist ethical tendency is present. Morality plays as high a part in both systems as it had in early Buddhism, though now the discussions are not of the ethics of monastic community but of the path of transformation of the ordinary man into a Bodhisattva.

The difference between the two schools most often cited is the insistence of the Mādhyamikas that Dialectic (philosophy) was necessary for enlightenment/salvation and the Yogācārin emphasis on the basic importance of meditation (*Yoga*). The Yogācārins agree with the Mādhyamikas that Reality (*Vijñaptimātra*) is śūnya: beyond all intellectual categories, ungraspable by language. But the Yogācārins go further and characterize Reality as Pure Consciousness (*Vijñāna*) and as the Highest Soul (*Paramātman*). The Sūnyavādins had considered everything that might reasonably be said about Reality and rejected it as inadequate. The Vijñānavādins argued, however, that even if all *views* are rejected as conducive to illusion, we still cannot reject as unreal the *consciousness* of those views.

Illusions and dreams, argue the Vijñānavādins, prove that consciousness can have a content without the existence of a corresponding object 'outside'. If, with the Sautrāntikas, we infer the existence of the 'original' (the thing "out there") from the existence of the 'copy' (the idea we have of it), we will end up with a lot of metaphysically useless baggage—things-in-themselves that will always remain essentially unknowable. Consciousness should be viewed as "self-contained", as giving rise to the varied contents from its own inner potentiality (*svaśakti*) and according to its own immanent laws of development.

A basic implication of such a viewpoint is that if it makes no sense to talk about things 'outside' of my consciousness, then it makes no sense to talk about things 'inside' either. 'Subjective' and 'objective', they agreed with the Mādhyamikas, are mutually dependent and relative concepts. Therefore, they are not labels for distinct and ultimately real metaphysical entities. Looked at from one point of view, Reality (consciousness) can be characterized as subjective, from another viewpoint it is objective. But if the division of consciousness into 'subjective' and 'objective' is misleading, conducive to illusion, we've obviously got a problem. Our whole language is predicated on this (false) dichotomy. What we need, therefore, is a new way of talking, a new 'model' for consciousness. So enters the Vijñānavāda concept of the *ālayavijñāna* (great storehouse of consciousness), one of the most puzzling conceptual devices ever conceived.

When pondering over the often incomprehensible 'explanations' of the *ālayavijñāna* it is useful to remember one thing. The Vijñānavādins agreed with the Mādhyamikas that Reality could not be grasped by the intellect. Assuming that this agreement was sincere the theory of the *ālayavijñāna* must be seen as just that, a theory, an *attempt* (perhaps unsuccessful to explain the phenomena of consciousness without reference to the false subject/object duality through which they are most often viewed.

The Vijñānavādins agree with the Mādhyamikas that from the ultimate standpoint there is no real difference between *Samsāra* and Nirvāna. They, however, discuss the three, rather than the two, aspects of Reality:

1. *Parinispanna*: The transcendental 'ground-reality' upon which all phenomena are superimposed (the movie screen).
2. *Ālayavijñāna*: That which superimposes the phenomenal world upon the *parinispanna* (the projector).
3. The phenomenal world: the imaginary subject/object duality superimposed (the movie).

Thus all phenomena, our perceptions of things 'without' as well as 'within', are the illusory manifestations of the *ālayavijñāna* and are not ultimately real. We must rid our consciousness of the false subject/object duality we impose upon it through Yogic practices until we become one, through Pure Knowledge, with Reality.

NOTES

Part One

1. Joseph Needham, *Science and Civilisation in China*, vol. 2, *History of Scientific Thought* (Cambridge: Cambridge University Press, 1956), p. 238 (hereafter cited as *Civilisation in China*).

2. Prem Sunder Bose, trans., "Sarvasiddhāntasaṁgraha" in *A Source Book in Indian Philosophy*, ed. Sarvepalli Radhakrishnan and Charles A. Moore (Princeton: Princeton University Press, 1957), p. 234.

3. Edward Conze, *Buddhist Thought in India, Three Phases of Buddhist Philosophy* (Ann Arbor: The University of Michigan Press, 1967), p. 182 (hereafter cited as *Buddhist Thought*).

4. Chandradhar Sharma, *Indian Philosophy: A Critical Survey* (New York: Barnes & Noble, Inc., 1962), p. 142.

5. Donald J. Munro, *The Concept of Man in Early China* (Stanford, Calif.: Stanford University Press, 1969), p. 50.

6. Ibid., pp. 127-128.

7. Fung Yu-Lan, *A History of Chinese Philosophy*, trans. Derk Bodde, 2nd ed., vol. 1, *The Period of the Philosophers* (Princeton: Princeton University Press, 1952), p., 399 (hereafter cited as (*Chinese Phil.*).

8. Needham, *Civilisation in China*, passim.

9. D. C. Lau, trans., *Mencius* (Baltimore: Penguin Books, Inc., 1970), p. 24.

10. Needham, *Civilisation in China*, pp. 190-191.

11. Lau, *Mencius*, p. 35.

12 Surendranath Dasgupta, *A History of Indian Philosophy*, vol. 1 (Cambridge: Cambridge University Press, 1922), p. 160n (hereafter cited as *Indian Phil.*).

13. Fung, *Chinese Phil.*, p. 226.

14. Dasgupta, *Indian Phil.*, p. 257.

15. Needham, *Civilisation in China*, p. 285.

16. Dasgupta, *Indian Phil.*, p. 257.

17. Tang Chun-i, "The Individual and the World in Chinese Methodology", in *The Chinese Mind*, ed. Charles A. Moore (Honolulu: East-West Center Press, 1967), p. 272.

18. Fung, *Chinese Phil.*, p. 127.

19. Ibid.

20. Ibid.

21. Ibid., pp. 181-182.

22. Ibid., p. 115.

23. Ibid., p. 99.

24. Ibid., pp. 285-286.

25. Ibid., p. 285.
26. Ibid., p. 313.
27. Ibid., p. 75.
28. Ibid., p. 73.
29. Ibid., p. 75.
30. Ibid., p. 92.
31. Ibid., pp. 120-121.
32. Ibid., p. 145.
33. Ibid., p. 286.
34. Ibid., p. 287.
35. Ibid., p. 326.
36. Ibid., p. 330.
37. James Legge, trans., *The Sacred Books of China, The Texts of Taoism* (Part One), The Sacred Books of the East, ed. F. Max Müller, vol. 39 (New York : Dover Publications, Inc., 1962), p. 139.
38. Fung, *Chinese Phil.*, pp. 68-69.
39. Ibid., p. 71.
40. Ibid., p. 371.
41. Ibid., p. 392.
42. Kenneth W. Morgan, ed., *The Path of the Buddha* (New York: Ronald Press Co., 1956), pp. 28-32 (hereafter cited as *Path*).
43. Eliza Gregory Wilkins, *The Delphic Maxims in Literature* (Chicago: University of Chicago Press, 1929).
44. Fung, *Chinese Phil.*, p. 367.
45. Donald J. Munro, *The Concept of Man in Early China* (Stanford, Calif.: Stanford University Press, 1969), p. 51.
46. Dasgupta, *Indian Phil.*, pp. 58-59.
47. Eric Voegelin *Order and History*, vol. 2, *The World of the Polis* (Baton Rouge: Lousisana State University Press, 1957), pp. 312-319.
48. Maneckji Nusservanji Dhalla, *Zoroastrian Civilization* (New York: Oxford University Press, 1922).
49. Ibid., p. 228.
50. Fung, *Chinese Phil.*, p. 321.
51. Ibid., pp. 324-325.
52. Kewal Motwani, *Manu Dharma Śāstra* (Madras: Ganesh & Company, 1958).
53. Conze, *Buddhist Thought*, p. 92.
54. Morgan, *Path*, p. 414.
55. Ibid., p. 112.
56. I. B. Horner, trans., *The Collection of the Middle Length Sayings* (*Majjhima-Nikāya*), Pali Text Society Translation Series no. 30, vol. 2, *The Middle Fifty Discourses* (*Majjhimapannāsa*) (London: Luzac & Company for the Pali Text Society, 1957), p. 16.
57. Ibid., pp. 16-17.
58. Fung, *Chinese Phil.*, p. 92.

59. A. V. Williams Jackson, *Zoroastrian Studies: The Iranian Religion and Various Monographs*, Columbia University Indo-Iranian Series, A. V. W. Jackson, ed., vol. 12 (New York: Columbia University Press, 1928).

60. Dhalla, *Zoroastrian Civilization*. pp. 31-33.

61. Eric Voegelin, *Order and History*, vol. 1, *Israel and Revelations* (Baton Rouge: Lousiana State University Press, 1956), pp. 234-236.

62. Fung, Chinese Phil., p. 31.

63. Morgan. *Path*, p. 45.

Part Two

1. Daniel Henry Holmes Ingalls, *Materials for the Study of Navya-Nyāya Logic*, ed. Walter Eugene Clark, Harvard Oriental series, vol. 40 (Cambridge : Harvard University Press, 1951), p. 33 (hereafter cited as *Materials*.)

2. Fung Yu-Lan, *A Histroy of Chinese Philosophy*, trans. Derk Bodde, 2nd ed., vol. 1, *The Period of the Philosophers* (Princeton: Princeton University Press, 1952), p. 269 (hereafter cited as *Chinese Phil*).

3. K. N. Jayatilleke, *Early Buddhist Theory of Knowledge* (London: George Allen & Unwin Ltd., 1963), p. 334.

4. Troy Wilson Organ, "The Silence of the Buddha"., *Philosophy East and West*, vol. 4, no. 2, July 1954, p. 126.

5. Richard McKeon, ed., *The Basic Works of Aristotle* (New York: Random House, 1941), p. 1288 (hereafter cited as *Aristotle*).

6. Cho-yun Hsu, *Ancient China in Transition* (Stanford: Stanford University Press, 1965), p. 156.

7. Wing-Tsit Chan, *A Source Book in Chinese Philosobhy* (Princeton: Princeton University Press, 1963), p. 260 (hereafter cited as *Source Book*).

8. R. Shamasastry, trans., *Kauṭilya's Arthaśāstra*, 8th ed. (Mysore, India: Mysore Publishing House, 1967), pp. 11-12.

9. Ibid., pp. 37-38.

10. Ibid., p. 39.

11. John C. H. Wu, "Chinese Legal and Political Philosophy", in *The Chinese Mind*, ed. Charles A. Moore (Honolulu: East-West Center Press, 1967), p. 223.

12. Joseph Needham, *Science and Civilisation in China*, vol. 2, *History of Scientific Thought* (Cambridge: Cambridge University Press, 1956), p. 23 (hereafter cited as *Civilisation in China*).

13. Fung, *Chinese Phil.*, p. 290.

14. Ibid., p. 297.

15. Jadunath Sinha, *A History of Indian Philosophy*, vol. 2 (Calcutta: Central Book Agency, 1952), p. 223 (hereafter cited as "Vol. 2").

16. McKeon, *Aristotle*, p. 229.

17. Needham, *Civilisation in China*, p. 528.

18. Chan, *Source Book*, p. 160.

19. Ibid., p. 161.

20. Friedrich Solmsen, *Aristotle's Smyste of the Physical World, A Comparison with his Predecessors* (Ithica, N. Y.: Cornell University Press, 1960), p. 146.

21. Philip H. Wicksteed and Francis M. Cornford, trans., *Aristotle, The Physics*, The Loeb Classical Library, vol. 1 (Cambridge: Harvard University Press, 1929), pp. 419-421.

22. Sinha, vol. 2, p. 237.

23. Ibid., p. 236.

24. Shwe Zan Aung and Rhys Davids, trans., *Points of Controversy or Subjects of Discourse* (*Kathā-Vatthu* from the *Abhidhamma-Piṭaka*) (London: Luzac & Company for the Pali Text Society, 1960), pp. 393-394.

25. Needham, *Civilisation in China*, p. 288.

26. Wing-tsit Chan, *An Outline and an Annotated Bibliography of Chinese Philosophy* (New Haven, Conn.: Far Eastern Publications, 1969), p. 177.

27. Fung, *Chinese Phil.*, p. 259.

28. Ibid., p. 260.

29. Ibid., pp. 305-306.

30. Hugh Tredennick, trans., *Aristotle: The Metaphysics*, Books I-IX The Loeb Classical Library (Cambridge: Harvard University Press, 1933), Book III passim.

31. Ingalls, *Materials*, p. 53.

32. T'ang Chun-i, "The Individual and the World in Chinese Methodology", in *The Chinese Mind*, ed. Charles A. Moore (Honolulu: East-West Center Press, 1967), pp. 271-274.

33. John Herman Randall, Jr., *Aristotle* (New York: Columbia University Press, 1960), pp. 69-72.

34. B. D. Basu, ed., and Nandalal Sinha, trans., *The Sacred Books of the Hindus*, 2nd ed. rev. (Allahabad, India: Sudhindra Nath Basu, 1923), Intro., passim.

35. Hellmut Wilhelm, *Change, Eight Lectures on the I Ching*, trans. Cary F. Baynes, Bollingen Series no. 62 (New York: Pantheon Books Inc. for Bollignen Foundation, 1960), pp. 17-18.

36. Ibid., p. 18.

37. Hugh Tredennick, trans., *Aristotle, Metaphysics II* Books X-XIV The Loeb Classical Library (Cambridge: Harvard University Press, 1935) Book XII, p. 151.

PRONUNCIATION : SANSKRIT AND PĀLI

a as *u* in *rut*
ā as *a* in *father*
e sometimes as *a* in *made* (Veda)
e sometimes as *e* in *pet* (Theravāda)
i as *i* in *sit*
ī as *i* in *machine*
o as *o* in *go*
u sometimes as *oo* in *boot* (Buddha)
u sometimes as *u* in *put*
ū as *u* in *rude*
ai as *ai* in *aisle*
au as *ou* in *house*

Unlesss otherwise noted consonants are pronounced as they are in English except:

ṅ as *ng* in *sing*
ñ as *ñ* in *señor* (Spanish)
ś as *s* in *sure*
g always as *g* in *gun*
s always as *s* in *sit*
c always as *ch* in *child*

A consonant followed by *h* is to be aspirated except:

sh as *sh* in *sheet*
ch as *ch* in *church*
th sometimes as *th* in *thumb*
th sometimes as an aspirated *t*

A consonant with a dot beneath it is pronounced as the English consonant but with the tip of the tongue near the roof of the mouth, except:

ṣ as *sh* in *shine*
ṛ as *ri* in *writ*

GLOSSARY

abhāva : non-existence, negation, absence

Abhidharma : see sketch on Buddhism

adharma : opposite of dharma, demerit, non-virtue; rest, motionless

adṛṣṭa : unseen force or power, potential form; destiny

advaita : non-dual, absolute

Advaita Vedānta : an Upaniṣadic-based school developed by Gauḍapāda and flowering in the 9th century philosopher Śaṅkara

Advaitin : a non-dualist; a Vedāntin

ahaṃkāra : ego, individual

ahiṃsā : non-injury

ajīva : non-living, non-spirit, unconscious

ajñāna : ignorance

ākāśa : space, ether

ānanda : supreme joy, bliss

anātman : (Pāli, *anatta*) : Buddhist view of "no soul"

antaḥkaraṇa : the internal organ or sense

antaryāmin : inner controller

apūrva : positive force resulting from performance of a ritual

Arhat : the ideal saint of the Hīnayāna schools

artha : wealth

Arthaśāstra : the major work by Kauṭilya

asatkāryavāda : a theory of causation which holds that the effect does not pre-exist in the cause

āśramas : the Hindu stages of life : student, householder, retirement, renunciation

Aśoka : an Indian king (ca. 249 B.C.) noted for his peaceful reign and for spreading Buddhism

āvaraṇa : veiling, barrier, concealment

avatār : an incarnation of deity

avidyā : ignorance

Bhagavadgītā : one of the most popular Hindu sacred texts, rather eclectic, dating between 200 B.C. and 200 A.D.

Bhagavān : God as an object of one's devotion

bhakti : devotion, active service

bhāva : Being

bhoga : experience in the world

bodhi : intelligence, wisdom, enlightenment

Bodhisattva : the ideal saint of the Mahāyāna schools

brahmacarya : celibate student

Brāhmaṇas : the ritualistic part of the Vedas

Brahman : Ultimate Reality; God

Brahmin : member of priestly caste

buddhi : intellect, intelligence; consciousness

cakra : psycho-physical center of the body; "wheel"

cāritra : right conduct

Cārvāka : early materialistic Hindu school

ch'i : vital force, breath, air

chih : matter, substance; to cause; law, regulation; to govern, restrain

ching : quiescence; permanency, constancy, rule

Chuang Tzu : see sketch

chung : loyalty, faithfulness

cit : pure consciousness; thought

citta : intelligence, mind

darśana : intuitive vision, insight; system, school; philosophy

deva : presiding deity, minor god sometimes comparable to "angel"

Dhammapada : a Hīnayāna sacred text

dharma (Pāli, *dhamma*) : law, duty, virtue, merit, order; body of teachings; element; motion

Dharma-chakra : the Wheel of the Law turned by the Buddha; Wheel of Righteousness

Dhūrtta : one of the two schools of Cārvāka

dhyāna : meditation

dik : space

dravya : substance

duḥkha : suffering

fa : law, regulation: model, method; to imitate

gṛhastha : householder

guṇa : quality, attribute; the three constituents of *prakṛti* : *sattva*, *rajas*, and *tamas*

Han Fei Tzu : see sketch

Hīnayāna : earlier Buddhist systems, see Buddhist sketch

ho : correspondence; harmony
hsiao : filial piety
hsin : good faith, one of the Five Constant Virtues
hsing : human nature; punishment; form
hsu : emptiness, vacuity
hsuan : mystery; profound, secret
Hui Shih : one of the Dialecticians, noted for his paradoxes
Hsun Tzu : see sketch
i : righteousness
Īśvara : Lord, God as determinate, *saguṇa* Brahman
jaḍa : unintelligent, inanimate, unconscious; material
Jainism : see sketch
jāti : class; caste; birth, rebirth
ien : humanity, humanness, benevolence, human-heartedness, virtue
jīvanmukta : one who attains emancipation while still living
jñāna : consciousness, knowledge
kaivalya : 'isolation', emancipated state, aloneness, detachment
kāla : time
Kalki : an Avatār of Viṣṇu yet to come
kalpa : cosmic cycle
kāma : pleasure, desire, love
karma : action; the results of good or bad deeds
kleśa : affliction
kriyā : action, activity, acting
kṣaṇa : moment, instant
kṣaṇavāda : Buddhist doctrine of momentariness
Kṣatriya : warrior caste, noble
Kumārila : see sketch on Mīmāṁsā
li : law, principle; good form; ritual, ceremony; reason; decorum
Lieh Tzu : a Taoist philosopher, traditional author of the *Lieh Tzu*
Lokāyata : Cārvāka
Mādhyamika : see sketch on Buddhism
Mahābhārata : great Sanskrit epic containing the *Bhagavadgītā*
Mahāvīra : founder of Jainism
Mahāyāna : later Buddhist systems; see Buddhist sketch

Maitreya : the Buddha to come
manas : mind
Manu : author of the Code of Manu (ca. 1000 B.C.)
mārga : path, way, process
māyā : ultimately unreal; illusion
Mencius : see sketch
Mīmāṁsā : see sketch
ming : destiny, fate
Mo Tzu : see sketch
mokṣa : emancipation, liberation, salvation
mukta : liberated person
Nāgārjuna : see sketch on Buddhism
Naiyāyika : adjective form of Nyāya; see sketch
nāmarūpa : name and form; mind-body complex; appearances
niḥśreyasa : the highest good
nirguṇa : without attributes, qualityless, indescribable
nirvāṇa (Pāli, nibbāna) : the emancipated state, salvation, (heaven), quietude
nivṛtti : cessation, inactivity; contemplative
Nyāya : see sketch
Parama-Puruṣa : Cosmic Person in the Vedas
pāramārthika : relating to ultimate reality
paramātman : the true self; Supreme Spirit
parikarma : yogic purificatory practices
Patañjali : founder of Yoga school
Piṭakas : refers to the three divisions of the Pāli Canon : Sutta-Piṭaka, Vinaya-Piṭaka, Abhidhamma-Piṭaka
prajñā : Wisdom, knowledge, insight, intuition
prakṛti : original, uncreated matter or substance consisting of the three guṇas (in Sāṃkhya)
pralaya : periodic dissolution of the world; cosmic involution
pramāṇa : means of acquiring valid knowledge; means of cognition; measure
prāṇa : vital breath, life, vitality
prāṇamaya : astral body
pratītyasamutpāda : the chain of endless causation; dependent origination
Pravṛtti : activity, effort; volitional resolution; energy

Purāṇas : "ancient stories"; literature which develops the Hindu trinity of Brahmā, Śiva, and Viṣṇu

puruṣa : spirit, soul, *ātman*; man, person

puruṣārthas : the ends or goals of human endeavors

rajas : one of the three guṇas; activity, pain, restlessness

Ṛg-Veda : oldest of the four parts of the Vedas; most ancient of Indian sacred literature, variously dated between 1400 B.C. and 4000 B.C.

ṛṣi : sage, seer

sādhana : spiritual discipline or exercise; means; accomplishment

saguṇa : qualified, determinate

sākṣi : the subject, perceiving consciousness, the witness, spectator

samādhi : concentration, trance; highest stage in yogic meditation

Sāṃkhya : see sketch

saṃsāra : cycle of death and rebirth; the continuing transmigratory rounds through mundane existences and deaths.

saṃskāras : old habits from past experiences; potencies resulting from past lives

Saṃyutta Nikāya : one of the works in the *Sutta-Piṭaka*

saṅgha : monastic community; brotherhood

sannyāsa : one of the four *āśramas*; renunciation, mendicancy

Sarvāstivāda : Buddhist school; see sketch on Buddhism

sat : Being; existence

satkāryavāda : a theory of causation holding that the cause is inherent in the effect

sattā : Being; existence

sattva : one of the three *guṇas*; light, goodness, harmony

Sautrāntika : Buddhist school; see sketch on Buddhism

Shang Ti : a Chinese anthropomorphic god

shen : spirits

shih : power, authority; scholar

shu : altruism; statecraft, methods

skandhas : aggregate of elements

Śūdra : outcaste; farmer, laborer

sukha : pleasure, happiness

śūnya : empty, void

Śūnyavāda : Buddhist school; sketch on Buddhism

Suśikṣita : one of the two schools of Cārvāka

sūtras : aphorisms expressing the essence of the teachings of a school

syādvāda : the Jaina doctrine that all knowledge is relative

tamas : one of the three *guṇas*; ignorance, inertia, darkness

Tao : Way; cosmic order, Nature; the moral order; ineffable Reality

Tao Teh Ching : short, aphoristic work attributed to Lao Tzu containing the earliest formulation of Taoism

tapas : ascetic discipline

Tathatā : "thatness", "suchness", Ultimate Reality

teh : power, virtue; Tao as manifested, Tao particularized; character

Theravāda : Hīnayāna; see Buddhist sketch

Ti : Lord, God; deities

T'ien : Heaven, Supreme Power; Nature

Tīrthaṅkaras : the twenty-four "ford-finders" or prophets of Jainism

Tripitakas : "three baskets", the three *Piṭakas*

triratna : "three jewels" of Jainism : right faith, right knowledge, right conduct

Upaniṣads : the last part of the Vedas containing monistic speculations and providing the basis for Vedāntic philosophies

Vaiśeṣika : see sketch

Vaiṣṇava : religious sect treating Viṣṇu as the personal deity while advocating absolutism

Vaiśya : merchant caste

vānaprastha : hermit; retirement

vāsanā : seeds from past expriences; dispositions; unconscious impressions; potentialities resulting from *karma*

Vedānta : see sketch

Vedas : most ancient of Indian sacred literature

vidyā : true knowledge

vijñāna : consciousness, cognition, thought

Vijñānavāda : see Buddhist sketch

vikṣepa : distraction, projection; a power of *māyā*

viśeṣa : particularity

wen : refinement
wu : non-Being; matter, things
wu wei : non-assertion, spontaneity, naturalness, accomplishment without effort
yi : righteousness
yin-yang : passive and active cosmic principles, contrasting yet complementary
Yogācāra : Vijñānavāda; see Buddhist sketch
yu : Being; "the mother of all things"; space; desire

INDEX